Justice, Dissent, and the Sublime

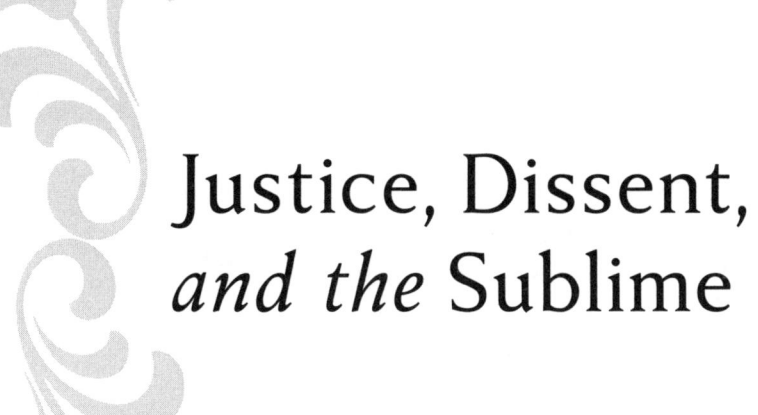

Justice, Dissent, *and the* Sublime

MARK CANUEL

The Johns Hopkins University Press
Baltimore

© 2012 The Johns Hopkins University Press
All rights reserved. Published 2012
Printed in the United States of America on acid-free paper
9 8 7 6 5 4 3 2 1

The Johns Hopkins University Press
2715 North Charles Street
Baltimore, Maryland 21218-4363
www.press.jhu.edu

Library of Congress Cataloging-in-Publication Data

Canuel, Mark.
   Justice, dissent, and the sublime / Mark Canuel.
       p. cm.
   Includes bibliographical references and index.
   ISBN 978-1-4214-0587-2 (hdbk. : alk. paper) — ISBN 978-1-4214-0609-1 (electronic) — ISBN 1-4214-0587-3 (hdbk. : alk. paper) — ISBN 1-4214-0609-8 (electronic)
   1. Aesthetics in literature.   2. English literature—18th century—History and criticism.   3. English literature—19th century—History and criticism.   4. Justice in literature.   5. Sublime, The, in literature.   6. Romanticism—Great Britain.   I. Title.
   PR448.A37C35 2012
   820.9′007—dc23   2011047314

A catalog record for this book is available from the British Library.

Special discounts are available for bulk purchases of this book. For more information, please contact Special Sales at 410-516-6936 or specialsales@press.jhu.edu.

The Johns Hopkins University Press uses environmentally friendly book materials, including recycled text paper that is composed of at least 30 percent post-consumer waste, whenever possible.

Contents

Acknowledgments vii

Introduction 1

CHAPTER 1 Beautiful People 14

CHAPTER 2 Justice and the Romantic Sublime 40

CHAPTER 3 The Reparative Impulse 63

CHAPTER 4 Biopolitics and the Sublime 94

CHAPTER 5 Aesthetics and Animal Theory 121

Notes *147*
Index *171*

Acknowledgments

I am grateful for the questions and comments from several audiences who heard parts of this work as it unfolded—at meetings of the North American Society for the Study of Romanticism and the Modern Language Association, at the English Department Colloquium at the University of Illinois at Chicago, at the Eighteenth- and Nineteenth-Century Cultures Workshop at the University of Chicago, and at the Columbia University Society of Fellows in the Humanities.

I want to add particular thanks to Jennifer Ashton, Lauren Berlant, Jessica Berman, John Bugg, Jim Chandler, Ralph Cintròn, Jenny Davidson, Lennard Davis, Stephen Engelmann, Andy Franta, Lisa Freeman, Linda Gregerson, Sharon Holland, Oren Izenberg, Justin Joyce, Anna Kornbluh, Kevin Lamb, Zach Lamm, Michael Lieb, Sandra Macpherson, Dwight McBride, Walter Michaels, Davide Panagia, Larry Poston, Christina Pugh, Richard Sha, and Sarah Zimmerman. They commented on arguments, suggested reading, read chapters, or offered encouragement as the book progressed.

Thanks are also due to Matt McAdam, my editor at the Johns Hopkins University Press, for his early and continued support for the project, and to Colin Jager, the reader for the Press, who offered extraordinarily detailed insights on every chapter and helped to make this book better. Joanne Allen's copyediting corrected many errors and infelicities in my writing. Rob Kaufman gave the manuscript a complete reading that was both generous and rigorous, and I have only begun to think about some of his comments. Mary Beth Rose helped sharpen and expand arguments throughout the book; she also patiently listened to—and thoughtfully engaged—my arguments even in their earliest and sloppiest stages.

Parts of chapters 1 and 2 were published in an earlier form as "Doing Justice in Aesthetics," *Representations* 95 (Summer 2006): 76–104.

I dedicate this book to my many teachers from whom I continue to learn, including Lynda K. Bundtzen, Sharon Cameron, Jerome Christensen, Frances Ferguson, Jan Glitzenstein, Leo Grant, Larry Graver, Paul Holdengräber, Mary Poovey, Chris Pye, Willard Spiegelman, Karen Swann, and Betty Winograd.

Justice, Dissent, and the Sublime

Introduction

I begin with one of the most obvious features of Mary Shelley's celebrated novel *Frankenstein; or the Modern Prometheus* (1818, rev. 1831). The monster, we're told over and over again, is ugly. Surely his creator, Victor Frankenstein, describes him in a way that wouldn't exactly make him stand out in a lineup: he has yellow skin, stringy hair, watery eyes, and thin lips.[1] Still, as Victor reports (and others concur later), "no mortal could support the horror of that countenance," and his bodily movement renders him "such a thing as even Dante could not have conceived" (51). The "deformity" of the monster's "aspect" is "more hideous than belongs to humanity" (85); worse than a "mummy . . . endued with animation" (50), he's a "wretch," a "filthy daemon" (65), a "devil" (84).

The absolute certainty that the monster is "hideous," matched with the absolute vagueness about exactly what makes him so hideous, only magnifies the importance of policing the boundaries around what proper humanity looks like. Perhaps it's almost as obvious that this anxious insistence on the monster's ugliness underscores the degree to which Shelley's celebrated novel is really also very much about beauty and about the function that beauty serves in forming human relationships. Hideous though he may be, the monster is supposed to have "beautiful" features, and thus his ugliness—what makes him appear an altogether different "species" (46)—is a failure of resemblance to the whole from which his parts derive. The central characters in the novel attest to the numerous windfalls that accumulate from successful resemblance and recognition. They continually report on being soothed into loving affection by one another's beauty; "pretty" children are drawn to other pretty children (56); the monster's recognition of his own deformity is all the more affecting when contrasted with the "lovely creatures" (97) he observes in the cottage of the DeLacey family and with the "beautiful creatures" in the Frankenstein family unit (121). It is only the blindness of old Mr. DeLacey that momentarily makes it possible for the monster to be included in their beautiful domestic space, from which he's violently banished by the father's lovely children and the "lovely stranger," Safie (99).

In each of these cases, beauty functions as a description of persons but also, and more importantly, as a signal of their likeness to one another. Beauty is thus a description of persons and a motive for sympathy-generated social relations that create "mutual bonds" (103), exhibiting what Percy Shelley in his preface to the 1818 edition called "the amiableness of domestic affection" (5). A community of lovely beings, that is, enlarges to accept other lovely beings with an equally lovely symmetry. Critics such as Paul Youngquist have shrewdly noted this aspect of the novel's normative aesthetics for quite some time. They have noted, that is, how the aesthetic of beauty creates exclusions that result in human society's rejecting the monster.[2] But it might even be said that the monster, once he understands that his horrific deformity makes him an outcast, to a certain degree only further underlines the exclusive aspects of beauty. For when he asks Victor to create a mate for himself, the "hideous" creature asks for his features to be replicated symmetrically. The new creature will be like himself, thus "exciting the sympathy of some existing thing" (124). There will be a kind of beauty in the replicated deformity; the attraction that creates communities is based on likeness.

Throughout chapter 17 of the novel—in which the monster approaches Victor with the demand that his maker create a mate for him—Victor puzzles over the difficulties that arise from the monster's demands. Supposing the monster continues in his quest for "sympathy" with man once he has his mate, and supposing he is disappointed in that quest by meeting with "detestation," wouldn't a companion simply aid him in "the task of destruction" (124)? Victor's qualms trace out the logical implications of communities grounded in sympathy. From his perspective, it seems that the only solution to the monster's dilemma would be a world in which similar individuals could be grouped but not mixed, so that that no one would either inflict or suffer the pains of rejection.

But negotiations with the monster don't end here. Indeed, they take on an altogether different character that emphasizes a different aesthetic approach to other beings and also a different moral-political perspective associated with that approach. The end of the chapter represents Victor's reaction to sublime images in nature—the stars, the passing clouds, the dark pines (126). The scene inspires a sense of "wonderful solemnity" stirring Victor's "strange thoughts" (126). In contrast to accounts of human beauty in the novel, the moment described here emphasizes an inward movement that delineates nothing other than Victor's sense of estrangement itself, his separation from all those around him. (Curiously, that estrangement foreshadows his ultimate recognition that making a mate for the monster might simply induce the creatures to "hate each other" [140].) At the same time, however, that sense of sublime separation also ratifies a new kind of connection. In a passage that Shelley added to the 1831 edition of the novel, Victor affirms an "adoration" of those with whom he has no "sympathies" or "companionship" (127).[3] And this sense of separated connection is precisely what becomes associated with his commitment, momentary though it is, to do his "duty" to the monster by adhering to his "abhorred task" of creating a mate for him (127).

The sublime moment of separation linked to an adoration beyond sympathetic companionship corresponds to moral-political pulsions throughout the chapter that repeatedly show Victor to be "moved" by the monster's words: a shuddering and recoil, followed by an assertion of the cause of "justice" (124), encouraging him to yield to the monster's demands. This is not the result of an identification with the monster, though. Victor feels as distant from him as ever. Instead, Victor's own estrangement from other beings moves him to reconfigure his obligations to them. In this pivotal scene, then, the novel vividly contrasts two different aesthetic modes, with different moral-political implications. On the one hand, the aesthetic of beauty both impels and solidifies an account of "virtues" that, as the monster puts it, are dependent upon living "in communion with an equal," allowing him to "feel the affection of a sensitive being, and become linked to the chain of existence and events, from which [he is] excluded" (125). On the other hand, the sublime moment connects to a different account of relationships, an account linked to a commitment to "justice" that is due, as Victor puts it, "to [the monster] and my fellow creatures" (125), even though the creatures that are one's fellows (just like the monster) are radically separate from him.[4]

The combating perspectives fiercely vie with each other throughout the rest of the novel. In the final chapter, Victor continues to ponder the "greater claims to attention" from those of his own species, contrasted with the feeling of being "bound towards [the monster], to assure, as far as was in my power, his happiness and well-being" (184). Two different modes of binding are at stake. Much as Victor attempts to gravitate toward the "greater claims" of those most like him, the claims to likeness remain increasingly strained; the monster effectively trumps them by insisting on the very obligations that Victor denies, punishing him for withdrawing what is "in [his] power" to give (184).

༺༻

I AM SUGGESTING THAT THE NOVEL is invested in something quite nearly the opposite of an aesthetic representation of political community based entirely on sympathy and nurture, as some critics have suggested.[5] More than that, however, I begin with *Frankenstein* in order to point to a prominent line of thinking in Romantic texts that contrasts sharply with a recent prevailing, and I would argue mistaken, attempt to conjoin the aesthetic of beauty alone with commitments to justice and other similarly desirable political ends. In the past ten years or so, numerous theorists and politically oriented critics have devoted significant attention to the way that beauty—because of its emphasis on proportion, symmetry, and mutuality—recommends social justice, reciprocity, or other politically redemptive structures and behaviors. Like *Frankenstein* itself, the present work argues strenuously against that claim. It urges a reconsideration of another kind of connection between aesthetics and social justice, one founded upon the sublime rather than upon the beautiful. I take Immanuel Kant's account of the sublime's privileged association with just societies as my starting point for that claim. And turning to still other texts from the Romantic period (including Samuel Taylor Coleridge and Charlotte Smith), I show how the sublime's perspective on justice, in contrast to beauty's emphasis on sameness and replication, foregrounds asymmetry, complaint, and disagreement.

I make these arguments in five chapters. The first two concentrate explicitly on aesthetic writings, analyzing the work of contemporary writing on beauty and figuring out why the aesthetic of beauty has become hegemonic in our time. In chapter 1, I show how the aesthetic of beauty has emerged as the most influential aesthetic discourse in the past ten years. What's surprising about this trend is not only that the category of the aesthetic has been significantly narrowed in relation to its historical breadth but also that many critics and theorists—I take the work of Elaine Scarry, Wendy Steiner, and Peter DeBolla as my primary examples—have invested beauty with an exalted social purpose. Like a much broader range of writing that I also address, from Dave Hickey's *The Invisible Dragon* (1993) to Roger Scruton's *Beauty* (2009), these writers claim that beauty's emphasis on symmetry, communicability, and shared emotion provides a model for ideal social relations, relations described in terms of justice or mutuality.

Arguments about the general political import of imaginative forms can be traced back at least as far as Plato's *Laws* (360 BC), wherein the duty of the poet is to shape verse that supports, without derivation, the "intrinsic rightness" of the state's laws.[6] The recent discourse of beauty and justice, however, is most vividly illuminated by its tendency to reproduce problems within the aesthetic of beauty that are acknowledged and explored in writing from the eighteenth century, which emphasizes but also constricts the role of beauty in the cultivation of political life. The social value of the beautiful, in accounts by the likes of Joshua Reynolds in his *Discourses* (1769–90), is less attributable to justice than to the disciplined acquisition of gentlemanly "elegance and refinement."[7] Current writing on beauty, repeating these constraints, can only view justice in terms of the recognition and repetition of uniform identities. This writing consists, I argue further, in a distinctive updating of eighteenth-century aesthetics for postmodern biopolitical purposes. Situated in an increasingly corporatized academic environment that has lost incentive for political dissent, the new discourse of beauty enforces a new form of cultural eugenics, making justice coextensive with the replication of subject-consumers.

Chapter 2 counters the discourse of beauty and its emphasis on replicated identities and looks back to another, very different discourse from the late eighteenth century: that of the sublime. Kant's discussion of the sublime in his *Critique of Judgment* (1790) conveys one of the period's most resonant accounts of an aesthetic standpoint on justice that he also traces out in his *Groundwork of the Metaphysics of Morals* (1785), the *Critique of Practical Reason* (1788), and *The Metaphysics of Morals* (1797). Moving in two directions simultaneously, the sublime's imaginative work is subjective and dissociative even while it provides a larger connection to others through its appeal to an assumed, but never enforced, use of reason. I turn also to the example of Byron's *Manfred* (1817) to show how Byron, like Kant, employs the sublime not as a simple model of just social arrangements but as an attempt to represent what I call a *reparative* perspective on justice. Manfred's sublime distance from conventional sources of authority provides an aesthetic vantage point that prepares the way for his pointed critique of capital punishment, which produces "other crimes / And greater criminals."[8] According to the perspective provided by the sublime in these works, argument, dissent, and modification take precedence over conformity and replication. The Romantic sublime, then—which I believe anticipates the arguments of John Rawls and some other political theorists—aesthetically conveys the possibility of a just inclusion of persons despite significant discrepancies in the weight and priority they give to different kinds of rights and resources.

From the very beginning, this book addresses the larger concern of how and why anyone thought that aesthetics had something to do with political organization to begin with. Critics and theorists, to be sure, have been comfortable with viewing the relationship between aesthetics and ideology for quite some time. Whether aesthetics is seen as inherently ideological (as in Terry Eagleton's *Ideology of the Aesthetic*, 1991) or as a utopian possibility that is not merely limited to ideology (as in Theodor W. Adorno's *Aesthetic Theory*, 1970), the question in these accounts has tended to revolve around the discussion of whether, or to what extent, aesthetics is or is not political.[9] My aim here, however, is to consider the actual work that aesthetics does. If Sheldon Wolin is right to say that all political theories depend to some degree on "imagination," which communicates the political "vision" of the theorist,[10] I address contending instances of possible roles for aesthetics in the pursuit of political justice in more particular terms. Whereas one tradition of thought (informed by the aesthetic of beauty) would make us believe that aesthetics provides a politically relevant experience because it provides a model for subjectivity, a far less well known countertradition (informed by the aesthetic of the sublime) frustrates that claim. The position I elaborate on here suggests that aesthetics provides a politically relevant experience because it conveys a sense that disagreement and dissent can be committed to, and bound by, a larger organization of relations. What is at issue, then, is not the role of aesthetics in political theory or political criticism but the tendency to view the political work of aesthetics solely in terms of picturing modes of being for the sake of replication. If what we do as critics or theorists is limited by the range of possibilities that we can imaginatively configure, then the urgency of the task of reexamining aesthetics can hardly be overestimated. The political-aesthetic logic of beauty does not merely facilitate literary and political theorizing; it controls and limits it.

Although this is not a book about contemporary theories of justice, its argument about the aesthetic component in thinking about moral and legal structures necessarily engages with some prominent perspectives. The oscillating structure of the sublime yields a connection with an account of justice based upon argument, complaint, and repair, an account that combines general rights with allowance for particular rights and seeks to make room for human desire and passion alongside reason. Although opponents of John Rawls's work routinely criticize his unyielding and unrealistic commitment to justice as impartiality, I suggest that many aspects of his work permit more allowances than his critics suggest, and many aspects of Kant's work that I emphasize can be traced forward to Rawls's. Moreover, I also stress aspects of this argument that coincide with other views, such as Stuart Hampshire's claim that "justice is conflict."[11]

At the most general level, following Kant's account, this perspective leads me implicitly to argue against the notion that the limitations of justice are "constitutive," therefore discrediting the attempt to seek out just social arrangements. Thus, although I have no reason to argue against Wendy Brown's or Mary Ann Glendon's claims that rights frequently leave larger structural inequalities intact,[12] the position outlined here (which is not far from Brown's or Glendon's) actually emphasizes the need to be vigilant in stipulating and enforcing new rights. At the same time, more particularly, I argue against two contending views of justice. Although thought about social justice obviously extends far beyond them, I concentrate on these views above all because they are of the most importance in politically motivated work in literary and cultural studies. One view, outlined in legal scholarship by the likes of Michael Sandel and in literary studies by critics such as Lynn Hunt, understands justice based on shared values and sympathetic identification.[13] Martha Nussbaum provides a compelling condensation of those perspectives in *Poetic Justice* (1995). She claims that the realist novel took a leading role in constructing "empathy and compassion in ways highly relevant to citizenship."[14] The second view, defended by the likes of Iris Marion Young in legal studies and pursued most consistently in the work of the contemporary philosopher Jacques

Derrida, bases justice on difference and a concern for otherness. Young urges a "positive sense of group difference" that would permit an "ideal of a heterogeneous public";[15] Derrida commits himself to justice to reckon with difference not merely at the level of groups or individuals but within individuals themselves. The respect for "singularity," he writes, makes justice "incalculable, it requires us to calculate with the incalculable."[16]

The first view, with its emphasis on a sense of social structure that reaches deeply into shared consciousness, makes it hard to see how opposed standpoints could coexist within the same framework; the second, with its emphasis on and celebration of difference, makes it hard to see what actual impact difference or otherness might have on a shared framework of social cooperation. The position that I associate with Kant's work and that I connect to other Romantic texts creates possibility for revision in order to secure greater economic and political opportunities for participants in a society. Unlike in justice as sympathy, these rights are the result of contending viewpoints; unlike in justice as recognized difference, differences are relevant precisely insofar as they impact a structure that accommodates those contending viewpoints. In that regard, the arguments I make here coincide with Michael Ignatieff's suggestion that "at best rights create a common framework, a common set of reference points that can assist parties in conflict to deliberate together."[17]

My argument goes beyond the initial concern with writing on beauty. The first two chapters together argue that writing on beauty occupies a primary place in today's broader intellectual landscape. Young's claims that norms of aesthetic ugliness lead to political "aversion" and exclusion and Judith Halberstam's corresponding urgent call for a transformative "transgender aesthetic" only begin to hint at the political-aesthetic stakes of the work I address here, even when those stakes are not openly acknowledged.[18] The next two chapters show how politically inflected theory of the last decade envisions answers to problems of social justice almost exclusively within the aesthetic mode of the beautiful, in which politics is conceived according to replicable and imitable models for human thought and action. Chapter 3 discusses two strands of critical theory—queer theory and cosmopolitan theory. I take both to be modes of postmodern critical analysis that often depend explicitly upon the logic of beauty. Despite their great differences, I show how their assumptions are profoundly compatible. Queer theory (in the work of Eve Sedgwick and Michael Warner, which has influenced a range of more recent texts) attempts to build general political positions from particular experiences. Cosmopolitan theory (in the work of Amartya Sen and Kwame Anthony Appiah, among others) infers particular experience from general principles and relationships. I show how they address problems of social justice by proposing a normative formation for individual political subjects; it is no coincidence that the political-aesthetic commitments of these works are conveyed by making literary characters, or the turns of literary narrative, available for mimetic replication at the level of individual queer or cosmopolitan subjects. I end the chapter by discussing two conversation poems by Samuel Taylor Coleridge that frame a different response to the issues raised in the theoretical texts. Rather than mapping individuals and communities onto each other, Coleridge reimagines the structure of those relationships. In "The Nightingale" (1798), the speaker estranges those with whom he is intimately related; in "Fears in Solitude" (1798), he does something like the reverse, drawing into closer contact those who seem most remote from him. The poems marshal their aesthetic forces to imagine revised social obligations and to critique customary sympathetic bonds.

Coleridge provides one instance of how a range of Romantic writings beyond Kant's work engage questions of aesthetics with questions of justice. While Kant introduces some of the claims that I carry forward in the rest of the book, I use his work mainly for its philosophical clarity. I have little stake in launching a claim about the actual influence of his work on the other writers I discuss, even though René Wellek long ago showed how widely translated, published, and discussed Kant's work was for an English audience by the last decade of the nineteenth century and how clearly it influenced some strains of Coleridge's thought.[19] Such a strong claim about influence hardly seems essential, since the connection between justice and the sublime was made by many others besides Kant. In his *Enquiry Concerning Political Justice* (1793) William Godwin speaks frequently of the relationship I study. "The man who vigilantly conforms his affections to the standard of justice," he writes, is filled with "the sublime emotions of tranquility."[20] Claude-Adrien Helvétius, who exerted a powerful influence on Godwin and other political theorists of the day, speaks of the just magistrate as one inspired by "sublime ideas" to seek the "general good" of a people.[21] Mary Wollstonecraft's treatise on the French Revolution refers to the "sublime theories" of religious toleration and civil liberty;[22] John Penn's *Further Thoughts on the Present State of Public Opinion* (1800) relates the aesthetic of the sublime to a sense of desert, "a principled resistance to oppression," a resistance to tyrannical declarations of war combined with a commitment to the "restraints of law" (among a host of other moral and social virtues).[23] The connecting thread in all of these instances—I emphasize general connections to Kant despite important distinctions among these accounts—is not to be found simply in the rhetorical consistency of describing political commitments as sublime. Rather, the aesthetic of the sublime is repeatedly associated with a commitment to a position of complaint or dissent coupled with a commitment to broader social cooperation and interaction.

Still further, though, the reparative standpoint on juridical law, and its association with the aesthetic of the sublime, can be found in a number of Romantic writers, whose works allow me to explore different dimensions of the argument that I make in the first two chapters. I address these issues as they arise primarily in Romantic lyric poems and occasionally in works that, like *Frankenstein*, are passionately indebted to lyric poetry. As in the works on philosophical aesthetics that I analyze in these pages, I consider moments of the sublime to be rendered nowhere more vividly than in lyric poems. But I do not point to the sublime in lyric poems merely because poems provide instances of an aesthetic mode; indeed, much of what I suggest is that that the poems do not serve as imitable or repeatable examples. Instead, the lyric poems I examine shift attention from differentiated internal states to external addressees and still larger patterns of sociality; they frame the sublime transport between internal meditation and external connection, dramatizing a specific kind of relationality without replication.[24]

By concentrating steadily on the sublime in Romantic works, I do not mean to obscure the fact that Romantic writers from Wordsworth to Keats were indeed interested in the aesthetic of *beauty* and used that term frequently in their writing. I claim, however, that in many respects the political-aesthetic significance of the sublime, as in *Frankenstein*, frequently exerts a critical pressure on the aesthetic of beauty. Still more—the final chapter provides an example with a reading of Shelley—this critical pressure often results in a notion of beauty, important as the word is in the Romantic lexicon, that (as some critics have noted before) pushes beauty itself closer to the dissenting aesthetic of the sublime. The claims I make in that closing argument could easily be extended, say, to Keats's account of beauty in "Sleep and Poetry" (1816), where beauty turns inside out: the poet's "strange influence," yielding an equally "strange / Journey" in thought and rhyme, dissents against and revises the beauty he receives from tradition.[25] While acknowledging beauty's presence in Romantic texts and its proximity to the discourse of the sublime, then, I nevertheless insist on the distinctiveness of the sublime's countervailing influence, because it emphasizes and accentuates the position of radical disagreement while retaining a notion of (shared) reflective judgment.[26] Thus, while it is always possible to show how intimately related the sublime and the beautiful are, and while this is an argument that I wouldn't disagree with, I would still insist that we miss a crucial opportunity if we ignore the sublime's distinctive contribution to political-aesthetic thought.

Chapter 4 continues to argue that without this critical pressure the political limitations of much current critical theory can be linked to their dependence on a restricted form of imagining or representing the political through the aesthetic of beauty. I understand the postmodern discourse of beauty in chapter 1 as the preeminent discourse of biopolitics because of its emphasis on modeling appropriate identities restricted along the axes of race, nationality, and sexuality. Chapter 4, moving in a complementary direction, shows how even biopolitical *critique* (from Giorgio Agamben to Slavoj Žižek) continues to be dominated by the aesthetic of beauty. Strangely, whereas many intertwined aesthetic and political philosophies of the eighteenth century provide a blueprint for the biopolitical connection between individual rights and national belonging, the critique of biopolitical regimes ends up repeating the problems of the biopolitical predicament itself. I turn to Charlotte Smith's poem *Beachy Head* (1807) to give an alternative view of the connection between aesthetics, nations, and rights. While the poem pays homage to traditional English "Norman Yoke" ideology, it formally and rhetorically unsettles that homage; its protective standpoint on slaves, solitaries, and shipwrecked foreigners asserts rights for others in the absence of social, national, or racial belonging.

Shifting back and forth from the aesthetics of contemporary political theory to the aesthetics of Romantic writing, this book engages not only with current trends in political theory and literary criticism but also, even more specifically, with the characterization of Romanticism subtly embedded within those trends. Although my insistence on the relevance of Romanticism to contemporary issues may at first seem eccentric, my argument in a sense repeats a backward glance within political theory itself, which—from Hannah Arendt to Giorgio Agamben—has tended to see Romanticism as an inaugural moment in the history of exclusionary forms of nationalism and other similarly conservative ideologies.[27] The present work does much to confirm the general importance of the Romantic age, while making an altogether different point about how this turning point contained an impulse toward critique within itself.

Still more, this book, even while it launches its principal polemic with regard to the political and aesthetic theories of the present day, makes consistent interventions in the interpretation of Romantic texts themselves. While exposing the priority of beauty in recent critical theory, and while looking at a contrasting logic in Romantic writing, I frequently put myself at odds with prominent critical accounts of the period that tend to be implicitly or explicitly invested in associating Romanticism with a somewhat conservative form of political aesthetics. Theresa Kelley's *Wordsworth's Revisionary Aesthetics* (1988) speaks consistently of the tendency of Wordsworth's poetry to privilege the beautiful as a means of resolution and control over the energies of the sublime.[28] Jon Mee's *Romanticism, Enthusiasm, and Regulation* (2003) shifts the aesthetic to a more obviously political register to show how Romanticism's normative poetics are committed to an exclusion of "innovating attempts to transform the world."[29] More recently, Denise Gigante's *Life: Organic Form and Romanticism* (2009) registers complete agreement with the current theoretical interest in beauty in that she identifies Romanticism across the disciplines of science and poetry with a "sense of beauty defined scientifically as life—and life defined aesthetically as beauty." In broad agreement with Mee, she argues that the beautiful life forms at the center of her study regularly exclude monstrous or threatening ones.[30] In many ways, while contrasting with these important and prominent accounts, my emphasis generally agrees with Orrin Wang's troubling of the tendency in criticism of the Romantic period to invest itself in "sobriety," that is, to invest itself in showing how texts of the period tame imagination and enthusiasm within a dialectical progression to higher knowledge and maturity.[31]

The fifth and concluding chapter examines the rights of animals in the Romantic age, showing how a crucial tension arises within the privileged relationship (outlined in the previous three chapters) between the sublime and social justice. I show how writers such as Coleridge and Shelley imagine a world ordered according to a sublime form or spirit that rules all human and animal beings regardless of similarities or differences among those beings. At the same time, however, the necessary connection between juridical forms and dissent or complaint underlines the importance of a common language that is rarely found or posited between nonhuman and human animals. I thus show how important it is throughout the eighteenth and nineteenth centuries to accompany notions of sublime political aesthetics with more sympathetic views of nonhuman animals, views that emphasize the similarities between human and animal being. From Anna Barbauld in "The Mouse's Petition" (1773) to Sarah Trimmer in *Fabulous Histories* (1786), writers inevitably view the capabilities of animals in terms of their adherence to the logic of beauty, that is, in terms of their anthropomorphic resemblance to humans in their actions and affiliations. The tension between these perspectives informs debates about animal rights to this very day. For if a commitment to utterly independent animal flourishing characterizes the work of some theorists of animal rights (e.g., Nussbaum), nonetheless an inevitable suspicion remains that such rights can only be understood in terms of "anthropomorphic" human sympathy. And according to that latter view, animal being (as in Akira Lippit's work) needs to be "remembered" in order to assure a proper commitment to their well-being. In closing, I show how for two hundred years the discussion of animal rights has foundered over a constitutive tension between abstract rights without consistent foundation and sympathetic understanding without consistent legal commitment. In its very distinction from other forms of (human) animal rights, it underlines the urgency of adopting a new mode of aesthetics for envisioning human justice even while it poses a distinctive and profound challenge to it.

CHAPTER 1

Beautiful People

It would be both right and wrong to say that aesthetics has returned as a subject of urgent scholarly inquiry since the early 1990s. It would be right in the sense that recent critics—Peter de Bolla, Denis Donoghue, Umberto Eco, Elaine Scarry, and Wendy Steiner, to mention a few of the most notable ones—have taken an interest in what might be defined broadly as aesthetic pleasure. That interest is explicitly formulated as a return to, or a return *of*, a way of experiencing art or nature that has been lost, forgotten, or suppressed. It would be wrong, though, in the sense that such recent work actually encourages a peculiar blindness to the terms of the discussion in which it ostensibly participates. Renewed commitments to defining and defending aesthetic pleasure center mainly on the question of what constitutes a certain restricted type of pleasure, namely, the experience of *beauty* in art or nature; they therefore eschew other familiar but related categories of evaluation, such as the sublime or the picturesque. This narrowing of attention may be interesting in its own right, but more surprising is the tendency among the same writers to favor beauty primarily because of its social or political relevance. With the spirit of having made a new discovery, writers on the subject have tended to claim that the experience of beauty is unique because it encourages some version of mutuality, equality, or justice among persons.

I suggest that these recent accounts, both in their narrowed aesthetic claims and in their extended dimensions, continue to be bound up with problems they refuse to acknowledge: they continue to be conditioned by the same normative definitions of persons and their pleasures that have been attached to the discourse of beauty at least since the eighteenth century. (By *normative* I mean that states of mind and body are attached not only to explicit prescriptions but also to an implied or unspoken social value of those states.) My argument proceeds in four parts. In the first three, I consider the general shape of these current analyses—and defenses—of the experience of beauty. I then go on to suggest that the discourse of beauty in its contemporary incarnation is less effective at accomplishing its stated redemptive mission than at rehabilitating a time-honored category for rather different purposes. It demonstrates and protects the new terrain of the postmodern public intellectual, a trained professor in the art of taste who defends his or her position within and outside the academy by packaging cultivated experiences for a wide readership.

Recognizing Beauty

Many of the recently published works on beauty approvingly include some version of the announcement that "beauty is back."[1] The nearly obligatory gesture, especially in this particular phrasing, suggests not that beauty has returned because we have returned to it as the result of logical argument but that it (or in at least one instance she) has returned as a personified figure that we should happily welcome in the form of articles, books, exhibits, and conferences dedicated to the subject. The expression "beauty is back," then, is not simply an attractive rhetorical gesture; it conveys at least one way in which beauty's return—better understood as the return of certain scholars to the question of beauty—surreptitiously builds an account of persons and interpersonal relations into its most basic intellectual assumptions. Indeed, the return of beauty is inseparable from some commitment, variously described, to beauty's social impact. Its return is the occasion not only to feel stirred once again by a particular pleasure long known as aesthetic but also to heal troubled social relations by heeding beauty's forgotten but oddly familiar call.

Although I refer occasionally to the wider range of writing that participates in this ongoing trend, my focus is mainly on three of the more complex and interesting works among them, Elaine Scarry's *On Beauty and Being Just* (1999), Wendy Steiner's *Venus in Exile* (2001), and Peter de Bolla's *Art Matters* (2001). In many ways, the treatments differ radically and seem to resist comparison. Scarry's is in the form of a manifesto, for instance, whereas Steiner's is in the form of a history; Steiner sees beauty as an embodied personal (usually female) presence in art, whereas de Bolla sees it as a varied set of affective responses to art. But these accounts actually share important features that help to expose a set of critical protocols animating the much wider and still proliferating range of politically inflected writing on beauty. The three works are exemplary in their commitment to linking the aesthetic of beauty and social justice, as well as in their tailoring of social justice to imperatives emanating from the popular media marketplace, in which new writing on beauty so shrewdly asserts itself.

One of the central assertions in Scarry's book is that objects and persons that we consider to be beautiful tend to be symmetrical and therefore exemplify the balance and proportion for which we strive in just social arrangements. A summary of this kind, though, might not only oversimplify the argument but also obscure its important initial claims that beauty is a highly particular experience—despite the capability for that experience to be generalized among different objects of attention.[2] Early on, Scarry repeatedly describes our sense of beauty as something that cannot be easily repeated: "beauty always takes place in the particular" (18), it is "unprecedented" (23), and so on. In fact, it is so particular that accounts of the beautiful become accounts of unique autobiographical experiences. When the author muses at length about admiring an owl "stationed in the fronds" of a palm tree (20), her point is ostensibly not to offer it as a model for anyone else but simply to claim that the experience occurred for one person in one place at one time.

Such a claim seems to be reinforced by the suggestion that beauty's "decentering" power can bring us into a radically different world (112), as if beautiful entities not only adhere to their own separate rules and standards but also resist our attempts to identify what those rules and standards might be. This is a common observation in recent accounts of beauty, launched with pointed urgency in order to separate beauty from traditional, presumably overly theoretical accounts of "the beautiful," which constrain our appreciation of objects. To speak of the beautiful is to violate beauty's claims to particularity, to nonreplicability.

But later in the argument, Scarry compromises this direction and indeed greatly simplifies it, solving the mystery of what binds together all these experiences of beauty. "Symmetry," she writes, is "the single most enduringly recognized attribute" of beautiful objects and persons (96). This disambiguation is crucial: beauty is "recognized," implying that we are not accidentally struck by objects but cognize them through their conformity to a notion of symmetry, of constituent parts that balance or mirror one another. *Symmetry* is defined in the *Oxford English Dictionary* by terms most often emphasizing resemblance rather than difference—*regularity, congruity, agreement,* and *exact correspondence*.[3] We hardly need to look there, though, since the examples furnished here all demonstrate these meanings. The skin to be admired on a body is a "smooth surface" without interruptions or excrescences; a flower is beautiful because it has petals that are identical in various positions (100–101). In retrospect, the more mysterious beauty of objects and persons described earlier in the text—from young boys and redbud trees to vases and poems—seems considerably less mysterious, capable of being understood as a kind of pattern recognition guided by a more or less simple concept.

This criterion—symmetry as a replication of similar parts—comes to seem all the more important once Scarry makes beauty an analogy for just social arrangements. She makes no sweeping claim for beauty as a cause for fairness or justice, but it is the concretely available instance of the balance found in just institutions and policies: it is said to make "manifest" or "sensorially visible" what could plausibly serve as a model for justice, even if the model is not put into practice (101). There is something inescapably *social* about beauty in Scarry's account, primarily because of the impulse toward the "distributional" that she attributes to it (80). Distribution is described in a number of ways, but most prominent is the emphasis on copying and resemblance: "beauty," we are told, "prompts a copy of itself" (4). Once perceived "involuntarily" by a beholder, beauty is "voluntarily extended" with the "same perceptions" at work in the original experience (81). While beauty urges us to make new things, those new things must resemble something already in existence, whose beauty, we now see, is dependent upon its symmetry. Thus we are urged to seek out and produce copies of beautiful objects and persons even where and when they may not be immediately visible.

If there is any doubt about the social relevance of this impulse, by Scarry's incessant analogies between making art—the copying of beauty, that is—and bringing infants into the world through heterosexual reproduction (4, 46, 71, 90) will put that doubt to rest. Her more open analogy between beauty and justice exists alongside a far less explicit but consistent emphasis on generation. Even the Tanner Lectures at Yale, from which Scarry's book was adapted, are credited with admirably "wishing to bring new lectures . . . into the world" (133). The reproductive model is of course a traditional one, familiar to us in various permutations from Shakespeare to Hume to Mary Shelley and beyond. But the use of this tradition enforces a particular view of what a tradition as such might actually mean for us. Although it's certainly true that Scarry occasionally makes discrete references to the love between boys and men in Greek culture, they have nothing like the paradigmatic value of heterosexual reproduction. We are informed simply as a matter of social fact that people seek "mates that they choose to love" and that "their children" appear as the biological instance of beauty's distribution in the world (109). Heterosexual coupling and reproductive sexuality thus demonstrate not beauty itself (although presumably the urge to reproduce would be much less urgent for the less beautiful) but the principle of distribution, through which beauty is brought into the world. The inevitable consequence of this reasoning for aesthetics is that even while beauty at some points seems to recommend a "standard of care" for a wider range of things and persons (66), it is significantly straitjacketed by the biological analogy into a standard of care applicable only to members of a group that more or less resemble one another.

It might be said that the earlier, apparently whimsical observations about palm trees coincide with this logic. For it ultimately becomes clear that Scarry is the latest scion of a cultural legacy, from Homer to Hopkins, that has also appreciated them; to find palms beautiful is not only to be struck by them but also to realize and fortify one's armorial bearings in an honorable lineage (21–22, 49).[4] Making the distribution of beauty look like a version of biological heredity, furthermore, is inseparable from Scarry's concern with future generations, who we supposedly hope will love beauty the way we do and will therefore cast a look of appreciative recognition upon us as "beauty-loving" as well (118). The point is not simply that we hope future populations will find happiness, in other words. We wish upon them specific resources—including Vermeers and forests—for feeling pleasure in ways that resemble our own (123, 124). Those resources have been decided by the taste—a "vote"—of those that preceded our own choices (123), and because of that vote, and our commitment to uphold its outcome, we attempt to preserve those resources far into the future (123). It may be true, then, that "self-interest," as Scarry argues, is not served by beauty (123). But this is because self-interest has been traded for social interest, an interest in extending the beauty of populations through biological reproduction and in extending the life of beautiful objects by ensuring their preservation for future beautiful people.

Whatever is social about beauty, though, is also deemed to be not simply social—not simply any model for relations between people—but actually just.[5] The connection is made at a rhetorical level by linking the two connotations of the word *fair*. To be "fair" is to be both beautiful and equitable—thus *fair* constitutes "a two-part cognitive event" linking beautiful or fair objects to just or fair social arrangements (92). Further, the relationship depends upon the logical importance of symmetry in both aesthetic and legal realms: if symmetry is the most commonly recognized attribute among beautiful things and persons, it is also connected to "equality" under the law, or what John Rawls identifies as "a symmetry of everyone's relations to each other" (qtd. in Scarry 93).

Surely the most provocative aspect of the shift from beauty to justice is the nearly perfectly redundant movement from symmetry among individuals to symmetry in social arrangements. For if beauty appears to be social insofar as it inspires a repetition of sameness, the need to produce just institutions appears to be virtually eliminated or at least much less urgent. Rawls, repeatedly (and sometimes problematically) invoked in this argument, takes as his guiding assumption that the challenge of achieving social justice in the present day—and at least since the eighteenth century—consists in acknowledging the disagreement in ethnic, sexual, and religious backgrounds or preferences among participants in political communities. I address this aspect of Rawls's argument later, but for now it will suffice to say that the "conflict of interests" that Rawls and many other political theorists take to be fundamental in our political landscape is made absent here.[6]

I am saying that the basic recognition of conflicting orientations is "made" absent because Scarry extends beauty's emphasis on homogeneity at the level of empirical perception to an emphasis on homogeneity at the level of social organization. Nowhere in the argument is this demonstrated more clearly than in one of the text's most specific and vivid renderings of justice: the Athenian trireme, propelled by 170 oarsmen "generally from the lower classes," rhythmically striking the water "in time with the pipeman's flute" (104). With its symmetrical structure and its oarsmen who were "full citizens," the trireme was in "almost complete correspondence" with Athenian democracy (104). The example on one level reveals the persistence with which Scarry's view of justice depends upon internal replication, upon multiplying similar individuals with similar tasks. What's almost too obvious is that those similar Athenians embody the other, unspoken meaning of *fair*: light- or white-skinned. On another, less obvious but equally interesting level, the example makes democracy stand for justice, collapsing politics and law, democratic representation and equality. Surely it could be faulted for this. But the collapse, which essentially suggests that justice includes no one outside the author's own political heritage, no one outside a Western democratic tradition that resembles her own, is perfectly in line with the logic I've discussed so far. Justice is imagined here on the model of a political culture passed on from parent to child; it extends the right of inclusion to repetitions of identities, to members of the same family.

Beauty's Look

Discussions of beauty are seldom able to ignore the influential definitions that Immanuel Kant supplied for it, and an explicit treatment of his work is one important link between Scarry's work and Steiner's *Venus Exiled*. For Scarry, Kant stands as the exemplar of a philosophical tradition in which the sublime became an interloper in beauty's domain. The very idea of the sublime introduced artificial divisions between the "principled, noble, righteous" character of the sublime and the "compassionate and good-hearted" character of the beautiful (84). *On Beauty and Being Just* responds by recovering the territory lost to the sublime; beauty thus wins back a higher "moral" and "metaphysical" value that Kant had seemed to take away from it (86). Steiner does something different: the Kant she argues against is wrong precisely because he is too metaphysical.[7] Quoting Tobin Siebers's account of the *Critique of Judgment*, she asserts that for Kant the beautiful in art is an "analogue to freedom"; it is a "vivid symbolization of autonomy" and thus only provides the possibility for a "beautiful we," a community held together by the "common autonomy of its members" in "glorious separation" from one another.[8] The "disinterested interest" in the beautiful that is quintessentially Kantian, and that Scarry frequently attempts to defend, is written off in Steiner's argument as a "total failure, in which expert and layman, avant-garde and bourgeoisie, man and woman, have lost all mutuality" (92–93).

Steiner's project is sympathetic to Scarry's connection between beauty and justice. As the previous quotation suggests, Steiner's aim in supporting beauty is to enhance the "mutuality" in aesthetic experience between various groups marked in various ways, at least between different classes and different genders. Beauty, writes Steiner, is an "interactive experience" that "provokes desire and love and a striving for equality" (11).[9] However, her careful avoidance of a word like *justice*, with its philosophical baggage, signals a different route toward a related goal. Beauty does not need to be redefined as much as it needs to be reappreciated. Despite the argument against Kant, the more consistent suggestion here is that no one was ever really wrong about what beauty is; they were simply wrong to reject or marginalize it in their quest for aesthetic purity or abstraction.

It thus turns out that the multiple and contradictory ways in which eighteenth-century aesthetics describes beauty as feminine—soft, seductive, ornamental, and so on—are a fundamental resource for Steiner's polemic. The bundling of a gendered term with these multiple images and evaluations, that is, allows the figure of woman in art to function as a "symbol of beauty" long established by the nineteenth century. In fact, so persistent is the conflation between woman and the wider subject matter of art generally that the presence of woman in art is virtually coextensive with the definition of art itself (34–35). Steiner's real interest, however, is in the "exile" of beauty from modern art, which means the exile of woman; her traditional implication in "ornament, charm, and gratification" makes her inappropriate for what twentieth-century artists consider to be "a pure aesthetic experience" (29). In their efforts to make their art more "sublime," modern artists push the female figure to the margins, identifying her with everything contingent, sensual, or merely pleasing—in short, everything that is not art (35).[10]

In one sense, then, the female figure in art is highly metaphorical: it stands for a range of other representations (of flowers, say, or animals, or landscapes) conventionally considered beautiful. Without that figurative value, it would be hard to understand how Steiner could see woman as the essential and defining element rejected by modernists, rather than just one subject among many. This would be interesting enough, since it appears as though one could read a convention of exclusion not as a definition to be overcome but rather as a blueprint for future interpretation. But there is more. For in another sense, *Venus Exiled* simultaneously insists on viewing a female figure not merely as an abstract representation of art but as a representation of women *outside* art. "Of course, a painting is not a person," Steiner warns, but her argument depends at many moments upon the equivalency that it rejects as apparently too naïve (92). Otherwise, it would be impossible for us to talk about the degree to which a subject's "femininity" could be "swamped by other factors" in art (xvi), the degree to which women are subordinated, that is, to the modernist's obsession with "color, texture, scale, and line" (62).

More precisely, though, this logic encourages us to see woman in art not only as an abstract symbol of beauty, and not even as a stereotyped image, but as a more or less convincing approximation of what real women are, act like, and look like. Our sense of what a real woman is allows us to see how a representation both is and is not like a woman outside of the work; we are able to distinguish between the represented woman and "other factors" separable from her. It is only by these means that Steiner can identify a woman *as* woman versus woman as a formalist fantasy of "sanitized geometry" (48), as a deformed body with "a hundred tits" (50), as an "African fetish object" (52), or as any number of things that a woman cannot, must not, be. What is required in the viewing of art is an attention both to how woman is represented in it and also to the reality of that woman, the "thought of the female model as a flesh-and-blood person subject to moral and existential vicissitudes" (79).

This important move clarifies exactly what Steiner means when she refers to art's power to communicate. (The idea receives further elaboration in Steiner's *The Real Real Thing* [2010], on the power of models in art to incite "mutuality, reciprocity, and egalitarian justice.")[11] Art communicates by representing a "flesh-and-blood person," a person who appears not simply as an object to be viewed but as the most vivid rendering possible of a psychological subject pressured by "moral and existential vicissitudes." One might wonder why anyone needs art at all. It might seem that if art should aspire to communicate on the model of flesh-and-blood persons, a painting would get in the way. But this does not entirely capture the scope of Steiner's argument, which makes the very idea of a real woman dependent upon a standard produced, at least in part, by art itself, since art itself renders an appropriately communicative subject. The flesh-and-blood person to whom she refers is a person with certain qualities that condition the kind of "mutuality" she is thinking of.

Thus in her recurring discussion of Eduard Manet's celebrated *Olympia* (1863)—we may compare its paradigmatic importance with that of Scarry's trireme—it becomes clear that mutuality depends not simply upon a communication between persons but upon a specific kind of look from a specific kind of body. The novelty of Steiner's reading of the painting resides in her impressive disavowal of a conventional account of its implied male viewer, as an objectifying male consumer of the prostitute's body and therefore an objectifying (male) consumer of the representation of that body. Rather than objectify that body, Steiner reads against formal and historical cues to grant it the status of a subject, one that looks back at the viewer in order to confirm a "blatant acknowledgement" of art's "communicative ideal" (91).

If at first it seems that the account opens the door to lesbian desire, Steiner closes it not only by minimizing the importance of her own gender but also by founding such an ideal upon a much more generalized "human intersubjectivity" (94). At the same time, though, the communicative ideal imagined here—as generous as it may initially seem—suffers significant constraint from other conditions of communicability. Communication in art, for Steiner, means communication between persons, which means a communication between direct expressions from bodies that more or less resemble the author's own. Nowhere is this more obvious than in the way Steiner extends her view of communicability only to the white woman in Manet's painting, ultimately reserving little comment for the black maid. She only casually acknowledges the maid's presence and clarifies in a footnote (one that puts race in exile to avoid upsetting the general claim about communicative ideals) that "the painting must strike us as racist in setting off Olympia's beauty against a black servant" (257n). Racism is central rather than marginal here, however, at least in Steiner's account of the work. For even though it is impossible to see the white figure in the painting as anything other than an object (or subject) constructed for us as beautiful, it is also impossible to see that notion of beauty as anything other than racialized.[12] If beauty involves communication, it is communication that cannot involve the black woman, the silent intermediary or messenger between the model and the absent (implicitly white) viewer, whether that viewer is a male client treating Olympia as an object or a professional critic treating her as a flesh-and-blood subject.

Beauty's Attitude

In their accounts of the social importance of beauty, Scarry and Steiner come from different directions but then converge. In one account, beautiful symmetries require specific identities; in the other, beautiful specific identities form the basis for larger symmetries. In both, the mutuality or equality that might characterize the relations between bodies ends up looking like a communication between two identical parties; the redemptive power of beauty thus becomes restricted to repetitions of sameness and coordinating exclusions of difference. Peter de Bolla, in *Art Matters*, adopts a position that might seem to avoid these alternatives, since at many points he takes time to reject accounts of aesthetic experience that depend upon either a normative account of beautiful objects (the eventual point of Scarry's argument) or a normative account of the person who views them (the starting point of Steiner's position).[13] Instead, the experience of beauty—described as an "aesthetic response" (27) of mute wonder elicited by works of art—occurs somewhere between object and subject: we neither "have" such an experience nor "make" it (14), since it is a feeling simultaneously produced by works of art and felt as a private affect "knowable only to me" (15).

De Bolla's book, because it ranges so widely in its attempt to describe this "unknown or unknowable" feeling, may appear to differ in its aims from Scarry's and Steiner's explicit interest in defining beauty (14). Nevertheless, de Bolla himself repeatedly calls upon beauty as a way of summarizing the qualities in art that inspire the feeling toward which he gestures. In his three central examples, Barnett Newman's paintings possess the "elemental beauty" characteristic of all "timeless" works of art (28); Glenn Gould's performances of Bach are "shimmeringly beautiful" (93); and Wordsworth's poetry has a "childlike beauty" (105). And these expressions only begin to imply the more profound way in which his account—in both its explicit aesthetic and its implicit political claims—is thoroughly consistent with recent writing that more obviously addresses the aesthetic of beauty.[14]

According to de Bolla, aesthetic responses properly understood can only be found in art, and not in nature (8–9). While he distances himself from Steiner's mode of viewing beauty as a specific figure in art with a purely personal connection to the beholder (9–10), he also has little interest in Scarry's mode of viewing beauty in terms of symmetrically organized objects. Still, the particular way in which he attempts to define the aesthetic in terms of art's intimate connection to the beholder leads to the true alignment with the positions from which he might appear to differ. De Bolla consistently identifies the "aesthetic" with an experience understood as "affective" (3), but he also turns to art because it (unlike nature) provides an appropriate model for that human affect. While not simply a concept, that is, art withholds its absolute truth, while inducing a replicable "sense of wonder" (16). Works of art are thus saturated with reserves of knowledge so deep that any encounter with them must continually prompt the author to ask what hidden reserves of knowledge are contained in the work—"What does the poem know?" he asks when reading Wordsworth (126)—but then to insist that the question cannot be answered. Not being able to answer the question turns out to be more than an epistemological barrier; it is a kind of aesthetic gain, since (in what seems like an explicit recapitulation of the pathetic fallacy) the inaccessible or obscured knowledge embodies and recommends a replicable attitude about that knowledge: a "mutism" (19), "sensitivity" (43), or "serenity" (47), in short, a state of attention that is neither too detached nor too inquisitive. And thus works of art, having not only knowledge but also an attitude about their knowledge, finally offer themselves up as if they were living beings requiring a specific form of "accommodation" from the viewer in order to achieve a requisite level of "intima[cy]" with themselves (24–25). A work of art, de Bolla writes, "teaches us how to approach it. The image, to some extent, teaches us how to look, the music how to listen, the poem how to read" (26). And de Bolla invests art even more generally with a "power to prompt us to share experiences, worlds, beliefs, and differences" (15), reminding us of the incitements to justice that are found throughout the treatments of beauty by Scarry and Steiner.

Because of this relationship between art and beholder—one in which a work of art teaches a viewer not only how to treat the artwork but also how to teach others—the act of "witnessing" art is an experience that is "specific" and "unique"(27, 139). But it is also a moment of shared affective connection, in which there is a sense of reconciliation or accommodation between the two. Further, beyond this intimacy, the experience of witnessing art, as he describes it in his discussion of the paintings of Barnett Newman, is "involving and inclusive" (40) in a way that proceeds to inflect a definition of "public space" (38). "Different subjects with different expectations, aims, and objectives" (35) occupy that public space because of their embrace within a single "regime of looking" (36). An intimate encounter, in other words, miniaturizes, in its replication of affect, a larger "social and shareable" experience in which the publicness of a public is defined precisely in terms of a shared sense of wonder or devotion (40). The individual body, in its encounter with an artwork, simultaneously becomes a "social body" (41), since individual and social mirror each other.

Both the logic and the consequences of de Bolla's argument emerge with particular clarity in the commentary on the pianist Glenn Gould's 1981 recording of Johann Sebastian Bach's *Goldberg Variations* (1741), since the appreciation of art becomes inseparable from an appreciation of a replicable attitude prompted by reminders of the performer's physicality in that recording. By gravitating toward specific human attributes embedded in the music's performance, in other words, de Bolla transforms performance into an occasion to recommend an experience—"a particular way of being" (90)—to be shared by others. Gould's audible signatures—heavy breathing, muttering, singing faintly heard in the background of his recordings—are neither impurities to be ignored nor eccentricities to be fondly admired. That is, they are not to be considered as elements to be included in or excluded from an account of form; rather, they are directions to inherit Gould's own embodied practices of attention. We listen to Gould not in order to listen to Bach but in order to be like Gould, approximating his "extraordinary musical intelligence" as we listen to Bach as Gould plays him (77). Listening to Gould listen to and play Bach, furthermore, requires us not merely to understand a particular person's perspective but to occupy a replicable "ecstatic" psychological formation (80). That formation is precisely what's required when we view a painting by Newman or read a poem by Wordsworth. We don't need someone to interpret the painting or read the poem, however, because such works already manifest or imply the recognizable human attributes audible in Gould's recordings and also prompt, with their "low, whispering voice" (28), a corresponding tranquil attitude of "wonder" in readers (87). Readers, viewers, or auditors model themselves collectively after objects of aesthetic appreciation, which are like people themselves in their embodiment and encouragement of identical attitudes.

The Biopolitics of Beauty

By considering these recent important works by Newman, Gould, and Wordsworth, I do not mean to imply that such accounts of the beautiful are merely prejudicial on the basis of race, class, gender, and so forth. I do not mean to imply that they should become more inclusive by accepting a greater diversity of objects or persons as beautiful. This is what Isobel Armstrong wants when she calls for a more "populist" aesthetics redescribed within the domain of "ordinary" experience.[15] And this is also the kind of response adopted by disability studies; for Siebers, for instance, "disability aesthetics embraces beauty that seems by traditional standards to be broken."[16] Although I do not disagree with the motivations behind these claims, I would instead suggest that the current engagement with the discourse of beauty *requires* the restrictions and inclusions that I ascribe to them. Such restrictions and inclusions are not problems with any specific rendering of the beautiful; they both demonstrate and argue for beauty's problematic internal logic.

It's hardly surprising that we could turn virtually anywhere in the important recent work on aesthetics and find that the return of beauty is inseparable from an emphasis on the importance of shared identity. The three recent works discussed above map out a terrain on which virtually the entire field of recent work on aesthetics can be located. For instance, Dave Hickey's *The Invisible Dragon* (1993), an early and influential example of the trend I'm describing, understands beauty as a purified "contractual alliance" with an image; the beautiful in art is experienced like an "old friend," confirming a set of "shared values" between art and viewer and between viewers.[17] More recently, John Armstrong's *The Secret Power of Beauty* (2004) continues to think of beauty as a demonstration of and incitement to "kinship" and "recognition"; art "achieves what we long to find, but cannot lastingly achieve, with another person," even while it simultaneously recommends the very kind of kinship that one should strive for.[18] And Elizabeth Prettejohn, in *Beauty and Art* (2005), emphasizes the attention beauty gives to the "reciprocal relation between art object and viewer" but does not question this as a basis for "progressive politics."[19]

In all of these instances, beauty is considered as an aesthetic representation and encouragement of some kind of justice, contractualism, or mutuality. But treatments of beauty that might at first glance seem critical of this line of reasoning surprisingly end up endorsing it. Jeremy Gilbert-Rolfe praises beauty for its irreverent "challenge to art's seriousness," but, rather as in Steiner, the excessive and uncontrollable quality that he ascribes to beautiful images ultimately coagulates into utterly conventional human attributes. For him, beauty is "feminine," "frivolous," "irrelevant," and epitomized by photographs of glamorous fashion models.[20] In the volume of essays entitled *Beauty Matters* (2000)—we can only smile at the repeated attempts to boost beauty's dubious political credentials by including the word *matters* in titles, in imitation of Judith Butler or Cornel West—Eleanor Heartney's foreword advises the reader that "beauty seems in need of rehabilitation today as an impulse that can be as liberating as it has been deemed enslaving."[21] Even so, the essays themselves seldom rise above asserting new norms for what counts as a beautiful body or object to pressure the logic of normativity itself.

Even a critical perspective like Douglas Mao's, which deliberately opposes Scarry's emphasis on heredity and birth by proposing a more just emphasis on beauty achieved through "earning"—beauty that is produced through labor—does little to offset the general importance of shared identity in her argument.[22] This kind of theorizing on beauty has troubling implications in that beauty continues to sponsor notions of ideal political community that severely restrict membership to those who symmetrically replicate and share the same heritage, looks, or attitudes. But this aspect of the argument is seldom, if ever, acknowledged in current writing on beauty, a fact that seems especially odd considering that the submerged emphasis on shared identity I'm describing has informed writing on art and taste for quite some time. In the most compelling examples from the eighteenth century, in fact, the discourse of beauty more or less explicitly directed its efforts toward securing a gendered sense of national or racial identity. I concentrate mainly on a single instance among many—Sir Joshua Reynolds's *Discourses* (1769–90)—to illustrate my point.[23] Reynolds's discourses on art arose from his lectures at the Royal Academy, of which he was the first president. They focus on painting above all and bear the mark of the specific pressures felt by Reynolds and others to provide a level of artistic instruction that would rival that of Continental schools. An English academy would reach the heights of a grand European tradition, while also adding luster to a national tradition.

Claiming that great art is to be produced by copying classical models, Reynolds—like Scarry—identifies the beauty of such models in part with their "symmetry."[24] To be sure, he departs from the more rigidly conceptual definitions of symmetry, or "harmony," in aesthetic theory by insisting on the association of beauty with "weakness, minuteness, or imperfection" (106). He argues in *The Idler* (1759), moreover, against judging artworks according to inflexible "Rules" imposed by connoisseurs and critics.[25] These qualifications are also significant as a way of distancing English art from its rigid French and other Continental rivals, at least as Reynolds and others in his cohort, such as Samuel Johnson, perceived them. Even so, he notes in the *Discourses*, the most imperfect subjects of artistic rendering possess "a kind of symmetry or proportion." Though appearing to deviate from beauty, a figure "may still have a certain union of the various parts, which may contribute to make them on the whole not unpleasing" (109).

Reynolds here seems to be echoing the kind of claim that Francis Hutcheson makes about the notion of beauty as "Uniformity amidst Variety."[26] Whereas Hutcheson in far more general terms connected taste to respect for God and in turn to "national Love, or Love of one's country,"[27] Reynolds goes much further by making his support for an English academy join the production of refined art with the production of refined individuals. Following classical models in art (a practice adopted by Steiner in her continual and almost unswerving dependence on conventional "masterworks" of Western European art [109]) is inseparable from the enterprise of forming the bodies and tastes of English society. There is a "general similitude that goes through the whole race of mankind," Reynolds claims, but this similitude is precisely what makes it possible to discriminate between "what is beautiful or deformed" or "what agrees with or deviates from the general idea of nature" (190–91). By these means, "contentions" and "disputes" become minimized amid the exclusive circle of "gentlemen" in the academy, all of whom hold "mutual esteem for talents and acquirements" (317). The kind of mutuality and equality imagined in the *Discourses*, in other words—analogous to present-day advocacy for beauty—is guaranteed by unending mimesis: by copying properly cultivated subjects (analogous to de Bolla's social bodies) from classical models to form an artistic academy and by distributing copies of those cultivated subjects to enhance the "elegance and refinement" of a national public (79).[28]

Although in one sense it may be true that Reynolds's subject here is more consistently art and taste rather than beauty, beauty nevertheless commands the logic. The emphasis on proportion amounts to nothing less than a "rule" (108), he insists—his hesitation about such codification notwithstanding. This rule of symmetry or proportion is coextensive with an "ideal beauty" (103); it is a rule that in turn promotes new instances of beauty. Beauty becomes the thing that is shared between one artist and another and between artists and the national public.

It is this connection of beauty with a standard or rule that Edmund Burke seems to oppose in his *Philosophical Enquiry into the Origin of our Ideas of the Sublime and Beautiful* (1757) despite his close association with Reynolds and his apparent influence on the *Discourses*.[29] Burke appears far more decisively to disconnect beauty from notions of "proportion," "mensuration," "calculation," or "geometry" (93).[30] At the same time, though, his repeated association of beauty and (among other things) smooth, gentle variation in surfaces begins to operate as its own kind of rule or "common cause," of beauty (121). And it turns out that even the taste for beauty itself, under the influence of this common cause, likewise exemplifies a certain degree of cohesion, for the "principle" of taste is "the same in all men" (21); it is "common to all" to such an extent that deviations from that common taste are viewed to be a "defect in judgment" (23, 24). Burke clarifies this generally social value of beauty when he asserts that the "personal *beauty*" of women—"the sex"—provides the attraction necessary to induce generation in the species (42). The still more explicitly political value of beauty comes to the fore most clearly in Burke's *Reflections on the Revolution in France* (1790), which prizes beauty as a way of attracting and maintaining proper domestic affections—a properly modulated social "love" and cultivated "manners"—which in turn are the foundation for English citizenship. "To make us love our country, our country ought to be lovely," he writes.[31] Furthermore, in the face of the threatened dissemination of revolutionary principles, Burke continually expresses his own love of "justice" as "grave and decorous" (178), embodied in a love for beautiful people and things presented for the reader's admiration: hearths, altars, armorial bearings and ensigns, ancient portraits, and a beautiful French queen.[32]

If the deviation from rule in Burke tends nevertheless to enforce a "general similitude" among "mankind" as we find in Reynolds, Kant's account of the beautiful in *The Critique of Judgment* lays out even more explicitly why it is that judgments about beauty tend simultaneously to exemplify and reinforce collective social judgments even when they do not overtly appear to do so. As much as Scarry and Steiner seem to oppose Kant, their work demonstrates, just as its predecessors in the eighteenth century did, what Kant calls an "empirical interest" in the beautiful and what de Bolla more openly demonstrates in his insistent effort to render his experience communicable and thus "available to others" (140). The beautiful "interests only in *society*," Kant writes, because we "communicate our *feeling* to all other men, and so as a means of furthering that which everyone's natural inclination desires."[33] For him, judgments of the beautiful are by no means defined by this sociability; in fact, they cannot be defined by it. Such judgments upon the "purposiveness" of an object—a "harmony" of imagination with concepts (24)—only arise in "private sensation," which we "imput[e] . . . to everyone" (51, 50). And thus "universal communicability" is only a presupposition, or an "idea" (51).

We do not actually require others to feel the pleasure that we merely impute to them.

The trouble is that the communication arising from sociability so urgently solicits the use of concepts of the understanding that our feelings become readily attached to them, making our communication an attempt to codify pleasure and assimilate it to the pleasures and desires of others (think here of the "top ten" lists of movies, books, or things one needs to see before dying). Communicable pleasure may thus become a version of social modeling in which experience is always anticipatory and echoed, always demanding a repetition in us and inviting a corresponding duplication in someone else. It is precisely this tendency that leads to the socially exalted status of the "refined man," honed by aesthetic education; his refinement likewise prepares the one who feels and communicates a sense of beauty for community with others, for "love and familiar inclination" (139).[34]

Despite the resonance of eighteenth-century aesthetics among the most recent writing that I discuss, there is comparatively less interest lately in the sublime, that other well-known mode of experience inherited from the same era.[35] It is either explicitly or implicitly rejected, set aside either by eliminating its distinction from the beautiful, casting it as an enemy to the beautiful, or simply ignoring it entirely. Certainly this recent erasure is not very surprising, considering the viewpoint that many New Historicist critics (I use the term in the broadest possible sense) adopted in the 1980s. De Bolla's own account in *The Discourse of the Sublime* (1989) shows how sublime "excess" is controlled by a resort to "common subjectivity" or "society." Howard Caygill's account gives the sublime a somewhat larger role, casting it as a consciousness of the "violence of legislation" even though it works mainly to support a sense of "proportion between finality and human freedom" that lies at the heart of human "culture."[36] In either argument, the sublime is a negative force that must be subordinated to the interests of a more placid (and beautiful) form of social life.[37]

The strategies of beauty theorists imply, in broad agreement with New Historicist accounts, that the sublime has been, and continues to be, associated with violent and asocial power, theoretical abstraction, and traditional notions of masculinity. The welcoming back of beauty has therefore coincided with an attempt to equalize feminine beauty with masculine sublimity or to champion beauty over its masculine adversary. The particular vantage point that the contemporary discourse of beauty has on the sublime is not simply the result of an intellectual conviction (regardless of that discourse's unacknowledged compatibility with important New Historicist readings); we would be utterly mistaken to see beauty's return to academic parlance as the result of a scholarly debate.[38] Nor can its prominence amount merely to a sense that the sublime has "already been done," although that sentiment is not entirely at odds with what I am about to say about the rationale informing the accounts of recent beauty theorists.

I want to suggest here that the sublime's marginalization in current writing on aesthetics gives us an opportunity to understand how those works have arisen within the context of certain institutional and political obstacles and opportunities, and they cannot be evaluated accurately outside them. Recent works on aesthetics are not simply repetitions of an eighteenth-century discourse, in other words, but repetitions with a difference—taking on a peculiar shape that marks them as participants in conditions characterized by institutional and political demands specific to our own historical moment. While I want to draw a parallel between current writing on beauty and eighteenth-century writing on beauty, then, my goal is twofold: to emphasize an unacknowledged continuity between the two and also to insist on a shift that marks the attempt in contemporary beauty theory to address present political and economic conditions.

In two important essays, "Morality and Pessimism" and "Public and Private Morality," both published in 1978, Stuart Hampshire makes a connection between philosophical abstraction and the "abstract cruelty in politics" practiced by the United States in the Vietnam War.[39] Against the uniformity of philosophical "political calculations," Hampshire embraces the value of diverse and often incompletely formulated moral and political convictions.[40] True moral convictions, he believes, arise from a multiplicity of discontinuous local manners, customs, and communal traditions. The "ineliminable conflicts" that arise between these diverse convictions, and between such convictions and all institutional attempts to control them, amount to a decisive rebuke to militaristic discourses of calculation.[41] Opposing the merely "rational aims" behind "cool political massacres," Hampshire makes moral philosophy virtually interchangeable with antiwar resistance.[42]

It would not be much of a stretch to see writing on the sublime from roughly the same period as participants with Hampshire's work in the same arena of political commitment.[43] Literary historians like Ronald Paulson explicitly connect the eighteenth-century discourse of the sublime with revolutionary sympathies, but we can discern an even more powerful impulse to connect the sublime to a force that is essentially, rather than contingently, radical and oppositional.[44] When we read the great statements on the sublime from the 1970s, such as Harold Bloom's rendering of the literary sublime as a bold rejection of the power of the "precursor" or "parent" poem, it is hard not to see at least the potential for developing the political possibilities lurking behind the generally psychoanalytic apparatus supporting his account.[45] Thomas Weiskel goes even further in affirming the imagination's power of "usurpation," suggesting that the sublime "provided a language for urgent and apparently novel experiences of anxiety and excitement which were in need of legitimation."[46] Neil Hertz, in a book that appreciatively revises Weiskel's position, repeatedly sets up the sublime as a momentary disruption of a nostalgic or conservative appreciation for "great literary works . . . and the traditional culture out of which they sprung."[47]

To read the work of recent writers on beauty is not simply to register its distance from the politics of the Vietnam War. It is to register its place within an academy that takes a different view of its relation to politics in an even more general sense. Denis Donoghue's *Speaking of Beauty* (2003) openly equates the "return of the beautiful" with the decline of the "'politicization' of literary studies." Aesthetic appreciation can once again take hold of a field in which "scholars who write about gender, race, and sexual disposition" previously held sway.[48] This scornful withdrawal from politics has the air of popular attacks on the supposedly radical politics of academics from the 1990s; the outrage over the title of Eve Sedgwick's 1989 MLA paper on Jane Austen—"Jane Austen and the Masturbating Girl"—is only one of the more striking instances of that trend.[49] But this withdrawal from politics is itself a politics; the banality of the statement is exceeded only by the banality of the attempt to stifle it and all other theoretical claims.

Although the extremity of Donoghue's position, explored elsewhere not only in his relentless defenses of "aesthetic distance" but also in his explicit retreat from the "battlegrounds" of politicized literary study, cannot be taken as representative of the positions of all writers on beauty, his views support aspects of theirs even while lending their tones more sharpness and stridency.[50] Even if it may be difficult to claim that the general interest in beauty is simply politics in disguise, I would still suggest that the meaning of that interest can be most clearly delineated by accounting for its emergence within an academy that—as Bill Readings and Masao Miyoshi have claimed in different ways—has drifted away from its traditional support of a national culture (in a manner reminiscent of Reynolds's academy) and at the same time established a symbiotic relationship with multinational corporate enterprises, whose sustaining influence shapes the arena for moral, political, and aesthetic argument.[51] Corporate power is not visible merely as brute force, but rather as a subtle restructuring of dependencies, resulting in a rearticulated institutional landscape with muted opportunities, incentives, and rationales for protest. The changes in that landscape's terrain—complicit with the curtailed voice of a radical left in the United States and Western Europe, with implicit approval of repressive regimes abroad, and (conversely) with the bipartisan support for U.S. military intervention in supposedly unstable political situations across the world—are most visible in the academy's shift from an emphasis on public criticism to "industrial management," from independent inquiry to partnerships between "research institutions and the business community."[52] In this terrain, in other words, there is at least the beautiful appearance of widespread, mimetically replicating consent. And as Eric Cheyfitz has cogently argued, this emerging political-aesthetic sensibility leads not only to changes in the university structure that go unchallenged by its members but also to a collusion between state and university power structures in which protest and complaint about political issues far beyond the university's walls are stifled or censored.[53]

The partnership to which I refer means that the new war in the academy is not characterized as an opposition to the reigning political reason of the nation's leaders. It is a quiet, defensive war against obsolescence. The academy does not struggle against a monolithic political rival, as Stuart Hampshire understood it; it marshals its workforce against other players within and outside itself for a stake in the global economy (hence the lack of motivation for arguing against political regimes that further its expansion), an economy that steadily threatens to narrow the opportunities for jobs, publication, and other means of profit or recognition for today's scholars. It is more or less clear that the careers of the writers I have mentioned so far are not endangered by these circumstances; the point is that each of these critics and theorists establishes a commanding position within such circumstances rather than merely reacting to them. Writing on beauty thus makes no attempt to overcome or disguise academic and scholarly credentials as if they were a handicap; indeed, academic credentials entitle the authors to exercise a voice that speaks for cultural literacy and that articulates the norms that are to shape its audience. Writing on beauty therefore both enacts and defends the goals of the postmodern public intellectual, styling itself as a source of commentary that is as popular as it is authoritative.[54]

There is another way of saying this. Writing on beauty—more so than the products of traditional "stars" in literary theory, with restricted audiences—represents a crucial and innovative imaginative bridge between the contradictions in contemporary academic humanistic disciplines, which John Guillory has so eloquently described, between high theory and vernacular, popular discourse.[55] It does this in the midst of, while it is enabled by, its winnowing out of dissent and complaint, a formation of an elite discourse that simultaneously attempts to bridge the widening divide between liberal education and the wider public. Perhaps this achievement is best exemplified by the fact that current writing on beauty is basically untheoretical and unpolemical; or at most the polemic is intentionally softened. Work on beauty by academics thus takes a supervisory, authoritative role in a discourse that nevertheless logically resembles the trove of books on beauty by and for nonacademics, such as Ruth Gendler's *Notes on the Need for Beauty* (2007). Adversaries, in virtually every instance, are gently pushed aside or ignored entirely. Donaghue is perhaps the most outspoken in denouncing "political" critique in order to silence it. Arthur Danto's *The Abuse of Beauty* (2003) seconds the motion with a persistent equation between attending to beauty and "being philosophical": philosophy becomes synonymous with a politely authoritative manner that disengages itself from virtually all recent opinion on the subject.[56]

Their serene erasure of contenders only falls into line with the works on beauty that precede them. De Bolla rarely faces counterarguments of any kind in much detail; relevant accounts appear in notes that acknowledge a "growing body" of work, even though that work never ruffles the surface of the chapters that have submerged it (152). In Scarry's account, the political critique of beauty, rather than being delineated with any complications, is quickly caricatured—the adversaries are unnamed—and then diminished, its varied arguments being called a minor "quarrel" that the author can hush up to avoid seeming "bad tempered" (59–60), as if the stakes of argument had been reduced to a problem of manners. Steiner treats political critiques of beauty only slightly differently. It is true that she cites opponents like Andrea Dworkin, whose novel *Mercy* is an example of the "clash of contemporary sexual ideologies" surrounding the subject of beauty (147). But there is little need to treat Dworkin's position—that women can be victimized by conventional signs of beauty, thus perhaps troubling Steiner's wish to infuse beauty with woman's "agency"—with any sustained attention. For the allegorical structure of beauty's exile and return that sustains Steiner's narrative makes it possible to view arguments against beauty as a passing churlish mood that is now vanishing as we cheerfully welcome beauty back.

The point here, then, isn't even that these writers ignore politics; it is rather that ignoring politics testifies to the authors' collective effort to dislodge their work from a specialized set of conversations that might restrict their audience.[57] Eco's *History of Beauty* (2004), devoid of any reference to competing accounts, is the most extreme instance of the way each work strangely aspires to be the first word on its subject,[58] although new candidates, such as Roger Scruton's *Beauty* (2009), continue to appear. Beauty books, moreover, repeat one another's arguments without acknowledgment: Ian Stewart's *Why Beauty Is Truth* (2007) repeats the symmetry argument in Scarry; Prettejohn repeats the emphasis on recognition in Steiner; Alexander Nehemas's *Only a Promise of Happiness* (2007) echoes the celebration of shared affect in de Bolla.[59] In each of these cases, the goal is not to respond to other views but rather to ignore them, as if they aimed to become—in their hushed reduction to polite banter and their flawlessly elegant presentation—the beautiful objects they so lovingly describe.

In the competition for recognition in the marketplace, recent writing on aesthetics addresses itself to economic exigencies by shaping itself into a particularly viable, because eminently consumable, discourse. At the same time, it is not simply a shallow bid for popularity among other competitors, which range from William Bennett's anthologies of great writing by conservatives to Bloom's reading selections for intelligent children and also include the vast sea of postmodern fiction whose plots obsessively pay homage to classical singers, famous paintings, and canonical literature. Writing on beauty, by encouraging the cultivation of the audience whose attention it simultaneously solicits, holds a unique place among these other publications, which merely participate in the art of refinement. The achievement of recent writing on beauty—we can't deny that it is a substantial one—is that it preaches what it practices; it defends the nexus of biopolitical imperatives that lend it support.

We might very well say that beauty, even beyond functioning the way it does in the academic context that Guillory describes, is nothing less than the preeminent discourse of a postmodern cultural eugenics, whose aesthetic strategies collectively mediate, according to the imperatives that David Harvey assigns to neoliberal governments, between dispersed subjectivities and social regulations, between an "alienating possessive individualism" and a cohesive "collective life."[60] Beauty theory's authoritative and normalizing voice reaches into the recesses of bodily sensation, effectively and brilliantly viewing it as merely private, particular, and disconnected, while insisting on its replication and symmetry. To acknowledge this as the logic of beauty is to explain why the love of beauty has come to be described in some instances not only as something that everyone has and shares but also as something that might repeatedly be understood as grounded in the natural sciences and the biological process of the body. The discourse of beauty has recently been linked not only to a process of naturalizing, that is, but to nature itself. The apparent vagaries and varieties of taste can be tidied up within a uniformity and determination visible at the level of biological and physiological organization. Thus Ian Stewart talks about how "symmetry" is "fundamental to today's scientific understanding of the universe and its origins," while Denis Dutton speaks of our passion for beauty as an "art instinct."[61] To speak of beauty's connection to biopolitics, then, is to speak of the way in which a commitment to the normative replication of identity in the discourse of beauty has been extended into the economy of the body: beauty theory extends into a claim about the biological generation or determination of the body's pleasures.

In contrast to writing on the sublime, with its dedication to "urgent and novel experiences," the new discourse of beauty not only engages in the controlled battle for attention in the global marketplace; it amounts to a more concentrated defense of the effort to render disagreement into charming but inconsequential differences, enforcing relationship as the perpetuation of recognized likeness. Little wonder, then, that, for Leo Bersani and Ulysse Dutoit, beauty from Caravaggio to Proust can be summed up precisely as a play, or "movement," between identity and difference, a notion that coincides with Crispin Sartwell's attempt to accommodate the ideas of beauty in "every culture" even while consolidating those ideas to develop deeper similarities.[62] In their descriptions, enactments, defenses, and celebrations of the logic of beauty, texts such as those discussed in this chapter can allow little or no place for addressing relevant scholarship or theory on aesthetics. For the point is not to put forward contentious interpretations but to affirm beauty's inviolable heritage with the dazzling insouciance of a philosophical style.

As I have been suggesting all along, there is a powerful connection to be made between current writing on beauty and eighteenth-century aesthetics, but it is finally to Matthew Arnold to whom we might turn, leading us to a bridge between the work of Reynolds (and his contemporaries) and beauty theory in our own day. In many ways, writing on beauty assumes the role of a postmodern updating of Matthew Arnold's account of criticism as *"the best that is known and thought in the world,"* which is itself a recasting of one strain of eighteenth-century aesthetics.[63] Like beauty theorists, although more openly and knowingly, Arnold looks for his inspiration back to a prior age, to a moment when "ideas" rose above the "immediate political and practical application to all . . . fine ideas of reason."[64] These ideas are in turn the foundation of Arnold's view of "culture," which—described in terms of "beauty" and "harmony"—echoes eighteenth-century thought.[65] Arnold also marks an important step between eighteenth-century theorists and today's apostles of beauty, however; he displays a particularly heightened consciousness of the marketplace, especially insofar as working classes and religious dissent—"the rush and roar of practical life"—combine in a threat to cultural orthodoxy.[66]

Like Arnold, postmodern defenders of beauty have moved beyond the sphere of genteel cultivation found in the writers of the eighteenth century. But they have likewise moved beyond the merely defensive position of Arnold toward the commercialism and political dissent that he believed was threatening proper English culture. Arnold, looking back at the French Revolution, saw "practical life" and its political and economic turmoil as essentially disruptive for the project of national cultivation; he championed the likes of Addison and Burke, who resisted the "practice" and "politics" of the revolution with the might of "ideas."[67] The current leaders in aesthetic theory echo an eighteenth-century interest in beauty precisely to reframe the relation between aesthetics, politics, and the global economy altogether. The role of commerce now stands at the center of their implicit understanding of culture rather than at its margins. For that culture is devoted less to mediating between individuals and representative democracy (as we find in Arnold's anxious cultivation of legitimate citizens) than to fostering a neoliberal ethos of homogenized difference.[68] To defend that culture's forces is to defend a controlled but revitalized competition that incorporates, quells, and quiets—rather than excludes—the energies of dissent.

Thus we see, in admittedly broad brushstrokes, beauty's career since the eighteenth century. Having bolstered the admirable axioms of civic virtue in Reynolds, having passed through the crucible of class and race warfare in

Arnold, beauty is repurposed in the work of its postmodern champions to adopt more subtle though certainly still decisive means of asserting its norms. Current writing on beauty absorbs opposition into replicated sameness punctuated by inconsequential differences, while at the same time ignoring or quieting actual argument. The sleight of hand we find in these texts, of course, is to turn an interest in cultural preservation and purity inherited from the eighteenth century, and re-enlivened in Arnold's work, into an interest in justice. This is because writing on beauty defends, in the name of justice, equality, or mutuality, the replication of subject-consumers.

CHAPTER 2

Justice and the Romantic Sublime

I've said that recent writing on aesthetics has usually avoided the oppositional, dissenting position of writers on the sublime. If this is an "argument" that beauty theorists have had with the sublime, it is an argument that can best be understood with reference to the present political and institutional demands that this writing both defends and demonstrates. Returning to the subject of the sublime, specifically as Immanuel Kant describes it in the *Critique of Judgment* (although I will glance at other accounts as well for comparison and contrast), we can more carefully assess the costs of this avoidance. In one sense this is a recovery of Kant's thinking that does not simply endorse the views of the sublime to be found in critics like Weiskel and Hertz, discussed in the previous chapter; my purpose is to reconsider the sublime, including the scope and limits of its relation to justice. This reorientation will acquaint us with a new set of terms to describe the sublime's significance. It will also acquaint us with a description of justice that departs from the privileging of mutually reinforcing identities.

This recovery, while it aims to argue on the same plane as the current discourse of beauty and not simply discard aesthetics as generally irrelevant, does not attempt to directly claim Kant's aesthetics and politics for the present. It would make no sense to deny that many aspects of his thinking reflect the prejudices of his time.[1] And it would make just as little sense to advocate for Kant's philosophy as a blueprint or model for our own mental frameworks or political structures. Indeed, using aesthetics as an imitable model is precisely what I avoid, and I think it is precisely what Kant wants to avoid as well. Instead, I pursue a more modest goal: I reconsider a fundamental dimension of his thought that has not yet received proper acknowledgment by today's guardians of the aesthetic and thus recommend it at the very least as the basis for a more wide-ranging response to the inadequacies of the accounts of aesthetics and justice that I have discussed so far.

The Mind's Stormy Movements

Why Kant? Although acknowledging the historical specificity of Kant's work means in part to acknowledge its limitations, frequently emerging in racial and sexual prejudices, it also means to acknowledge its particular interventions and contributions. In fact, I believe that the second route can give a more nuanced interpretation than the first, which often risks judging his work by the benchmark of current politics. Kant's work emerges within a political climate of absolutism and a drive toward powerful national cohesion. This is how his work has often been contextualized, most usefully and convincingly by Caygill.[2] At the same time, his work emerges as a response to, and an attempt to accommodate, the insights of English empirical philosophy of the eighteenth century, which was frequently critical of political absolutism in its desire to locate the authority for experience in individual sensation, feeling, and reason.

These internally conflicted or paradoxical directions designate a crucial insight. Throughout his aesthetic, ethical, and juridical thinking, Kant combines a commitment to authoritative discursive and institutional forms with an even more rigorous commitment to dissent. Moreover, he adjusts the terms of his historical context: he wrests empiricism from its connections with habit and custom and opens structures of political authority up to the possibility of continual and productive revision.

I shall focus first on the mathematical sublime (§§25–27), since it's here that Kant makes the most relevant claims about the sublime's relation to moral (as opposed to juridical) law. For Kant, the sublime (*Erhaben*)—a feeling of awe inspired by the apprehension of overwhelming magnitude, primarily in nature—differs from the beautiful in that it involves a play between reason and imagination, removing imagination from the realm of immediately communicable concepts used in our experience and understanding of the world. The sublime, while ascribed to objects, is a feeling arising entirely within the subject; and here Kant seems to echo earlier theorists of the sublime such as John Baillie, whose 1747 *Essay on the Sublime* endows the "imagination" within the subject with a power to make even familiar objects "new," so that the "soul *sublimes* everything about her."[3] In the third *Critique*, the sublime arises "merely in ourselves and in our attitude of thought," and thus (as in Baillie) it is a "state of mind," rather than any object, that is sublime.[4] The sense of the "absolutely great" that defines the sublime is not to be derived from a "standard which we assume as the same for everyone," moreover, but rather from a sense beyond sense, or beyond a standard that could be applied to sensible objects in order to measure them (86). The imagination is unable to form a complete empirical intuition of what can only be apprehended as infinity, and its struggle to account for the uncountable calls for another faculty: reason, which can supply "comprehension in *one* intuition." The result is "*the bare capability of thinking* this infinite without contradiction" (93). The mathematical is related to the aesthetic not because it adheres to a norm of rationality but because it acts in tandem with the work of imagination in order to provide a form for formlessness—anticipating Dedekind's 1888 definition of infinity in terms of a single mathematical function that defines a class. As Frances Ferguson sums up this "formal account," the mathematical sublime responds to "the difficulties of arriving at any account of any *one* whatever outside a process of systematic formalization."[5]

It's the unusual way in which Kant connects this struggle, failure, and resolution to the capacity for "respect" for "bare capability" that requires our attention here. Because the single intuition appears as a result of a "law of reason," he explains, we experience the incapacity of the imagination subjectively to provide a single intuition even while acquiring a "respect" for the "rational determination of our cognitive faculties" (96). What we respect is the faculty of reason that makes oneness, the "*one* intuition," possible. But why is it entitled to such respect, respect that we do not have for, say, concepts of the understanding? The question seems particularly hard to answer given Kant's odd way of describing the sublime as a species of pain arising from the imagination's incapacity and consequent "violence" to the subject (99). At the same time, though, reason emerges as protector and guide, achieving respect not in the abstract but entirely through a *relation* between imagination and reason.

On the one hand, reason requires the imagination for its intermittent, fleeting manifestation. There is no other way to make sense of Kant's assertion that reason lends imagination a "correspondence" with reason's laws and makes those laws "intuitively evident" (97). On the other hand, reason is called forth or solicited by the imagination, which is "impelled in its apprehension of intuition" (97). Imagination's strenuous work, while unable to arrive at a numerical magnitude that is a whole, thus proceeds *in the shape of formality* without being pure form. Reason thus can deserve respect because it makes possible, and indeed requires, the free work of the subjective cognition "within us" while also giving us "*one* intuition," an intuition that is not anything like a doctrine or maxim of law but an unscripted feeling of lawfulness. Whereas the beautiful is purposive with respect to communicable concepts, the sublime is subjectively purposive, communicating only the fact of judging—or judgment—itself, a "consciousness of subjective purposiveness" (87).

In this sense, the feeling of the mathematical sublime, giving evidence for the shaping effects of reason, relates to the "dynamic" sublime in §28 (the feeling of might in nature) insofar as our faculties gain a mental "dominion" over nature to provide a concrete feeling of "humanity in our person" (101). At this moment Kant injects a palpably affective element into the discussion, in that the sublime involves an observation of nature as "fearful" without resulting merely in the subject being "afraid *of* it"; this is because of the subject's sense of a faculty of judgment despite external powers that might threaten him or her with submission (100, 101). Both versions of the sublime outlined here differ in substantial ways from the version in another celebrated account, Edmund Burke's *Enquiry*, familiar to Kant and to many of his German contemporaries. In the *Enquiry*, Burke understands the sublime most consistently as a "modification of power." Power is understood, as it is in the Kantian dynamic sublime, as "ideas" of "strength, violence, pain, and terror" that "rush in upon the mind." Such "ideas," furthermore, are linked to a particular physical threat of "rapine and destruction," and these "ideas" of threat in turn precipitate from actual threatening objects. The sublime effect of those ideas necessarily deteriorates when the "ability to hurt" is "stripped" from the objects, as in the case of an ox, whose extreme strength is modified by its status as an "extremely serviceable" animal. The same can be said of a horse, although

Burke quickly adds that although the horse is a "useful" animal for humans, it can nonetheless seem sublime in scripture; he quotes from the book of Job, chapter 39, to demonstrate the "terrible and sublime" aspects of the animal that "blaze out" from the passage.[6]

In many respects Burke's emphasis on the inherent qualities of objects follows a logic similar to that found in the work of John Locke, David Hartley, and other empiricists, according to which ideas in the mind are produced by sensations of the external world.[7] Still, what the biblical passage suggests to him is not simply that the book of Job manages to capture a threat that is actually within or associated with the horse, nor even that it proves God's infinite ability to invest all beings with power in relation to Job's "vile" finitude, although the latter interpretation would seem to be the point of the passage in its biblical context.[8] Burke's point does not seem to be that it is actually speech uttered by God, and the removal of the passage from its context is itself significant. Instead, the main drift of Burke's account might be closer to Kant's, even though Kant himself was at least as uneasy as Burke with the idea that animals like horses, which are useful to humans, could produce any aesthetic pleasure. The biblical text provides an entirely new and compelling description of the horse—as the imagination is challenged by multiple sense impressions—in "*one* intuition."

In the third *Critique*, this form-giving power of the sublime has something to do with the priority of the sublime in Kant's text more generally as a paradigmatic instance of aesthetic judgment. We might note as an instance of that priority that while the discussion of "beautiful art" involves an account of art as "designed" with "rules" that are made evident through the act of judging, this discussion nevertheless finds its way into the "Analytic of the Sublime" in §§ 44 and 45 (149–50). This importation has the effect of making the beautiful—that which is governed by a play between the imagination and concepts of the understanding—understood in terms of the sublime, so that art is beautiful because it can be seen "as if it were a product of mere nature" (149). And if beautiful art in one sense echoes the terms of beauty more generally because it "furthers the cultures of the mental powers in reference to social communication" (148), in another sense (insofar as it is viewed through the prism of the sublime) beautiful art yields something else. Art viewed in association with the sublime is art because it declines to impose the traditions of artistic "schools" or the requirements of pre-given "rules." At the same time, such art (as in the sublime) excites the viewing subject to feel as though that very independence from a rule were guided by a rule beyond a rule (148).

Another striking aspect of the sublime's position in Kant's text also deserves attention, namely, its demonstration of a "mental disposition" that is "akin to the moral." The relation the aesthetic bears to the moral in turn helps make clear why the aesthetic can be entitled to the "respect" Kant accords it (109). Here again Kant can be compared with his eighteenth-century predecessors. Burke warns against simplistic attempts to align beauty with virtue according to a "loose and inaccurate manner of speaking" (112). But beauty nevertheless plays a crucial role in the formation of gentlemanly manners, which form the core of civic virtues in both Reynolds and Burke. It's certainly possible to locate the traces of this prominent trend in eighteenth-century aesthetics in Kant, who suggests that judgments about beauty provide communicable instances or images of moral goodness. For example, in the *Lectures on Ethics* (1762–64) he refers to the "charities of a rich man" as an instance of a "tender-hearted ethic" that is "morally beautiful," just as he thinks of religion itself as a "beautiful" incitement to morality. Such instances, in which tenderness and good manners bind together both objects to be viewed and subjects who view them, provide an important contrast to the "sense of obligation," which is itself "sublime."[9]

Even though Kant's interest in moral beauty—admirable representations, that is, of moral conduct—is fleeting and perhaps even dismissive, readers such as Paul Guyer and William Connolly suggest a straightforward equivalence between beauty and morality in his thought.[10] Meanwhile, the account of Kantian moral beauty might also be interpreted as the perfect analogue for the link between aesthetics and ethics that Michel Foucault pursued late in his career, when he championed the "moralities of Antiquity," which made "one's own life . . . a personal work of art."[11] The personal work of art in Foucault has been viewed by some queer theorists as encouraging the collective political-aesthetic practice of a "sociality with others struggling for survival."[12]

Sublimity in Kant has a far more profound logical connection to the moral than does beauty. This is not because the sublime and the moral are merely the same, even though many eighteenth-century writers, such as Joseph Priestley, following Burke, invested heroic virtues with sublimity.[13] Rather than occupying themselves with human sensation and action directed by a law of reason, our faculties, in Kant's view, provide a sense of this direction only indirectly. Limited to a "mental disposition," the sublime does not provide the subject with maxims in accordance with the law but simply with a subjective feeling that is also a feeling for the *bordering* of that experience by the law. The oscillation between independence and dependence, between feeling as autonomy and feeling as an "instrument of reason" (109), therefore does not result in morality or in moral action; instead it suggests what it would be like to give ourselves a maxim freely supplied by the moral law—in other words, what morality feels like. Rodolphe Gasché offers a useful corrective on the tendency to overemphasize the relationship between beauty and morality in Kant when he accurately captures the *Critique*'s argument as follows: "the discovery of the mind's intellectual destination and determination at the expense of the sensible enables the sublime to serve . . . as an aesthetical representation of the morally good."[14]

Doesn't Byron's Manfred, that quintessential Romantic hero, enact something of what Kant is talking about? Byron renders the sublimity of Manfred's "lofty will" through his anguished contention with the world's "Mysterious Agency," his struggle to grasp the forces of nature, "the blest tone which made me."[15] This aesthetic register in turn becomes inseparable from the hero's insistent critique of rival moral-political authorities, from the world of spirits to the realms of domestic tranquility (represented by the chamois hunter) and the church (represented in the abbot). William D. Melaney, in his reading of the relationship between Kant and Byron, aptly calls these contending authorities "false agents of reconciliation."[16] Manfred rejects conventional understandings of guilt, punishment, repentance, and forgiveness, which in turn align themselves with conventional aesthetic categories as outlined by Burke in the *Enquiry*. Byron, that is, makes the spirit world in *Manfred* parrot the Burkean notion of the sublime as a threatening external power. The spirits cull their speeches from a catalog of darkness, earthquakes, storms, and rough seas, claiming to govern the world with their "command" (1.1.67), even as the trumped-up conventionality of their "lightweight rhetoric"—Peter Martin's resonant description—seems like a gloss on their own weakness.[17] The same can be said of the hunter and the abbot, whom Byron shapes into advocates of a beautiful and comforting, but conventional, domestic tranquility and spirituality.

Melaney claims that Manfred's antagonism merely reveals aesthetic and moral "disorder," and he thus agrees with many readings before him that have connected Byron's work with skepticism or atheism.[18] However, by rejecting all sources of reconciliation—a rejection heightened by Byron's revision of act 3, in which he accentuates the abbot's role as a voice of mercy and contrition—Manfred renders his imaginative flights as a kind of law-giving. He refuses to retreat from the guilt he has imposed upon himself for his unnamed crime. He refuses either to escape from, or capitulate to, the punishment that he feels is his "desert," a sense of desert that is inseparable from Manfred's sublime removal from conventional sources of authority (3.4.136). "Half dust, half deity," Manfred rejects a spiritual, and spiritualized, world, only to usurp its authority internally (1.2.40). To put it another way, the Byronic hero's apparent alienation and melancholy brooding actually coincide with a purified form of moral order, and this is undoubtedly the reason for the praise he wins from Friedrich Nietzsche, who writes that he "must be profoundly related" to Manfred.[19]

To return to Kant, if the sublime establishes a kinship with the moral on the terms thus far described, he elsewhere clarifies the kinship from the other direction—from the moral to the aesthetic. In the third *Critique*, he seems to recall a common eighteenth-century connection between the sublime and "irregular greatness, wildness, and enthusiasm of imagination," as William Duff puts it in his *Essay on Original Genius* (1767).[20] Kant expands on such a notion to state that "enthusiasm" is sublime, that the following of "unalterable principles" is sublime, that in fact "every affection of the *strenuous* kind" is sublime. In what is perhaps his most famous example, he states that the commandment against graven images in the "Jewish law" is sublime (112–15). All qualify for characterization as admirably "stormy movements of mind" (114). In the *Groundwork for the Metaphysics of Morals* (1785), just as in the *Critique of Pure Practical Reason* (1788), Kant lends a certain kind of support for these claims when he describes the operation of the moral law working within a person as an instance of "sublimity" (*Erhabenheit*).[21] Strictly speaking, what is sublime in the *Groundwork* is neither the moral law itself nor the "maxim" generated in accordance with the law's "formal principle"—the "categorical imperative," that is, to "act as though your maxim should serve at the same time as a universal law [for all rational beings]" (56–57). Instead, as we are now led to expect, the sublime experience is constituted by and through a paradoxical relation between them (56). The moral law (in contrast, for instance, to ethics that are founded on divine authority, as in Spinoza) is utterly individualized because possessed by "every rational being." It makes no difference to us whether other people are faithful to that law, and indeed it would not be such a law if its worth were to be determined by the extent to which others follow it. But it is "at the same time . . . universally legislative" (56–57). We presume that universal status even if we suspect, or even if we are told, that the moral law works differently somewhere for someone else.

Reading the statements from the *Groundwork* together with those from the third *Critique*, I'm struck by a certain kind of liberality or generosity in Kant's efforts to gesture toward different *kinds* of moral or religious bearings (ultimately any strenuous operation of affections) that might qualify as sublime and hence as akin to the moral. To be sure, the *Groundwork* has little or no interest in stipulating what the lines of kinship might be; it declines to supply empirical instances of belief that might be compatible with moral law. A concern with such instances would, after all, merely produce an account of what a "virtuous person" is and thus violate the claim that morality must be legislated freely by and in our selves.[22] The third *Critique* does tread gingerly in that territory, however, and the results are intriguing. It accentuates the paradox of the moral law by suggesting that plural moral dispositions might be compatible with the operation of reason's laws. All instances of the feeling of the sublime are accorded equivalent "respect." Even when Kant appears to restrict that sense of plurality—for instance, when he hastily dismisses "enthusiasm" as unworthy of reason's "approval"—it soon becomes clear that enthusiasm occupies a place on a continuum with morality rather than simply opposing it. The "satisfaction" of reason eventually can be earned with a broadly defined "tendency to morality within us" (112–15), a tendency he demonstrates elsewhere by showing that regardless of the "hopeless quality ascribed to their minds" by others, even hardened criminals may experience a sense of self-reproach.[23]

From the Moral to the Juridical

The move Kant makes here actually helps us to answer a number of challenging questions that critics have frequently directed toward his claims. For instance, how can the strenuous work of the moral law be anything other than a merely mechanical adherence to convention? Or, from the other direction, how can the universally legislative avoid contamination by the particularity of human sensation and desire?[24] From one point of view, Kant applies reason too inflexibly; thus Richard Rorty accuses him of denying the pull of particular "loyalties" in his pursuit of a universalized ethics.[25] From another point of view, Kant appears to be doing exactly the opposite—he is a wavering empiricist caught in the cross hairs of his own passions; thus David Lloyd accuses him of grounding his ethics in a variable taste.[26] Kant's answer to both would seem to be that by encompassing many possibilities within a single moral tendency, the moral law is capable of comprehending far more moral dispositions than some critics might think.

At the same time, however, Kant's implicit subject at this point in his discussion of a moral "tendency" has been transformed. It's not really the sublime, and it's not the moral. It's something like the juridical—the ability to illustrate, from the standpoint of a legislator rather than from that of a moral subject, what kinds of moral laws might count as lawful, that is, morally lawful, but from the legislator's point of view. From that point of view, aesthetically affected agents are granted the status of moral agents.[27] It should hardly be surprising, then, that the sublimity of different religions and moral perspectives leads Kant at precisely this moment to remark—from this legislator's perspective—on how some governments control their subjects by supplying them with "images and childish ritual" in order to contain "enthusiasm" and thus forcefully enhance social order (115).

With a hint of disdain typical of dissenting sensibilities pervasive elsewhere in his work and throughout Romantic writing, Kant at once acknowledges the workings of established religion—how governments not only compromise their subjects' liberty to believe but actually give them things to believe in— and exhibits the juridical vantage point of the *Critique* itself as *something other* than such an endorsement of normative beliefs.[28] He even goes so far as to suggest that a policy of inclusion might result in a kind of perpetual but controlled war, which is why he finds "a peculiar veneration for the soldier" even "in the most highly civilized state" (102). (This may be one of the places in Kant's text where we accept the gist of his argument while not necessarily accepting his admiration for militarism, no matter how controlled it might be.)

It's precisely in this gesture that we can grasp the full implication of what we might call Kant's "secularization" of the sublime. In one sense he shifts away from a traditional association between sublime experiences and worship of the deity—found, for instance, in the way that Joseph Addison connects the "Apprehension of what is Great or Unlimited" to "Devotion" in contemplation of God's "Nature."[29] And yet in another sense this secularizing of the sublime, denoted by a shift from worship of the deity to respect for reason, is accompanied by a capacious acceptance of sectarian perspectives. The point of this maneuver is not to identify moral agents with juridical law but rather to concede to them a generally (morally) lawful status qualifying them for inclusion in the *Critique*'s jurisprudential gaze. In the *Critique*, the sublime's link to questions of both morality and legislation is suggested only faintly and in very general terms; Kant restricts his concern solely to the question of what might be either excluded from or included in the polity. Still more can be said about the connection between the sublime, the moral, and the juridical, however. And taking these observations only a bit further, we can see how the sublime's kinship with the moral, once extended to the issue of legislation, reveals a connection between aesthetics and just social arrangements that does not depend upon the logic of imitation and replication that is so predominant in current discussions of beauty.

In their interpretations of Kant's claim that moral and juridical law are compatible, some views of or variations on his account suggest that the moral might simply be equated with the juridical. But that argument is not without problems. Jeremy Waldron points to opposing interpretations of Kant's moral philosophy that attempt to account for the connection between morality and legislation. According to one interpretation, Kant's categorical imperative lies beyond all conventional legislation by the state; if all govern themselves according to the moral law, the reasoning goes, it is unnecessary to think of any law beyond it. According to the other interpretation, the terms of the categorical imperative could be taken as the model for just legislation itself. Waldron revises both positions, reaching the conclusion that for Kant, individuals who follow the moral law will not necessarily agree with one another. The law, meanwhile, must govern over those subjects, providing "a hindering of a hindrance to freedom."[30]

This reading is both persuasive and useful, because it recognizes that Kant sees the operation of the moral law as incompatible with, yet working alongside, juridical law's power to prevent or settle disputes regarding the intrusions of one person's right upon another, intrusions arising as a consequence of owning private property and negotiating public spaces. Nevertheless, it is hard to ignore that Waldron seems to make it possible to tip the scale rather easily toward the merely coercive force of the law, so that what Kant is saying might sound rather conventional: that disputes about the justice or injustice of the law are ultimately settled by the power of the state, which determines the proper boundaries within which freedom is to be exercised.

It should be emphasized (even more than Waldron does) that Kant continually invokes a set of corrective contact points between individual moral agents—who are moved by their separate enthusiasms, principles, and affections—and the laws to which they adhere. A powerful contrast thus emerges here with Friedrich Schiller, who thinks of the aesthetic of the beautiful as a means of joining "free" individuals—through an appeal to the "common sense" of society—under the triumphant reign of a moral-political law. This makes such freedom (experienced, in Schiller's terms, through the sublime) only an "illusion."[31] The idea of the aesthetic as a political means of joining individuals through a *sensus communis* becomes crucial in Hannah Arendt's interpretation of Kant's aesthetics and its implication for his politics. Arendt quite clearly anticipates the work of Guyer and Connolly in viewing the aesthetic as a "common sense" producing a "standard" of "communicability."[32] But we must take note of the fact that the very idea of committing moral philosophy to the communication and enforcement of moral doctrines was, for Kant, nothing short of the "death of all philosophy."[33] Indeed, there is much to suggest that Arendt's view of the political significance of Kant's aesthetics is much closer to Schiller's beautifully seamless public mediation of autonomy than it is to Kant's political aesthetic of the sublime.

It should be remembered that Kant opposes revolt and revolution of all kinds, asserting in *The Doctrine of Right* (1797) that "the presently existing legislative authority ought to be obeyed, whatever its origin."[34] And he frequently and irregularly insists on distinctions between intention and action and between internally and externally generated duty, distinctions that tend to bolster claims among critics that Kant makes juridical law quite separate from moral law.[35] But dissent—in particular, dissent that takes the form of complaint, criticism, and refusal—occupies a prominent position in the political writings. Central to Kant's account of "enlightened" social order is, after all, the "unsocial sociability" that arises from conflicting claims among political subjects, claims that individually provide an index of value for political agents and collectively convey a political community's good health.[36] A paradox lies at the center of this thought: a social order that fosters the free development of an individual's "capacities" is precisely the one in which unsociability "threatens to break this society up"; in other words, the ideal social order nurtures agents of its possible dissolution, even while the agents of dissolution presumably accept that society because their very "existence" becomes most "valued" in it.[37]

It is not inconsistent with public duty, Kant insists in his famous essay "An

Answer to the Question: 'What is Enlightenment?'," to voice concerns about the "impropriety" or "injustice" of existing laws. A clergyman speaking in a public forum, for instance, might question or oppose the "mistaken aspects" of religious doctrines or the "inadequacies of current institutions," including his own church. A military officer might likewise complain about the injustices in military service, and a citizen might complain about the unfairness of taxation.[38] The central contention in all of these claims is that political subjects are required to adhere to specific functions attached to their civil obligations in order to achieve "public ends"—thus it is wrong for individuals privately to undermine or subvert the law's commands—while at the same time the very notion of "the public in the truest sense of the word" must invite the same citizens' commentary and criticism.[39]

Kant's commitment to a public is inseparable from his conviction that no public could adhere to an unchanging constitution or set of doctrines. It hardly seems important here for him to be concerned with the fact that different plaintiffs might not agree on what constitutes an impropriety or an injustice, as Waldron shrewdly points out. More to the point is the general endorsement of the correction of injustices, the righting of wrongs. Indeed, so vital is this endorsement to the conception of just legislation set forth in *The Doctrine of Right* that the "refusal of the people (in parliament) to accede to every demand the government puts forth as necessary for administering the state" functions as a fundamental support for the state itself—for security against corruption, betrayal, and despotism.[40]

The justice of juridical law, in other words, is not to be found in its identity with the moral law operating in any given political subject; we don't have a "respect" for juridical law that approximates our respect for a law of reason. Kant clearly differs from G. W. F. Hegel in this regard, for the latter views the state precisely as the "actuality of the ethical idea"; but he also differs from Thomas Hobbes's suppression of private morality with the law's "publique conscience."[41] Justice is not to be found either in the pure realization of or— its opposite—in cancellation of the moral law in order to achieve legal order. It is to be found in the visibility and availability of the means of correction. Justice as equal treatment before the law requires the engagement and testing of contrary standpoints, demands, and needs.[42]

Manfred ends up with this kind of corrective position. This is why it is so inaccurate for critics to view Byron's dramatic poem only in terms of a struggle for independence or an assertion of purely negative liberty.[43] Manfred repeatedly launches a critique of the excessive use of legal violence, "the torments of a public death" (3.1.90). He speaks of the retributive logic of the avenging Spirit, who comes to claim the "forfeited" life of the hero at the end of the play, as a logic that simply produces murder, punishing crimes "by other crimes / And greater criminals" (3.4.123–24). In this regard, Byron's character gives voice to observations that John Cam Hobhouse—friend, traveling companion, and parliamentary reformer—repeatedly made about instruments of torture and death during their Alpine tour of 1816, when Byron was writing his dramatic poem.[44] And Manfred also sounds very much like Byron himself in his 1812 parliamentary campaign against the death penalty for frameworkers convicted of "destroying or injuring . . . Stocking or Lace Frames" or any "machines or engines used in the Framework knitted manufactory."[45] Manfred, that is, echoes Byron's complaint against the "palpable injustice & the certain inefficacy of the bill," in which he asks, "Are there not capital punishments sufficient in your statutes? Is there not blood enough upon your penal code?"[46]

The critique of the excesses and illogic of the death penalty in *Manfred* does not arise from a position that merely seeks to escape the law; neither Manfred nor Byron in his parliamentary speeches seeks to undermine legal authority altogether. Instead, the critique of retributive penality emerges from Manfred's even more determined commitment to upholding a sense of juridical law. The critique, after all, aims at the *excesses* of "public death" and violent punishment rather than the idea of punishment in general. It cannot escape our notice, in that same vein, that the critique of punishment in the final scene of the drama follows swiftly on the heels of Manfred's "wildest flight" of imaginative expansion (3.4.43). In that moment, he meditates in solitude on "Nature" (3.4.3) even while he recalls a youthful moment of reflection on the ruins of Rome—ruins that provide Manfred with a sense that the "sceptered sovereigns . . . still rule / Our spirits from their urns" (3.4.40–41). Even as this sublime meditation so grandly unleashes itself from all constraint, it settles into a meditation on an imagined continuity of sovereign rule. Although in his letters Byron refers to the drama as "mental theater,"[47] Manfred's mental movements rigorously bind themselves to an external structure that they seek both to oppose and to modify.

Many readings of *Manfred* would suggest that this logic overturns, or at least compromises, the hero's autonomy or, worse, that it results in metaphysical incoherence. But it might be more accurate to say that Byron's drama contextualizes Manfred's meditations on selfhood, situating them within a juridical framework, with which they also contend. The role of suicide in this work adds an intriguing twist to this logic, since suicide both critiques the law and underlines its force. Manfred's own death at the end of the drama looks from one vantage point like the suicide that he attempted in act 1; now, in the final scene, he is his own "destroyer," not anyone's "dupe" or "prey" (3.4.139, 138). His death appears to be a refusal to concede to the violent imposition of authority, while reinforcing his own internal sense of "requital" and "desert" (3.4.130, 136). At the same time, though, Manfred's death is not unambiguously the suicide that the abbot supposes it to be when he urges him to "die not thus" (3.4.145). Manfred interprets his death, even while he is his own destroyer, only as a form of subjection, perhaps to the law of the sceptered sovereigns who rule his spirit from their urns. It is not that he kills himself but that "the hand of death is on me" (3.4.141), an externalization of the cause for his own death that is reinforced by the passive construction in the last lines of the drama, spoken to the abbot: "Old man! 'tis not so difficult to die" (3.4.151).

Manfred's impulse to be his own "destroyer" may seem, in a very troubling way, to repeat the death that is imposed upon him at the end of the drama. But the critical role of suicide is given a much sharper edge when Manfred recalls the negative side of Roman rule in act 3, scene 1. There his criticism of the bloody culture and political executions of ancient Rome is captured in his anecdote about Nero (Byron calls him "Rome's sixth emperor," Otho, rather than the fifth), who commits suicide rather than endure execution—"the torments of a public death" at the hands of the senators—or rather than accept the hand of "loyal pity" from the Roman soldier who tries to stanch his wounds (3.1.90, 92). The torments of a public death are vividly described by Suetonius in his *Life of Nero* (AD 121): the criminal, he writes, is pierced through the neck with a fork and beaten with rods, experiencing a "scandal" and a "shame" that fills the fallen emperor with "terror."[48] The soldier's loyal pity, which Manfred analogizes to the abbot's argument for "atonement" (3.1.84), offers only a false "fidelity" to the victim, since it operates entirely within the domain of the law's violent strictures. By contrast, Nero—with whom Manfred allies himself—makes suicide into a reaction to, and critique of, punishment as an instrument of terror and humiliation.

We should bear in mind that the subjects of capital punishment and suicide draw Byron into a complicated but ultimately illuminating relationship with Kant's writing. Kant approves of the death penalty as the only appropriate punishment for murder according to the *lex talionis*; he argues against suicide, moreover, in which the human subject is a mere object.[49] While the distinction in perspectives is truly important, there is an underlying, more profound connection between them. Kant's zeal for capital punishment and his distaste for suicide are clearly conventional approaches to legal and moral problems: he adopts a rigid adherence to a traditional form of punishment, just as he adopts a view of suicide that judges it (in equally traditional terms) to be "abhorrent" and thus against God's will (a position not unlike that of Socrates).[50] But he is far from consistent in his positions on both of these issues. In the *Anthropology* (1798) it is none other than the example of Nero that brings Kant to articulate a position closer to Byron's. He understands capital punishment, that is, as a punishment that deprives the subject of any ability to acknowledge that it is deserved. By committing suicide, Nero, rather than submitting to the punishment of death, chooses "to die a free man and carry the sentence out himself." By killing himself, moreover, Nero is able to die with "honor."[51] Kant hesitates to give too much credit to Nero here: the "morality" of his action, he says, "I do not claim to justify."[52] Still, this commentary, by not merely muting the critique of suicide but making suicide apply a critical pressure to a dishonorable and shameful punishment, connects more clearly with Byron's rendering, in which suicide is less significant for its abhorrent qualities and more so for its complaint against the terrors of the law. If Byron departs from Kant, in other words, he does so in a way that is thoroughly Kantian.

Disobedience, Correction, Repair

Manfred's relentlessly critical position provides the strongest justification for the comparison with Kant; we could contrast it with the urgent issue of metaphysical unity and reconciliation that is the subject of Goethe's *Faust* (1806), which Byron knew—Matthew Lewis read it to him—and obviously used as a source for his own drama. But Byron accentuates a wayward dissidence in the hero that is all but eliminated at the end of *Faust*'s part 2 (1832), when the hero's endless striving is finally put to rest by his redemption.[53] I cite *Manfred* as only one instance of a resistant approach to justice that animates a whole range of writing in the Romantic period. This writing explores and modifies energies that Jonathan Lamb associates with the legacy of Job's sublime disturbance of normative "standards of propriety" in eighteenth-century literature and that Peter Brooks associates with the melodramatic, and also sublime, "moral imagination."[54] Samuel Romilly implies that the reform of the death penalty would be guided by a "lenity" that would emerge from the ability of the British public to think of a mode of lawfulness beyond the merely accepted convention.[55] Wordsworth too, in *The Prelude* (1805), strenuously imagines a law beyond the law in his critique of the French Revolution; in his rendering, the revolution imposes a universal terrorizing "fear." Revolutionary terror, meanwhile, meets a retort in the poet's own more principled "visions" of pleading before "unjust Tribunals" with a "soul" plagued by its own sense of "treachery and desertion."[56]

The value of dissent and the concern for its expression that I have been discussing establish a powerful link between these views and Rawls's. Rawls's essay "The Justification of Civil Disobedience" (1969) lays particular stress upon this aspect of his account of justice and thus helps us to modify the view that Scarry attributes to him in *On Beauty and Being Just*.[57] Civil disobedience exerts a corrective pressure on the law—it is a "minority" opinion that basic principles of justice are being violated—at the same time that it acts according to a principle that would allow for the existence of a range of other simultaneous and conflicting pressures.[58] While attempting to "correct injustices" by "disobedience from infractions of the fundamental equal liberties," Rawls writes, "these liberties would . . . be more rather than less secure. Legitimate civil disobedience . . . is a stabilizing device in a constitutional regime, tending to make it more firmly just."[59]

Rawls, following and extending Kant, seems to use *legitimate* to refer to whatever disobedience would not conflict with the rights of others. Perhaps that reading of Rawls's intent is more generous than those of many readers. Stanley Cavell, for instance, argues that Rawls's view of public reason is unnecessarily strict, leaving out the opportunity for dissenting voices to be adequately heard in the "conversation" of justice; Melissa Williams more pointedly advocates a more politicized view toward group interests.[60] The common assumption that Rawls, like Kant, is hostile to the recognition and acceptance of difference should be questioned. In *Political Liberalism*, in fact, he suggests that legitimate disobedience might be broad enough to include "subversive advocacy" and revolutionary activity (345–46). And in his efforts to defend "public reason" as a mediation of disputes, he clarifies that commitment as generated from within different vantage points rather than an externally imposed norm (226, 241). By the same token, the "primary goods," which include "basic rights and liberties, institutional opportunities, and prerogatives of office and position, along with income and wealth" and are the product of a just social arrangement, are capable of expansion and revision over time (181). Even the concept of the "original position," which depends upon a "veil of ignorance" beyond which people set aside their distinctive commitments in order to stipulate the character of just institutions, is not meant to "overrid[e] our more particular judgments." Rather, Rawls asks that the original position be the function of a commitment to an ideal level of inclusion and abstraction, even though particular judgments, upon "reflection," may cause a readjustment of the abstraction itself (45–46).

In contrast to some of Rawls's critics, then, I suggest that what is Kantian about Rawls is not a cultivation of an inflexible sentiment or uniform rationality but the contrasting emphasis on complaint and dissent, an emphasis not entirely different from that of some interpreters of Rawls, such as Loren A. King, who states that "our encounters with other persons and ideas in a variety of settings may lead us to reformulate our values, interests, and aspirations in ways that may not have occurred to us prior to our encounters with other critiques, other perspectives, other beliefs and traditions."[61] Stuart Hampshire's claim that "justice is conflict," in that participants in just social arrangements "will sometimes collide with others who make contrary judgments," is entirely compatible with this view, even though Hampshire tends to see himself as more at odds with the Kantian tradition.[62]

My emphasis on the *nonidentity* between the moral and the juridical in this trajectory of thought from Romanticism to some contemporary political theorists, a nonidentity that is nevertheless the basis for an insistent and potentially conflictual relationship, necessarily puts my account here at odds with prominent views that immediately preceded Kant and that responded to his work. Kant's corrective relation between moral philosophy and legality contends with radically discrepant accounts in Hobbes and Hegel; it also contrasts with a whole range of different modes of mediating between individual and society, particularly insofar as that mediation, in its distinction from Hobbesian absolutism, emphasizes the cultivation of public sentiment. David Hume, for instance, views justice as "utility," which he defines as a "habit" or uniform social custom.[63] Although J. G. Fichte approved of, and appropriated, many aspects of Kant's philosophical departure from the account of law either as absolutist rule or as custom, his emphasis on majority rule as the determination of justice led him to view objection simply as an injustice that must be punished.[64] While there are important differences in these perspectives, in their significant variation they depend upon some notion of mutuality or shared value or conduct; they tend to eliminate the conflict and criticism built into the Kantian account.

More recent prominent views of justice have continued to foreground the importance of shared culture, beliefs, or values. Beyond the recent works on beauty discussed in the previous chapter, these include Michael Sandel's call for a "politics of moral engagement," Charles Taylor's commitment to community organized around a common view of a "good life," and Michael Walzer's emphasis on the "understandings shared among citizens" about core political values that shape personal freedoms.[65] Distinct from communitarian views, the one I am elaborating here, and to which I give a greater privilege, highlights the role of contest, complaint, and redefinition: the fruitful interplay among vantage points that contributes to justice as maximized opportunity. Opportunity, following Norman Daniels's view (in the context of healthcare reform) consists less in a distinct culture than in an "opportunity range," accommodating an "array of life plans" that persons in a just social arrangement can construct for themselves.[66]

The work of Sandel, Taylor, and Walzer, because of its emphasis on shared identity and attendant exclusion, might at first glance seem to provide a context for the work of beauty theorists. Scarry's, Steiner's, and de Bolla's accounts of politically advantageous structures modeled through the aesthetic of beauty certainly appear to echo those views. At the same time, though, their logic, more closely resembling the nationalist and elitist aesthetics from Reynolds to Arnold, insists even more fervently on viable community as shared identity. While in one sense resembling communitarian versions of justice, then, beauty theory takes that argument in a direction that speaks out most eloquently as nothing less than the preeminent aesthetic discourse of biopolitics. That is, whereas communitarian theorists think of shared aspects of identity as a necessary component of just societies, beauty theory equates ideal social arrangements almost exclusively with the production of biopolitical norms.

My argument about the importance of justice as staked out in Kant both intersects with and departs from Foucault's account of the eighteenth- and nineteenth-century rise to hegemony of *homo economicus* over *homo juridicus*, of economic man over juridical man, and his late interest in Kant's account of enlightenment as a permanent process of critique. Kant's view of legal right as a structure open to complaint and revision can be understood neither as the "spontaneous synthesis" of interanimating economic actors within "civil society"[67] nor with the more oppositional twist that Foucault makes to Kantian critique. In his writings on Kant and the Enlightenment, he shifts the weight of Kant's critique almost entirely to the level of the subject, an "ontology of ourselves."[68] Judith Butler appropriates and amplifies this later emphasis of Foucault's on the subject, describing her understanding of performative subjectivity as the "radical reoccupation and resignification" of norms.[69] If it is true, as Foucault claims, that the question of governmentality in the eighteenth century is understood in terms of a *rationality* rather than an adherence to *truth*, then the Kantian position aims to expand the number of contact points between those mechanisms of governmentality and the subjects within them. Kant's account of right neither coincides with nor merely opposes that rationality but instead aims to test and reshape it.

Sublime Complaint

Kant's view of a frictional relationship between morals and legislation, with its connection to and departures from competing accounts, finally brings us back to the question of the relationship between aesthetics and justice, which I have so far only implied in my explanation of Kant's text and other Romantic examples. For if the aesthetic of beauty envisions and impels the kind of logic that Foucault attributes to the biopolitical structure of "civil society," the sublime aligns itself more clearly with a position of dissent and complaint.

The implicit suggestion of the recent writing on beauty that I've been examining is that the nonidentity between differing moral perspectives and structures of justice either doesn't exist or isn't important; justice or mutuality in social arrangements either requires or arises from a harmony among identical or at least similar parts. Susan Stewart's brief but suggestive remarks on how the sublime produces a contrast between "individuality" and "the social as a whole" begin to hint at the crucial contrast I wish to make with the political aesthetic of beauty.[70] More precisely, the sublime, to appropriate and now slightly alter Gasché's terminology, could be called the "aesthetical representation" of an unharmonious harmony between conflicting commitments to justice. Instead of beauty's tendency to make experience a means toward furthering the inclinations of others, the sublime promotes a feeling that is simultaneously subjective and compatible with the disagreement and nonresemblance of others—with the incompatibility among, and nonheritability of, aesthetic experiences.[71]

It's true, then, that the sublime produces a certain sense of autonomy, because it urges us to see ourselves and others as ends rather than means. But autonomy in Kant's account does not seem to be merely opposed to the kind of reciprocity that Steiner takes to be at work in her defense of beauty, as much as she accuses Kant of proposing what she imagines to be a society of utterly disconnected individuals. Neither subjective nor collective, the Kantian sublime composes subjectivity and collectivity in relation to each other. And thus it would be more correct to say that Kant's interpretation of autonomy gives a different sense of what reciprocity might be.

On the one hand, it seems crucial for Kant to distinguish in the *Critique of Judgment* between the kind of freedom he claims to be at work in aesthetic judgments and attempts of persons to separate themselves from others out of a "fantastic wish" for solitude or a "misanthropic" contempt for humanity (116–17). On the other hand, the sublime is important in its connection to the issue of reciprocity not because it replicates what is already given to experience—it does not ask for de Bolla's sharing of feelings, attitudes, or identities otherwise determined—but because the subjectivity of feeling is compatible with the "bare capability" of sharing, not sharing a visibly unified idea of reason itself but sharing the activity of *morally* lawful but nonidentical reasoning. And that reasoning potentially forms the common ground for *juridically* lawful resistance and complaint. This is what is at stake in Manfred's alliance of the sublime with a protest against penal law, just as Byron's Childe Harold insistently imbibes the sublime scenery of Greece, which "defies the power which crush'd thy temples gone,"[72] and just as Percy Shelley's enthusiastic speaker in his "Mont Blanc" (1817) "interpret[s]" or "feel[s]" the voice in the "great mountain" as if it could "repeal / Large codes of fraud and woe."[73] In this same line of political-aesthetic thinking, Thomas De Quincey's praise of "just, subtle, and mighty opium" in his *Confessions of an English Opium Eater* (1821) links the power of "spiritualized" and "sublimed" passions to a revisionary "chancery of dreams," where wrongs are redressed, sufferings are assuaged, and "sentences of unrighteous judges" are "revers[ed]."[74]

The dimension of the sublime I address here—its potential for encouraging plural associations predicated on productive antagonisms—must be taken into account in order to revise the more strictly oppositional status assigned to it in the work of Weiskel and Hertz. That oppositional status receives sustained attention in Jean-François Lyotard's work and more recently in the work of Jean-Luc Nancy and Vivasvan Soni.[75] Often, these views (as in Weiskel and Hertz) avoid a detailed consideration even of Kant's own open and suggestive connections between the aesthetic and moral philosophy, or (as in Lyotard, Nancy, and Soni) they insist on aesthetics merely as an interruption or disruption of juridical discourses and institutional structures.

At the same time, I see the need for some adjustment to the arguments that historicist critics make from the contrary direction. As discussed in the previous chapter, critics such as de Bolla and Caygill tend to normalize the sublime. Terry Eagleton's treatment of Kant's aesthetics in general as hopelessly abstract and disembodied is yet another instance of a political interpretation of Kant neglecting or downplaying the oppositional energies that seemed closer to the center of deconstructive readings.[76] Strangely, Eagleton, because he insists on seeing all work in aesthetics as a potent affective source of "human bonding," reads Kant's aesthetics as an attempt to enforce order on social antagonisms, even though the point of the sublime, with its antagonisms that connect to justice, is entirely the opposite.[77]

The relationships I've been exploring must necessarily bring us to admit a certain kind of limitation on Kant's sublime even while we account for its relevance. It is not a replicable model or "analogy" for justice, as Scarry claims beauty to be; it cannot recommend a system of laws in the way that she imagines boys, flowers, palms, or paintings as a series of prompts to devise symmetrical social arrangements. Rather than operating as a model of physical or mental attributes, the sublime offers us what would best be described as an open and variable stance or posture toward justice. This position is at a decided remove from any decisive position on what the law of the land might be; it gives us a feeling of what following a moral law, rather than a juridical law, would be like. The aesthetic, like the moral, does not *need* to concern itself with justice; that's why Kant regards the corrective position of moral reasoning to be "meritorious" but not moral.[78]

This removal may also be viewed as its limited strength. For the sublime also gives us a feeling of what Kantian justice needs in order to be justice. Justice requires a corrective standpoint on the law and its accumulation of prejudicial inclusions and exclusions. That standpoint might lead to what Jacques Rancière defines—quite apart from the issue of aesthetics—as politics itself, which is a refiguring of space, "of what there is to do there, what is to be seen or named therein." In Rancière's work, That space is fundamentally paradoxical, configured as the "part of no part," an artificial construction that includes without merely representing. By contrast, the achievement of consensus, Rancière argues, "reduces politics to the police."[79] It is precisely that reduction that Kant derides in the third *Critique*'s account of oppressive religious regimes that attempt to legislate ritual. Rancière's attempt to privilege a highly specific form of the political is what I identify as a commitment to justice, a commitment that continually emphasizes a structural relationship rather than a replicable adherence to a code, norm, or standard.

It might be argued that what I describe as a standpoint on justice that allows for asymmetry is nonetheless a code, norm, or standard. But it seems far too easy and predictable to say that all attempts to revise a system of conventions are nevertheless dependent upon conventions. The standpoint I describe differs crucially from the mere enforcement of uniformity, because it stakes its most basic claim to justice on its ability to accommodate and solicit disagreement from contending perspectives. This distinguishes it from a view of justice that assumes that the terms are the result of collectively held values established in advance and codified into structures of cooperation. The Kantian aesthetic standpoint commits itself to submitting the groundwork of norms—crucial for communitarian theorists and for beauty theorists—to a rigorous test rather than a consistent affirmation.

From a more historical perspective, the corrective standpoint is one that John D'Emilio has described in relation to the career of Bayard Rustin, and one that Melissa Orlie identifies with the tradition of Anglo-American religious dissent (which, along with the teachings of Gandhi, influenced Rustin).[80] It is a position, Orlie argues, that is capable of accommodation to "socially produced necessities," while allowing an exercise of "enthusiastic imagination" for modifying structures of political power.[81] Kant's sublime therefore provides an aesthetic sense of that reparative standpoint. While it cannot give us a perfectly symmetrical image of laws or governments, it can give us a sense of community beyond communion—a sense of what it would be like to occupy a place in a just community, in which individuals differ in their corrective relationships to law, while at the same time engaging in the collective enterprise of correction.

CHAPTER 3

The Reparative Impulse

Kant's encouragement of the formation of a corrective standpoint on legal and political institutions and discourses might stimulate us to modify the terms upon which the "public" is understood and addressed by the postmodern public intellectual. Whereas the current discourse of beauty simply occupies and defends a position of authority, a corrective standpoint might dedicate itself to altering the structures in which that authority resides. This line of argument can accommodate the fact that not all participants will value the same freedoms, even as they collectively engage in the enterprise of correction. They participate, that is, in a structure in which their demands, which may be quite different during and after the deliberation process, are nonetheless systemically linked to one another.

What Kant calls "the public in the truest sense of the word" would not be considered in terms of trained and replicated subject-consumers, but in terms of free and equal persons whose demands upon a political community would be continually debated and revised. I am not suggesting that there is something inherently wrong with academics' appealing to a wider public, in line with Stanley Fish's suggestion that academics should confine themselves to a "narrow sense of vocation" because public concerns "belong to others."[1] Rather I am suggesting a different way of imagining such a public: as one that is less dependent on a logic of social modeling and more consistently encompassed and addressed as a forum open to debate.[2]

If the aesthetic of the sublime and the vision of justice it affords might lead us to another way of conceiving or addressing the "public," it is all the more urgent to address two contrasting ways of configuring publics in current critical theory: queer theory's frequent commitment to oppositional, nonnormative counterpublics and cosmopolitanism's frequent commitment to inclusive international or transnational cultures. The relevance of these public or counterpublic commitments to my argument, moreover, can be discerned in their aim to repair or correct political affiliations that are considered (within those theories) to be too normalized or routinized, and it becomes clear that I share some sympathies with these approaches. My aim here, however, is to show how the postmodern champions of beauty discussed in chapter 1 are the self-conscious defenders of a political aesthetic that motivates a range of seemingly disparate modes of critique. It turns out that many instances of queer and cosmopolitan discourses depend upon similar devotions to a strain of aesthetic representation in which, according to the logic of the beautiful, responses to and judgments about the world are not merely subjective but normatively encoded responses and judgments. Those responses and judgments are used to map individuals and social groups onto one another.

Such a claim takes issue not only with identity politics but also with the way the aesthetic has increasingly taken a decisive role in defining the extent and limits of communal participation across prominent theoretical perspectives. I take it as a central rather than a marginal point that the queer theorist often turns to the sum of queer experience as the "glue of surplus beauty,"[3] or views "beauty" as the welcome sponsor of a uniquely queer approach to "convention" and "habit,"[4] or turns to the formal properties of postmodern art as instances of how we should approach "gendered embodiment."[5] At the same time, I take it as a central rather than a marginal point that the cosmopolitan theorist just as often praises "the beauty and interest of a life that is open to the whole world,"[6] or models attitudes based upon responses to "splendidly cosmopolitan" collections of art,[7] or praises real and fictional characters, and the sum of their experiences, as imitable models of cosmopolitan identity. By claiming these features to be central within the argumentative terms of these discourses, I point to the aesthetic of symmetrical imitation and replication as the organizing principle for imagining and realizing political goals and ideals.

In this chapter I show, first, that influential currents in queer and cosmopolitan theories share a fundamental but undertheorized similarity and, second, that both theories often simply reinstate the dominant logic in beauty's ur-discourse of postmodern aesthetic and political theorizing, thereby replacing one set of imitable models with another. The distance of the theorists addressed here from the beautiful aesthetic of the eighteenth century is only an imagined advance on the political aesthetic that reigned in an earlier age; they more or less clearly echo the work of Reynolds and Burke. For a contrast to this pattern of aesthetic thinking, I turn at the end of the chapter to the conversation poems of Samuel Taylor Coleridge. In those poems, the speaker takes up the cause of justice to others as he attempts to give full scope to their varying but nevertheless coordinated thoughts, actions, and growth. Here, as in the writings of the theorists I describe, the aesthetic assumes a crucial role, providing in the poet's thoughts about communities an instance of what belonging feels like. But just communities are not anticipated by supposing a shared identity among selves and others. Rather, Coleridge's conversation poems from the 1790s, in a mode that Coleridge explicitly associates with the sublime, take familiarity as an occasion for insistent estrangement and strangers as an occasion for increasing obligation. Both impulses define the Coleridgean aesthetic approach to justice.

Queer Particularities

We must ask, Why is beauty the favored aesthetic of the moment? Why the return to a historical discourse of aesthetics with so little reflection on its history, with so little reflection on its limitations? And why does this return take place within politically inflected critical and theoretical discussion that might otherwise seem to have armed itself against the influence of debilitating constraints and conventions? Maybe the reason for the centrality of aesthetics at the most general level could be this: if Sheldon Wolin is right to say that aesthetic representations are crucial foundations for political theory in general because they yield the author's "vision,"[8] the politically oriented work I discuss here makes the aesthetic of beauty the guarantee of the scope of vision. That vision depends—even as it implicitly or explicitly argues for a notion of justice or fair treatment as a goal in political community—either on producing general political symmetries out of particular individualities or on working in the opposite direction to produce particular individualities from larger political symmetries.

But why this vision in particular? Why is beauty the most prominent aesthetic mode for orienting the ambitions of queer and cosmopolitan thinking? In a sense, the question can be answered in a way that extends the argument of chapter 1. That is, queer and cosmopolitan theory often appear to be as profoundly (even while covertly) invested in an aesthetic guardianship—recommending and preserving appealing models of being and behavior—as beauty theorists are. That might seem more than a bit surprising, given the open affiliation that queer and cosmopolitan critique occasionally have with methodologies of deconstructive criticism, which (as explained in the previous two chapters) seem most often to be concerned with the aesthetic of the sublime. But some nuance can be added to my earlier, starker contrast between deconstructive approaches to the sublime and the aesthetic of beauty. This nuance helps to explain why it is that recent postmodern approaches, while indebted to deconstruction in their appeal to difference and multiplicity, nonetheless echo (at first glance contradictorily) the preoccupations of today's beauty theorists.

Earlier I suggested that deconstructive readings of the sublime seem to champion resistance in a way that's lost in recent writing on beauty. While that is in some ways true, there is actually a deeper continuity that connects the deconstructive interest in the sublime with the more recent postmodern interest in beauty. Deconstructive criticism claims that the sublime is primarily an instance of failed mental, psychic, or linguistic power; the sublime is less about the interplay between faculties yielding the possibility of form and more about imagination as a purely empirical faculty that encounters its own limitations. Looking even more broadly at deconstructive accounts—from Weiskel and Hertz to Jacques Derrida and Paul de Man—we find that the resistant posture described in the previous chapters is rooted in the notion of material, and more specifically bodily, contingency. Hertz's suggestion that the eighteenth-century sublime in general is a materially contingent threat to normative mental "integration" and Derrida's more pointed claim that (in Kant) "everything is measured . . . on the scale of the body. Of man" are only two of the more obvious and succinct instances of this reasoning.[9]

Even though deconstruction rightly emphasizes the centrality of the sublime in Kant's third *Critique*, then, the emphasis on integration and normative scale as both necessary and unstable repeatedly makes the sublime appear surprisingly close to an instance of the beautiful. In Derrida's insistence on Kant's focus on a proper perspective for sublime experience—a "related" position, situated at a "middle place" or "correct distance" for achieving it—the sublime is not an experience of form developed from formlessness but rather an experience of form as always already supplied or communicated, a beautiful replica passed on from another's experience.[10] In de Man's reading of Kant, which steers his "radical formalism"[11] into a logic that is "entirely material,"[12] linguistic materialism finds its most sustained metaphorical expression in a contingently and randomly articulated and disarticulated body. For de Man, the sublime derives not only from a moment of bodily framing (as in Derrida) but also from the body itself, hence his persistent analogy between language and a (dis)figured corpse, so lucidly analyzed by Hertz in his essays on de Man's "lurid figures."[13]

So it is not entirely the case that writing on beauty has simply neglected writing on the sublime. The acclimation of beauty theory to the current political economy of the university and adjacent institutions is enabled by a deeper continuity between its fundamental assumptions and deconstructive accounts of the sublime. In addition, there is a powerful link between beauty theory and deconstructive aesthetics even more generally (i.e., beyond the sublime). Barbara Johnson's *Persons and Things* (2008), which views language as inevitably caught up in anthropomorphism, and anthropomorphism as an imperfect attachment to beauty's impossibly idealized form, is perhaps the most recent work of deconstructive criticism to make this general connection with clarity and resonance.[14] Beauty theorists simply take Johnson's logic of form as a limitation or constraint and turn this account of embodied form to its advantage; beauty, for them, is about bodies and identities. There is, finally, a line of continuity between deconstruction and current beauty theory that likewise includes New Historicist accounts of the sublime (like de Bolla's and Caygill's) from the 1980s. New Historicism, that is, interprets the general deconstructive emphasis on the materiality of the body as the more particular occasion to assert the body as a site of normalization and routinization. Current theorizing on beauty, in turn, establishes a continuity with this lineage (an entirely unacknowledged one) even while taming all of its polemical features. Beauty theory appropriates the commitment to bodily norms and finds in it a tranquilizing element that signifies at aesthetic and political registers.

Three things can be said, in summary, about the link between beauty and late-twentieth-century trends in theory. First, it appears that recent writing on beauty is in fact surprisingly consistent not only with New Historicism but also with deconstructive accounts of the sublime. Second, however, writing on beauty renders the deconstructive and historicist emphasis on human scale into an overt and determinist aesthetic program, just as it carefully arranges the excessively academic features of these perspectives within a more popular and accessible domain. Third, this appropriation and reorientation tenders something like an aesthetic retailoring and taming of theory and theoretical debate. Even though theorists such as Paul Bové have implied that deconstruction's insights are often less radical than it often seemed to claim, and even though the political consequences of the New Historicist exposure of power structures was far from clear,[15] the discourse of beauty ends up yoking the deconstructive and New Historicist emphasis on bodily materiality ever more securely to the search for shared values. Beauty theorists far more openly reconcile themselves to a quest for asserting normativity as a positive political ambition. Beauty discourse thus illuminates the drift of deconstructive (and post-deconstructive) theoretical practices, even while those practices fuel the proliferation of beauty discourse. This, I think, is why the discourse of beauty seems so central in the politically oriented critiques discussed here, which show their debt to deconstruction and its legacy not, or not merely, in their references to theoretical works of the past twenty years but rather (perhaps less obviously) in their deliberate aesthetic strategies.

The critiques discussed here do not always overtly or consistently gesture toward the aesthetic of beauty, but beauty's aesthetic logic nonetheless stands at the center of a theoretical enterprise that expands particular practices into larger patterns of affiliation. Consider Eve Sedgwick's account of a queer-identified "reparative impulse," a desire for compiling marginalized experiences and memories ostensibly to counter a dominant political culture that is "inadequate or inimical to its nurture" (159). One of the truly important dimensions of Sedgwick's argument in *Touching Feeling* (2003) can be found in her shrewd critique of the New Historicist "paranoid" style, one that privileges the power of critique with the exposure of a supposedly omnipresent power structure and takes its process of exposure to constitute a kind of liberation from it. She deftly demonstrates how a careful consideration of the historical shift from the 1960s to the present would seem to suggest, in the continued existence of widely exposed and yet tacitly accepted structures of domination that have yet to be dislodged, that the dazzling efforts of critics wielding a "hermeneutics of suspicion and exposure" have hardly been able to make the enlightened analysis of power structures coincide with their defeat (140). She thus reveals something sobering about that gesture of exposure: that it may be not only dated but theoretically dubious. How, she asks, can we guarantee that the exposure of power will necessarily inhibit its growth or diminish its abilities to impose violence (146)?

This part of the critique is convincing because it suggests that injustice is not to be removed simply through knowledge. At the same time, though, it is not obvious how Sedgwick intends queer experience to check the imposition of violence that exposure cannot dismantle. She wants "a wealth of characteristic, culturally central practices . . . that emerge from queer experience" to operate in a sense that is reparative in relation to systems of power or authority that limit those practices (147). But how does that work? A clue to the problem appears in the way that Sedgwick claims to want to "do justice" to that domain of "experience" identified as queer (147, 150). For Sedgwick, doing justice means taking note of the "additive and accretive" aspects of individual experiences (149). Doing justice in this sense does not mean removing violence or suffering; it means that recognizing the mere existence of something—simply recording or noting experiences in the manner of anthropological research—might do politically reparative work. At the same time, this logic registers the implicit claim that justice is fundamentally a matter of recognition; such recognition is both a cause and a consequence of forming groups with similar systems of value. Thus Sedgwick easily moves from individual to group experience: she shifts gears almost imperceptibly by talking first about "individual typology," a discussion that then flows seamlessly into "shared histories, emergent communities, and the weaving of intertextual discourse" (150).

The heightening of language resonating with literary theory—typology, intertextuality—signals the relevance of the aesthetic to Sedgwick's enterprise. But if the aesthetic dimension of reparative work described here does the work of justice primarily by emphasizing the similarities of persons within groups, it's not entirely apparent how queerness would be reparative rather than another limiting imposition of norms on new communities. Nor is it apparent how this reparative work could repair a present or prior injustice suffered at the hands of a constraining or limiting set of power structures. The only way that Sedgwick can make sense of the idea that accreted experiences can look like alternatives to dominant power structures is by insisting on their limitation and their marginality, the fact that they have been forgotten and need to be remembered. Even so, the sharing of experiences to form communities—the formation of communities around recognition—would still risk attempting to justify the imposition of uniformity merely with reference to their nonhegemonic position. For something to be reparative, don't conditions need to have improved? How Sedgwick's accumulated experiences can lead to a new and better mode of being—how attending to them can do justice beyond merely an exchange of knowledge among people who already have that knowledge and share experiences with people who already value them—is not clear.

Sedgwick's account appears in many ways to be an appropriation of an account frequently voiced in deconstructive criticism, of justice as a responsiveness to otherness and difference. In Derrida's writing on the law, justice emerges as the registration of difference itself: "the act of justice . . . must always concern singularity, individuals, irreplaceable groups and lives, the other or myself *as* other."[16] Here we might make the same point about deconstruction's vantage point on justice that we made earlier about deconstruction's account of the aesthetic. The spirit of Derrida's point can be said to inform Iris Marion Young's insistence on the politicization of culture against distributive rules of law, resulting in an "ideal of a heterogeneous public, in which persons stand forth with their differences acknowledged and respected."[17] Even here, though, we can hear the familiar ring of an eighteenth-century civic humanist discourse of cultivated respect. Young raises this to a still higher pitch when she speaks of the need to inculcate increasingly more respectful "cultural habits" and to further a "cultural revolution" in order to instill them permanently.[18]

While Sedgwick's argument connects to this continuum of deconstructive ethics and politics, it also positions itself in a corresponding continuum of queer theorizing that continually attempts to come to grips with the question of how an alternative, nonhegemonic way of life might make substantial alterations to political, legal, and economic structures, structures that are resisted even as they ostensibly provide advancement and protection. On one end of this continuum might be found Leo Bersani's ambitious and apocalyptic redefinition of sociability by shattering the self in its desire;[19] on the other end might be found Judith Halberstam's effort to translate the experience of queer subcultures into political "redemption" through "collaboration."[20] Sedgwick positions herself somewhere between these two poles, allowing a considerable weight to accumulate with accreted experiences without claiming that those experiences merely translate into an alternative political structure or full-fledged community. Even so, her account also can't articulate how accreted experiences would be "reparative" in the way that I described them in the previous chapter—it can't say what's being repaired and how.

A somewhat more comprehensive answer can be found in Michael Warner's *The Trouble with Normal* (1999), although Warner's tactic is more clearly to aesthetically embed the virtues of an ideal public within a queer counterpublic.[21] And this brings us even more squarely within what Patchen Markell calls a "politics of recognition."[22] Warner is more specific about the kinds of valuable yet ignored queer experiences to which Sedgwick may be referring—found in the queer subcultures of "drag shows," "club scenes," and queer-oriented "web sites" (67). And he also more steadily articulates precisely how those experiences may add up to something that resembles a form of justice, or to use Sedgwick's vocabulary, how those experiences might indeed be "reparative." Still, it is never apparent how the experiences recommended by Warner could offer a politics of "acceptance" or "dignity" that is entirely at odds with a logic of the "normal" to which they are ostensibly opposed (67).

Warner's argument thus repeatedly values a particular set of practices—sexual "autonomy" that has shrugged off normatively imposed "shame" and its inhibiting effects (16)—that in turn yield a general principle. In those replicable practices—in bars with drag queens and in S/M workshops—he says, the sense that one group oppresses another with stigma is assuaged by the understanding that stigma is something shared. "Everyone's a bottom, everyone's a slut, anyone who denies it is sure to meet justice at the hands of a bitter, shady queen, and if it's possible to be more exposed and abject then it's sure to be only a matter of time before someone gets there, probably on stage and with style" (34). Warner's claim, in other words, is that shame can be overcome by imposing it systematically and democratically; everyone's claim to respectability and dignity can be put in check. According to that view, queer experience is not simply an experience located within an individual that is summed up in retrospect; it is an experience of *shared* anti-hierarchical evaluation. Shame and "abjection" are thus the "bedrock" of queer life, in his words, enabling a "special kind of sociability" (35). In another version of this argument, Warner and Lauren Berlant view queer culture's intimacies as an extension of intimacy into the public sphere and thus as a critique of domesticity and privacy. Intimacies accumulate into a specific kind of "knowledge" fostered in "mobile sites of drag, youth culture, music, dance, parades, flaunting, and cruising."[23]

Warner talks in *Trouble* about a community that cultivates not merely particular experiences, then—the point here is not to say, as Sedgwick does, that queers merely have certain kinds of experience that might be accumulated and then shared—but rather a more robust procedure or rule. In his account of the "ground rule" of queer life—"get over yourself" or "put a wig on before you judge" (35)—specific cultural practices can provide replicable models precisely because they provide images of, or commitments to, procedural justice. Those practices are not simply the things you happen to do but are rather the instance of a rule for a larger set of relationships: the things you do are accompanied by a disciplining or taming of experience in relation to others. Queer practices are supplemented by the claim that they are equally distributed, a claim that is also and unavoidably stated merely as the theorist's hope. That is, Warner can only state that it is "sure" to be only a matter of time before one person's shame is matched or outdone by another's. So, while solving the problem of how we get from queer practices to an account of justice, Warner accentuates a problem of the relationship between queer life and the conditions of social justice, since the achievement of justice depends solely upon a logic of, he hopes, replicable identity—imitated beliefs, commitments, gestures, and practices.

One response to Warner's claims might come from a more or less empirical direction. As Dwight A. McBride so trenchantly shows in *Why I Hate Abercrombie & Fitch* (2005), the very scenes that Warner celebrates are the occasion for racist exclusion and other forms of obvious inequality. McBride shows us, that is, how odd it is that one could cruise a queer website and leave it imagining that exclusionary judgments had somehow been suspended or that shame is equally shared in order to instill a salutary form of "sociability."[24] But the serious objections that McBride's work raises may also point us in the direction of the larger theoretical thrust of Warner's critique, a critique that makes it seem that cultural practices are not simply communal (as in Sedgwick) but rather thickly layered with favored and predetermined principles of thought and action. Furthermore, in his view, those principles would be widely acceptable to others as just, a politically acceptable rule for everyone. But what is demonstrated is not merely the unproblematic extension of queer experience inductively into a rule; the very instability of this extension is reflected in the way that the entire logic is phrased, in Warner's own words, merely as a wish—a moment of sharing that is only "sure" to happen when "someone" repeats our experience, "probably on stage and with style." The skeptical ring in the apparent assurance reflects the limitation built into the notion of justice as replication. And as McBride shows, not everyone is sure to share those experiences equally.

Cosmopolitan Multiplicities

In some ways, cosmopolitanism appears to be queer theory's inverse. It is committed to a maximum inclusion of values rather than to a specific mode of life; it is abstract rather than particular. But even if cosmopolitanism might not at first glance seem to resemble the commitment to a reparative potential within specific cultural communities, fleeting resemblances in approach between queer and cosmopolitan theory reveal an underlying similarity. If we were to take account of Judith Halberstam's or David Eng's dedication to seeing queer communities embrace change, multiplicity, or intersectionality, we would recognize qualities that the cosmopolitan critic also places at the top of his or her list of attributes to be cultivated by global citizens.[25] Indeed, what queer theorists and cosmopolitans have in common, I would argue, is a commitment to viewing a specific domain of attitudes and practices as politically or socially valuable. While the problem with queer studies is that it frequently makes particular practices into a general rule for social justice, the problem with cosmopolitanism is that it frequently makes a general ambition to accommodate other cultures into a particular cultural attitude. Both see the solution to social problems as dependent upon our adopting new attitudes and beliefs.

To say that political critique of various kinds depends upon aesthetic representations may not be controversial; more controversial is my claim that the logic of the aesthetic of beauty in particular is not merely an external decoration for queer and cosmopolitan arguments but in fact deeply encoded within their motivations, adjurations, and demands. As hinted in chapter 1, Denis Donaghue's suggestion that beauty eclipses an interest in politics seems entirely misplaced. Probing further, we can see that a certain kind of postmodern political commitment is completely consistent with the aesthetic of beauty and is in fact dependent upon it. In queer critique, we continually note the presence and weight of particular images and characters—the drag queen and the sex performer, for instance—that are themselves taken to be images of justice or the means of furthering it. Kathryn Bond Stockton's *Beautiful Bottom, Beautiful Shame* (2006), following in the footsteps of Sedgwick and Warner, appropriates a nonconventional "debased" form of beauty that is the subject of queer "communication."[26] José Esteban Muñoz and Tim Dean, from clearly different but still related perspectives, have recently put aesthetic modeling (through queer club performances and bareback pornography) front and center as a communication of what Muñoz calls "an alternative economy of public sex."[27] In *Queer Beauty* (2010), Whitney Davis goes a step beyond all of these accounts in his compelling historical view of how queer communities over the past two centuries have embraced beauty as a way of issuing a "normative communalization of judgments of taste."[28]

While queer critique tends to follow the logic of Steiner's account of beauty, in which local identities—recall Sedgwick's emphasis on a "typology" (150)—form the basis for larger symmetries, cosmopolitan critique works in the other, complementary direction. Similar to the manner of Elaine Scarry's way of making an abstraction (symmetry) the basis for identity, cosmopolitans make multiplicity—a multiplicity with balance built into it—serve as a replicable norm. The complexity and heterogeneity of a national history, for instance, is taken as a schema to be imported into an individual, who does justice to him- or herself and others by replicating, and replicating perceptions of, further complexity and heterogeneity at the level of individual identity.

Queer theory's aesthetic mode most often resides in the performative citation of the particular—a character or event that emblematizes a larger commitment. The privileged genre in queer theory is drama, then: drag performances, sex shows, and so on, have a ritual function in representing queer culture's opposition to heteronormativity to and for itself. Even when discussing prose narrative, as in Sedgwick's *Epistemology of the Closet* (1991), narrative primarily issues in a dramatic relationship with the reader, who recognizes, in Sedgwick's reading of Proust, the queer closeted speaker: Proust provides the "*spectacle of the closet*" but also is himself a spectacle, a demonstration of "*the viewpoint of the closet*."[29] D. A. Miller, in his account of the "narrative authority and beauty of expression" in Jane Austen's novels, thinks of that authority and beauty as what the gay man seeks to imitate in a shared "genius for detachment," a dazzling critical removal from the conventions of the everyday world.[30] The celebrated impersonality of the narrator is an occasion for admiring queer imitation.

Following a slightly different but complementary logic, cosmopolitanism's aesthetic mode resides most often in the construction of narratives—histories of reception, influence, and social interaction—that individuals are urged to frame and adopt for themselves as emblems of complexity. Openly acknowledging that her work applies aesthetics to ethics and politics,[31] for instance, Julia Kristeva turns to texts such as Diderot's *Rameau's Nephew* for examples of identities that embrace "dislocation" and the "articulation of opposites"; these examples are aesthetic embodiments of the strangeness and foreignness within all selves (an argument that, we shall see, appears elsewhere in cosmopolitan theory).[32] Stephen William Foster understands cosmopolitanism as a specific kind of imitable "ability to interpolate diverse elements" of one's experience.[33] In a similar vein, Scott L. Malcomson's instances of "actually existing" cosmopolitanism can be located in well-traveled people who visit numerous places over time; these instances in turn are framed and aestheticized as a political ideal that might be approximated in the behaviors of others.[34]

Cosmopolitan theory frequently turns to Kant's celebrated essay "Perpetual Peace: A Philosophical Sketch" (1795) as an early example of its theoretical commitments, however much they may have changed in the more than two centuries since the essay was written. There, Kant commits himself to a cosmopolitan federation of states and draws up articles that would protect those states from going to war with one another. Even though Kant is criticized in various ways by contemporary theorists, however, it is surprising that cosmopolitan theory has not entirely accepted the essay's political-aesthetic valences on their own terms. He insists on the "state of nature" as a "state of war" between nations, and a "state of peace" therefore as a solution that must be "formally instituted" with the articles outlined in the essay. The ultimate institution of a federation of nations governed by those articles would be the outcome of practical reason.[35] Even though the maxims of war and peacemaking would be "universal" (115), Kant's aims in the essay are completely compatible with the logic traced out in chapter 2. That is, he underlines the importance of a dissenting, corrective vantage point on international law when he stipulates that philosophers should be consulted by, and "speak freely" to, the "legislative authority" of states (115); this comports with the general claim that moral right is a "limiting condition of politics" (117–18). We should hardly be surprised when Kant refers to the "republican constitution," dedicated to preserving "complete justice to the rights of man" (113) and thus necessary for a cosmopolitan federation of nations, as "sublime" (112).

In contrast to Kant's emphasis on the sublime vantage point of dissent within legislative authority, current cosmopolitan theory frequently emphasizes the cultivation of a specific set of attitudes and beliefs that sets local alliances at a distance. Martha Nussbaum, for instance, opposes "nationalism and ethnocentric particularism" to the cosmopolitan education she favors, an education that values "reason and moral capacity" rather than local alliances. Nussbaum's work, even while it claims to move beyond particularism, makes "reason and moral capacity" the result of an indoctrination that can only seem like another kind of particularism.[36]

For the most part, recent theorists have strived to rehabilitate cosmopolitanism from another, seemingly different direction, that is, precisely by insisting on the value of interconnected but nonetheless visible local or national cultures, which are not cancelled but rather included and transformed in a definition of cosmopolitan identity. Distinct from the queer theorist's emphasis on counterpublics, this strain of cosmopolitan discourse emphasizes interconnected publics. Thus Amartya Sen's *Identity and Violence* (2006) seems to differ slightly from many queer theorists when he insists that the key to avoiding violence and bloodshed is be found in our ability to acknowledge that all people have more than one identity. Although *cosmopolitan* is not the word Sen uses to describe his claims, he resembles cosmopolitans such as Ulrich Beck in that he explicitly locates value not in a particular culture but in what Beck defines as a cosmopolitan embrace of "alternative ways of life and rationalities."[37] Sen, that is, repeatedly announces as a mere matter of fact that all people "see themselves—and have reason to see themselves—in many different ways" (15). And that leads him to fault people with a serious misunderstanding when they assume, for instance, that Muslims can be defined only as followers of Islam. Instead of being defined by a "choiceless singularity," he says, Muslims, just like everyone else, are in fact diverse and complex in their interests and affiliations (16).

We might very easily complain about a basic unclarity in Sen's guiding assumption throughout his argument. It is never entirely apparent why multiple identities are better than a single identity. After all, if others were to judge each one of a person's multiple identities negatively, it's not obvious why that person would be better off if he or she acknowledged—and others acknowledged—many identities rather than just one. Couldn't a person be fanatically devoted to a particular combination of identities with as much exclusionary fervor as would characterize his or her devotion to one? Even if some aspects of a person's identity involved less fanaticism than others, what would forbid that person from prioritizing those identities so that religion—while accompanied by other defining characteristics—overrode the importance of them for him- or herself and for others?

When Sen says that "each of us can and do have many different identities" (45), the point of this unclarity in his argument becomes evident. For multiple identities are a matter of actual belief and practice, and even if we "can" have them, the shift to "do" seems forced at best. A given person might not actually have them, that is, might not adopt them, cultivate them, or publicize them. And a person who has multiple identities might not use them correctly: he or she might allow one of the identities to be "all-engulfing" (67). Sen may be right when he talks about the need to be skeptical about hard and fast divisions between the global and the local, and between one culture or nation and another (132); such arguments have been made many times before. But we can't rely upon the complexity of an individual identity in quite the same way that we can rely on the complexity of a nation's history. Indeed, the "conceptual weakness" (46) of viewing people in terms of singular identities might not really be a weakness if the very people being described in fact share the identical conceptual weakness about their own identity formation. When Sen takes a disparaging view of the "narrowly frenzied" terms in which adherents of some religions define themselves according to a "vicious mode of thinking" (172), the trouble with his view intensifies still further. That is, he launches his claims on behalf of a specific privileged way of viewing identity (as multiple identities that balance one another, rather than prioritized or singular identities); thus his way of viewing identity simply seems like a highly specific cultural preference for complexity over singularity. This cultural preference may not actually be better for anyone; it may merely reflect the author's sense that multiple identities are analogous to the actual complexity of national and world history.

Sen makes cosmopolitanism look like a highly constrained way of rendering the complexity of other people's identities. His argument, once it appears in *The Idea of Justice* (2009), seems especially ironic, since Sen wishes to argue against what he takes to be Rawls's restrictive account of "reason" and the "reasonable," but he only accentuates the problem he criticizes.[38] If the problem with queer theory is that it seems to say that queers should embrace their own specific identity—as if that identity might, by its own gravity, solve problems of exclusion or other injustices—the problem with Sen's account is that cosmopolitanism (which is central to his idea of justice) encourages us to take and recommend a particular viewpoint on other identities, a viewpoint that persons with those identities may not actually adopt for themselves. We can observe this problem throughout the most sophisticated thinking on cosmopolitanism, which makes the rigors of thinking about others look bizarrely routinized, as if a complex identity were a prescription for cosmopolitan citizenship.

In many ways Sen's account is a more rigorous thinking through of the claims to be found in Kwame Anthony Appiah's *Cosmopolitanism* (2006), in which cosmopolitanism at one level appears to involve an uncontroversial claim that the histories of groups, nations, and art objects are all more complicated than any claim to local, singular culture might have us think. But the emphasis on art objects in Appiah's account actually shows how crucial the aesthetic of beauty is even in Sen's work, that is, how the opposition to singular affiliations is secured by replicable images of balanced multiple attachments. Few would argue with Appiah's extensive discussion of artwork, such as when he cites works by Picasso, Stein, and Matisse that demonstrate their appreciation of African carvings to suggest that "good artists copy, great ones steal" (126). By that he simply seems to mean that the work of these important artists was clearly influenced by their contact with African objects. Appiah then shifts from an analysis of objects to a claim about "living cultures" that seem to be modeled upon those very objects: they are "mongrel, hybrid" cultures (129). This supports his urge to adopt a distinctively aestheticized version of an identity: "We do not need, have never needed, settled community, a homogeneous system of values, in order to have a home. Cultural purity is an oxymoron" (113). And from there he goes on to say in very much the same vein as Sen that "the odds are that, culturally speaking, you already live a cosmopolitan life, enriched by literature, art, and film that come from many places, and that contains influences from many more" (113). In other words, like Sen, Appiah shifts from a judgment about cultural richness to a claim that people should adopt that cultural richness as a kind of attitude or set of beliefs. The aesthetic representation is an absorption of all cultural influences, which are then read back onto the human subject as a recommendation for his or her own sense of identity.

The argument for cosmopolitan hybridity is based upon what people actually experience, without acknowledging its own dependence on a particular narrative construction, a construction uncritically accepted as more real than an illusory or fictive national or local identity. In important recent critiques of this position—for instance, by Pheng Cheah and Bruce Robbins—the meaning of cosmopolitanism shifts from a universally shared identity to a more particular virtue or quality of attention that characterizes the cosmopolitan critic. For Cheah, cosmopolitanism—or what he calls the "cosmopolitical"—requires consciousness of, and attention to, the ambivalent power of nation-states, which can either oppose or submit to the forces of globalization. Thus, nation-states can be neither transcended nor opposed; they instead demand a "responsibility" to the specific circumstances that constitute "given culture."[39] For Robbins, cosmopolitan theory requires "self consciousness," an attention to the "impurity" in one's *own* judgments, which still must follow "democratic, anti-imperialist principles."[40]

For critics like Cheah and Robbins, cosmopolitanism is not the actual or potential property of all people, as Nussbaum, Sen, and Appiah want it to be. It is rather an identity possessed by the theorist who adopts a specific attitude about the importance of complex or impure relations between identities (either in others or in one's self). Thus, even if this strand of critique moves the analysis beyond a simple recommendation for a replicable character type for all people in order to become cosmopolitans, these critiques of a less subtle brand of cosmopolitanism still think of cosmopolitan theory as an attention to some kind of local culture or relationship between local cultures. The issue of cosmopolitan identity is framed in a seemingly new but related way: cosmopolitanism, as Amanda Anderson points out, becomes an "art of virtue" that is shared among theorists, who are singled out as a group as separate from those who are characterized merely by their local identities or international alliances.[41] Anderson's own account of "critical cosmopolitanism," carefully pitched between local alliances and impersonal detachment, clearly conforms with this line of thought.[42]

The discourse of cosmopolitanism, then, in many of its articulations produces images of wide affiliations—national, international, global—and makes those images appear as if they could be applied as particular, as if they could characterize individual affiliations themselves. Although these arguments do seem different from the queer argument, they converge in one important respect. For while Sedgwick and Warner suggest that queer practices might recommend a kind of procedural justice, cosmopolitan critics often make the judicious acknowledgment of differences and tensions appear to be a commitment or set of commitments on the part of specific persons. In the critique of that position, cosmopolitanism is considered to be, not a universally shared identity, but rather a heightened awareness of what is shared and what is particular. But that looks very much like an identity itself, or at least like a shared awareness or "art of virtue."

There are important and notable exceptions to these versions of cosmopolitanism, one of which comes from Robbins himself. The self-consciousness that he praises may seem to be merely an admirable attitude, but elsewhere he suggests that this attitude may have more to do with institutional commitments than with beliefs held by individuals. In particular, Robbins argues for an extension of the welfare state beyond national boundaries. He recommends, for instance, that richer nations—he doesn't really say what makes nations rich—commit themselves to transferring funds to poorer nations through a tax on international financial transactions. Such institutional manifestations of cosmopolitanism would widen commitments to justice. At the same time, they would lift any personal burden for "extraordinary outbursts of love or compassion"; in other words, they would eliminate the idea of cosmopolitanism as collective identity.[43]

This alternative dismantles not only the view of cosmopolitanism as shared passion but also the view of it as awareness and self-awareness. We might even say that Robbins is not talking about cosmopolitan identity, but about international justice. They aren't the same: we don't need special knowledge of peoples in order to recognize that they need to be treated fairly, and we don't need to reflect deeply on our own position to acknowledge massive advantages at the expense of others and to acknowledge that one should do something about that inequality. Our position may motivate our concern, but the concern is not *about* the position.

Seyla Benhabib, in *Another Cosmopolitanism* (2006), also defines cosmopolitanism as international justice, but for her, international justice is an even more capacious and flexible set of laws in tension with national sovereignty and with more local systems of political and ethical authority. The tensions are productive, however. Through activism and "democratic iteration," local groups engage in a dynamic relationship with legal structures, and they can change the shape of those structures in order to yield "new political configurations, and new forms of agency."[44] Benhabib's broadly Kantian perspective might lead us to reconsider Warner's work, in particular an aspect of it that complicates his more openly stated emphasis on the necessarily political gravity of queer culture. Warner's argument in *The Trouble with Normal* may at first seem puzzling, as I earlier suggested, because of its emphasis on the critical, counterhegemonic value of a community's norms (which he attempts to clarify by claiming that queerness does not militate against norms but against normalization).[45] And the problem with that argument is that such norms can only hold that critical position as long as a community's relative lack of power can be sustained. Thus, from a certain perspective queer critique may seem to be a celebration of, rather than a polemic against, a group's disadvantages, as if the group's disadvantaged status were a requirement for sustaining moral-political value.

This position may not be very attractive, but then the main point is not to imagine one accretion of experiences as a privileged model for others.[46] Warner's stronger but usually more submerged claim is that queer sexuality, because of its visibility and malleability within a range of informal, expanding, and intractable intimacies, demonstrates the very public nature of sex itself: the position of all sexual agents within dispersed geographical and discursive spaces that either limit or facilitate their actions. Thus, Warner's work tends to be evenly divided between weak and strong claims. In an article in the "Queer Issue" of the *Village Voice*, for instance, he insists upon the importance of nonhegemonic difference, as if "queer girls who fuck queer boys with strap-ons" carried a specific political gravity on their own. In a similar vein, he argues that what marginalized people share is a "history of disruption." Both assertions imply that values, beliefs, and practices that stand outside the norm might attract us merely because their marginal status recommends them as imitable sources of value. But Warner intriguingly points to the way such positions might collectively contribute to building a "new world" in which "people differ and there's always something new to learn."[47]

Warner's stronger claim, in other words, is that queerness (only implicitly) makes a formal demand for expanded means of legal and institutional freedom and protection, currently denied by sexuality's closeting within a sanctified zone of domestic privacy. The real point of Warner's work, then, is to be found in his effort, consistent with a logic that I attribute to Kant, to press the corrective claims of queer thought and practice against an existing regime of regulations in order to propose an explicit shape—through activism fired by, in Melissa Orlie's words, "enthusiastic imagination"—for something entirely new.[48] That new entity, that new community, would not quite resemble queer practices, the ethics of queer life, or the practices and ethics of any particular life at all. It would consist in associational frameworks—educational, political, medical, legal—enabling an expanded range of actions that we perform, eye with anticipation, or leave behind.[49] It would be accommodating and variegated enough to fit just about anyone's present, future, or past.

Strange Familiars: Coleridge's Conversation Poems

Robbins differs from Benhabib and Warner in that he recommends an entirely rationalized economic approach to the problem of injustice; the strong claims in Benhabib's and Warner's arguments are, as in Kant, that injustice could be addressed from positions that do not follow any preconceived notion of rationality but that can nonetheless insist—from radically different standpoints—on an institutional means of procuring and acknowledging right. This is a position that I associate with Rawls's appropriation of Kant in his outline of the role of liberties in the conception of justice. Even while a just society strives for equality (in "primary goods") it must give ample scope to the centrality of basic freedoms. That view of justice acknowledges that an individual's ends may be inconsistent with those of other individuals and can be revised. He thus claims that the priority of liberty ensures that the terms of justice will not be predetermined or static: free persons "do not think of themselves as unavoidably tied to any particular array of fundamental interests; instead they view themselves as capable of revising and changing these final ends."[50]

This moral-political position is one that I have been associating with the aesthetic of the sublime, an aesthetic that does not model individuals or communities as much as it conveys a standpoint on communal interaction. This standpoint presumes that subjects might be placed in asymmetrical relationships with one another. I now want to cast the net wider than Kant to consider the work of Coleridge, whose conversation poems from the 1790s, which have an immediate bearing on some of the issues that arise in both queer and cosmopolitan theory as I have described them. In a prominent line of queer theorizing, I've been arguing, the accretion of particular experiences is said to have some alliance with the cause of justice, but it's not always clear how that accretion can yield new, broad social commitments. In a prominent line of cosmopolitan theorizing, the interest in broad political affiliations and histories is also connected to claims for justice, even though it is not clear how the theoretical abstractions yield more just conditions for individuals. These complementary ways of reading particularities into generalities, and generalities into particularities, can account for the prominent appeals to beauty, beautiful art, and imitable patterns in many of the texts discussed so far in this chapter. The discourse of beauty is not merely an aesthetic vehicle for their political arguments; it is the predominating representational logic through which these arguments achieve their coherence.

Turning from contemporary theory to Coleridge—like my turn to Kant and associated Romantic figures in the previous chapter—may at first seem somewhat untoward, but it should seem significantly less so once we acknowledge the association between the main concerns of queer and cosmopolitan theory and those of eighteenth-century political-aesthetic paradigms. This association has not been completely unrecognized in the annals of historicist criticism, where the focus has often settled on unearthing a late-eighteenth-century background for contemporary theory. Eric O. Clarke, for instance, explores the importance of Romanticism as a moment of heightened self-consciousness about androgynous identity; Andrew Elfenbein argues for a connection between queer sexuality and Romantic genius; Richard Sha still more pointedly shows how "sex in this period was unusually recalcitrant to material fixity" and thus finds a forward-thinking, liberating potential in Romantic "perversion."[51] The importance of Kant's essay "Perpetual Peace" even in current discussions, moreover, testifies to the endurance of eighteenth-century paradigms in today's cosmopolitan theory. Still more, critics such as Adriana Craciun, Peter Melville, Gerald Newman, and Esther Wohlgemut argue for Kant's era more broadly as a foundational moment for the history of cosmopolitan thought.[52] Wohlgemut, for instance, shows how a "non-unified formulation of nationness" challenged "more unified models" of the nation in the writing of Edmund Burke.[53]

Although these critics have gone to considerable lengths to reveal a precedent for queer and cosmopolitan theory, I turn to Coleridge to show that he approaches the issues at stake in queer and cosmopolitan theoretical positions precisely in order to strike out in a new direction. Coleridge's poems from the 1790s—in particular his conversation poems, within which a lyric speaker addresses one or more persons—do something that departs from the beautiful logic of queer and cosmopolitan theory. While distancing themselves from the play of sympathies that characterizes the aesthetic of beauty, the conversation poems make an effort to adopt a reparative vantage point toward others that insists on a rebuilt and strengthened sense of obligation. That strength of obligation is achieved, however, only by building a sense of asymmetry and estrangement into the poems' revised understanding of community. And that sense is conveyed, I believe, through their commitment to the aesthetic of the sublime.

The conversation poems can be said to be the lyric counterpart of Coleridge's sustained interest in exploring the extent and limits of religious toleration, an interest that likewise informs William Godwin's influential *Enquiry Concerning Political Justice* (1793). While he distances himself from Godwin when it comes to theological matters, Coleridge nonetheless shares his contemporary's opposition to established religion and its stranglehold on the British government and civil institutions. I have elsewhere described Coleridge's politics of toleration primarily as they appear in his prose writings.[54] To summarize that argument briefly, even though Coleridge changed his religious orientation during his career—first a Unitarian, he later defended the Anglican Church—his political positions cannot not be defined entirely by this change. It would be more correct to say that Coleridge, even when he defended the established church, was hardly a conservative; instead, the consistent thread that runs from the early to the later writings is his desire to sustain the energy of vibrant argument that he associates with religious dissent and to harness that energy even within the structure of the established church itself. The presence and visibility of dissent is connected in Coleridge's writing with the progress of intellectual enlightenment even as it is considered to be the cornerstone of all pursuits of justice—the opposition to political and religious tyranny, the campaign for the abolition of the slave trade, and so on. Coleridge insists on the right of "petition," the right to assert "common grievances," amid an impassioned defense of constitutional law.[55]

My suggestion that the conversation poems focus on forming alliances in the midst of dissent and estrangement contrasts with accounts of these poems that tend to emphasize them as exhibitions of the author's comforting and "generous spirit," his appreciation for a humanized "beneficence of nature," or his celebration of "private and limited community."[56] This is not to say that domestic relationships are not important in his poems, for indeed they are, but rather that their expected lineaments are insistently troubled and questioned from within. As a first instance, consider Coleridge's poem "To Charles Lloyd, on his Proposing to Domesticate with the Author" (1797), which even in its title announces the importance of domestic intimacy, although that intimacy is challenged throughout the poem. Addressed to the young Charles Lloyd, who had taken up residence with the Coleridges to be tutored by the author, the poem speaks of a walk taken by the two men in the Quantock Hills. The speaker and his companion mount a "path sublime" to a "lovely hill sublime," while the stunning vision of nature gives way to an impassioned complaint against combined injustices—"Want's barren soil" and "Bigotry's mad fire-invoking rage."[57] Although this is not one of Coleridge's better-known poems, its terms resonate in the conversation poems to follow. The self-conscious references to the sublime are the aesthetic counterpart of the poem's shifts between autonomy and separation on the one hand and institutional critique on the other. The sublime ascent in the poem, that is, enables a "social silence" (25) and separation between the speaker and his friend, while it also engages that speaker in a critique of unjust government policy against the poor and against religious dissenters.

"To Charles Lloyd" exposes the basic aesthetic and political coordinates that are pursued in different ways in some of the more celebrated conversation poems of the 1790s. Moving in one direction, these poems deploy the sublime mode both to celebrate and to undermine the expected comforts of domesticity. In "The Nightingale: A Conversation Poem," first published in Wordsworth and Coleridge's *Lyrical Ballads* (1798), Coleridge takes the structure of an established community in order to disrupt it and build new contours and commitments. The speaker begins with a characteristic gesture of literal and discursive air-clearing. "No cloud, no relique of the sunken day / Distinguishes the West," the poet says; the evening is free of "sullen light," "obscure trembling hues," and "murmuring" in the water beneath the mossy bridge on which the speaker asks his friend and sister (Wordsworth and Dorothy) to sit with him (1–4). Even the nightingale, called by Milton "'Most musical, most melancholy' bird" (13), cannot disrupt the speaker's pleasure in the evening's calm.

This pleasure is a register not merely of the poet's personal feelings and not merely of his assessment of nature itself; it is a measure of his outright rejection of a tradition that interprets the nightingale's song as melancholy, a judgment resulting from a pathetic fallacy. That melancholy, like the cloud itself—so charmingly called a "relique," as if clouds themselves were like the dust of ages—arose (the speaker surmises) from a young man fraught with a "grievous wrong," a "slow distemper," who attributes his own feelings to the bird (17–18). The problem is not simply that the bird's song has been interpreted as melancholy but rather that melancholy, in every succeeding poet who "echoes the conceit" (23), has made room for no other feeling. As if the conceit itself imposed an architectural constraint, Coleridge goes on to describe generations of readers themselves as inhabiting overcrowded spaces—"ball-rooms" and "hot theatres" (37)—where they become stifled by their own "meek sympathy," imbibing ancient poetic conceits as they "heave their sighs / O'er Philomela's pity-pleading strains" (38–39).

It is hard to disagree with Phil Cardlinale's suggestion that Coleridge apes Burke's *Enquiry* in these early lines of the poem precisely in order to subvert his account of the sublime.[58] This is certainly true when it comes to the poem's treatment of Milton, considered by Addison, Joseph Warton, Burke, and legions of others to be the quintessentially "sublime" English poet. Coleridge quickly makes Milton seem like the purveyor of an entirely false (because conventionalized) grandeur; but he is also most likely thinking of another poem about a nightingale, "An Evening Address to a Nightingale" (1779), by Cuthbert Shaw, in which the speaker compulsively associates the bird's song with "sorrow" and pleads with the reader to replicate that sorrow with the "tribute of a tear."[59] (Coleridge even quotes Shaw's poem in the preface to his 1796 volume of poems.) At one level, the speaker in Coleridge's treatment of the nightingale responds by thoroughly rejecting the tradition handed down from poets to readers who in turn become poets that would ask us to interpret nature according to a hardened affect, one that creates an automatic "sympathy" between past and present interpreters. At another level, that rejection leads the poet to commit himself to sharing in "Nature's immortality" (31) even while that immortality is enabled by his own work; the poet's song "Should make all Nature lovelier, and itself / Be loved like Nature" (34). The speaker thus sets himself apart from a poetic tradition in order not merely to return to nature but to devote himself to a "lovelier" version of it that is itself like nature. Writing poetry requires a distance from the poetic tradition at the same time that it requires the forceful assertion of a distinct position within the very natural scene to which the poet devotes his attention.

While critiquing Burke's sublime, then, the poem moves to a position closer to Kant's. There is no evidence that Coleridge knew Kant's work or even translations of it at this time; still, for the poet to wish his own song to become like that of the nightingale's is to insist on a place for poetry that is not terribly far from Kant's arguments in the third *Critique*'s "Analytic of the Sublime" about artistic genius and its capacity to produce "another nature, as it were, out of the material that actual nature gives it."[60] And this, moreover, leads to the poet's outlining a curious new position for his readers; they are to view his verse as they view nature itself: less as a container for their emotions and more as a paradoxical focal point of shared resistance to sharing. This logic compresses a way of thinking through the relations between viewing and listening subjects throughout the poem.

Seeking not to "profane" the nightingale with misleading conventions, the speaker adheres to the "lore" he has learned with his friends, that of the nightingale's joyous song as he disburdens "his full soul / Of all its music" (48–49). At first it might appear that Coleridge has shifted to a mode of elegant anthropomorphism that is just as poetic as the poetry he has rejected. But it gradually becomes clear that he means to display a very particular kind of intimacy and familiarity with the bird that increases in importance—and in complexity—as the poem continues.

In the next verse paragraph Coleridge shifts from the iconic nightingale to the nightingale in nature, and this, I would suggest, contributes to undoing and remaking the familiarity and intimacy that appear to be the context for the poet's musings. The poet trains his verse on the "lore" of the nightingale known to the poet and those around him, shifting away from the birds and birdsongs of literature to a grove full of singing nightingales near the "castle huge" (50). Their songs are well known by a "gentle Maid" (75) who lives near the castle and who "knows all their notes" (74). The Maid's geographical position (near the castle, left vacant by its "great lord" [51]) and empirical knowledge (knowing all the notes) in a sense make her an allegorical figure of the poem's shift away from allegory, from the world of romance to the "lore" of experience. But the Maid does not really achieve the emblematic quality of allegory. It is far from clear that her knowledge of the nightingale's song is to be *repeated* by others. She is therefore more significant in furthering the poem's effort to depict familiarity less as a replicable knowledge or disposition and more as a state of attention to, or engagement with, the nightingale and its "wanton song," a song that is itself "like topsy Joy that reels with tossing head" (85–86).

The speaker's turn to his "dear Babe" Hartley, "Nature's playmate" (97), elaborates on this understanding of familiarity and familiar "lore" (91). He reminisces about Hartley listening to the nightingales, recalling the comfort he gives his son, in a "most distressful mood," by bringing him to the "orchard plot" to alleviate his sobbing from "some inward pain": the baby laughs at the moon, which glitters in the child's "undropped tears" (104). The speaker approaches the end his meditation with a wish, similar to the address to Hartley in "Frost at Midnight" (1798), that his son will "grow up / Familiar with these songs, that with the night / He may associate joy," before closing with a final "farewell" to the nightingale and to his friends (108–9).

It should be noted that the speaker says "farewell" twice—once twenty lines before the final good-bye—and thus appears to separate himself from his friends even while in their company. The double farewell, furthermore, accompanies the speaker's acknowledgment of commitment to his friends, whom he will rejoin "tomorrow eve" (87), once again to hear the nightingales' songs. These details connect with my more focused interest here in the shift of attention to Hartley, which underscores the shift of attention from literary romance to nature as an aesthetic approach to a moral-political stance. That stance more or less explicitly rejects the association that Coleridge makes between romance and utterly fictive notions of human agency and injury that make the nightingale into an abstract emblem of, and incitement to, equally fictive states of melancholy and suffering. In contrast, it adopts a more complex perspective. Implicitly taking up the issue of justice, it outlines what the father owes to the son in his attempt to alleviate suffering and to secure happiness. And yet this maneuver depends upon an assertion of intimacy and familiarity that's simultaneously undercut by an insistent shuttling between separation and association. The poem offsets the notion that assertions of intimacy might require the replication of beliefs or attitudes, which would be cultivated in the child by the speaker and in the reader by the poem.[61]

How does this happen? The notion of familiarity has already been shown to be complicated by the fact that familiarity with nature is precisely what allows the speaker to cast off all-too-familiar cultural stereotypes, as if familiarity were a tool of defamiliarization. (It is worth noting here that Wordsworth's prose fragment on the sublime and the beautiful insists on a "preparatory intercourse" with an object in order to experience it as sublime.)[62] The father's wishing that his son might become "familiar with these songs" (108) might mean that he intends the son to retain a past association between the night's luminous imagery and his own pleasure: he may "associate" the "night" with "joy." But the father's wish for the son's familiarity with birdsongs might mean a number of other things as well, troubling any claims that the conversation poems are principally concerned with the speaker's direct communication of thoughts to, or actualization of thoughts in, a listener or reader.[63] The wish framed in these lines cannot dispel the poem's own realization that the son might reject the interpretation of the father, for instance, just as the speaker has rejected his own poetic forefathers. The son's familiarity with nature, after all, might contradict the father's, thus providing support for Peter Melville's suggestion that the conversation poems are as much about "hostility" as they are about "hospitality."[64] Just as important as any affective and emotional continuity in the poem's powerful conclusion is its sense of a formal "familiarity" with the sounds and images in nature, coupled with a reminder of a persistent and enlivening discontinuity, a discontinuity that may be encountered in the moment of the poem's interpretation by a reader. Nothing in the poem demonstrates the play between familiarity and discontinuity more clearly than the nightingale itself, which is less significant as a container for emotions than as a focal point for the attention of the Maid, the poet, his son, and his friends.

By making the sharing of aesthetic experience alternately seem both dispersed and formally convergent, Coleridge adopts the logic of the sublime and thus rejects the kind of aesthetic logic at work in Steiner and in queer theory. The full range of Coleridge's poems about domesticity, with their highly mobile, fraught, and transient relationships—other examples include "The Eolian Harp" (1796) and "This Lime Tree Bower My Prison" (1797)—demonstrate affiliations that might certainly be called queer. But those affiliations are less important for extending local experiences to other bodies to produce new symmetries and more important for fracturing alliances, while nonetheless asserting obligations, from within.[65]

In still other conversation poems, Coleridge adopts a more public voice and addresses more "cosmopolitan" issues of Britain's place among other nations. Here too, though, his concern is to outline an obligation beyond British shores that simultaneously critiques the idea of political action motivated by sympathetic identification. In "Fears in Solitude: Written in 1798, during the Alarm of an Invasion" (1798), the speaker takes the occasion of a threat of a French invasion on British shores to assert a powerful connection between the speaker's own nation and its enemy (1,400 troops had landed in Fishguard in 1797 only to surrender two days later, and plans were brewing in 1798 for Napoleon to land in Britain). Whereas "The Nightingale" begins with intimacy and decomposes it, "Fears in Solitude" begins with the speaker's solitude in a "small and silent dell" (2) and then draws him out of himself into a larger set of public affiliations. That gesture both depends upon and is informed by the speaker's urgent questioning of Britain's traditional but falsely and hypocritically conceived national integrity.

The initial calm of the natural scene with which the poem opens quickly dissolves in the wake of the speaker's attempt to raise his readers' consciousness of having "offended very grievously" against the speaker's (and the nation's) "human brethren" (42, 32). The poet-speaker labors not simply to raise an alarm against the nation's enemy, then, but to rouse his audience to a sense of its wrongs, to a sense of how it has "offended" others. This engages the speaker at two levels. First, bearing some similarity to the critique of melancholy sentiment in "The Nightingale," the poem launches a profound attack on the ways in which British communities of sympathy, with their basis in religious uniformity, have typically blinded their members to the effects of their actions. Their "sweet words / Of Christian promise" (64) have little meaning in the eyes of the poet; they "gabble" over religious "oaths" that "all must swear" even though everyone means to "break" them (72–73). False religious uniformity does not merely cover over malicious intent, furthermore; it disguises violence in a beautiful cloak of sympathetically shared virtue. For the speaker continues his invective by showing how the nation's military actions accompany a litany of "holy names" (101) and "adjurations of God in Heaven" (102), all of which are meant to justify unjustifiable harm to persons who lie beyond the nation's boundaries.

Second, the critique of false community within the nation extends to advocacy for a new account of relations with those beyond it. Mary Favret accurately describes the way some Romantic-era literature uncannily registers the effects of war as a "constant dread" and "disquiet" even while attenuating those effects beneath barely ruffled, beautiful textual surfaces.[66] It's certainly true that the speaker's audience in Coleridge's poem is, as Favret claims, "dissociated from the ongoing war,"[67] but the whole point of the speaker's critique of a falsely imposed uniformity is to assert a more vivid sense of connection between the poet's audience and their "brethren." Even though the speaker urges British patriots to fight the French—to "render them back upon the insulted ocean" (147)—the poem goes far beyond a merely expedient defense of the poet's "native isle" (39). Indeed, speaking of an "insulted ocean" rather than an insulted island or insulted nation only begins to suggest the many ways in which the integrity of the native isle diminishes in importance compared with a more general sense of international justice. The speaker asks the reader to see France not merely as an enemy demonized in opposition to the falsifying rhetoric of "holy names" but rather as a victim of British aggression, and a victim that might require a penalty. The poem thus urges Britons to repent the "wrongs" it has inflicted on France (152). British patriots should return not with "drunken triumph" but rather with "fear" (151)—fear, that is, of a counterattack from a "vengeful enemy" (199), justly deserved because of Britain's own actions. And at the same time, the poem urges them to view the wrongs against France within the context of multiple wrongs to others. At home in the speaker's own country, Britons have robbed themselves of "freedom" and "life" as they drink up "Pollutions from the brimming cup of wealth" (62, 60); abroad, they have harmed "tribes" with "slavery and pangs" (50), deadly "vices, whose deep taint / With slow perdition murders the whole man" (51–52).

It can't escape our notice that Coleridge elsewhere—in *The Friend*—takes an interest in arguing against the idea that "cosmopolitanism is nobler than Nationality, and the human race a sublimer object of love than a people."[68] While not dismissing it entirely, he asserts that a "Law of Nations" that would be the outgrowth of cosmopolitan thought "is not fixed or positive in itself"; it is legitimate only when it arises from the "conscience" (291). This kind of cosmopolitanism, he argues, must be the outgrowth of "a circle defined by human affections, the first firm sod within which becomes sacred beneath the step of the returning citizen" (292). There are complications in this apparent retreat to domestic intimacy as the impetus for widened affiliations, however. We have already come to realize that for Coleridge the "human affections" are characterized by a purposeful estrangement, largely because the love of one's own "people" is viewed as sublime—"sublimer" than a whole "race." And if it is true that a cosmopolitan sense of right arises only from the "conscience," it might very well be said that Coleridge, in "Fears in Solitude," fashions the poem itself as the attempt to arouse that conscience, to sound an "alarm" to the English nation to abide by an expanded sense of justice and right. Conscience exerts its powers in Coleridge as a critique of the very same conventionalized domestic sympathies that appear to stand at its base.

As in "The Nightingale," this assertion of corrected affiliation is urged upon the reader precisely through an experience of the sublime. In "The Nightingale," the sublime moment emerges in the poem's shift from the confinement of closed spaces and romance conventions to the plurality of nightingales in nature. In "Fears," the speaker ends the poem with one of Coleridge's most compelling landscape descriptions, in which he leaves the "soft and silent spot" with which the poem began and moves to the "brow" of a "heathy" hill on the way "homeward" (208–10). This shift to a mountain view, as Richard

Holmes points out, punctuates many of Coleridge's poems and signals a removal "not merely from the restraints of domesticity, but from a narrow English culture."[69] At this moment in "Fears," a "burst of prospect" confronts the "startled" speaker; it is a "prospect" that is utterly removed from social influences—yielding a view of the "shadowy main" and "elmy fields" (215, 218)—even while, viewed as a "huge amphitheater" in the speaker's mind, it "seems like society" (217, 218). Viewed in this way, the "prospect" also seems to be "conversing with the mind . . . giving it / A livelier impulse and a dance of thought" (220). It is this "dance of thought" that allows the speaker to return in thought to the domestic space—to the "lowly cottage" where "my babe / And my babe's mother dwell in peace" (225–26) and, at a small distance, the "mansion of my friend" (223; this is Alfoxden, Wordsworth's home). But the dance of thought also allows him to connect to a wider view of "society" that is more general than the poet's domestic environment. And thus the gesture toward the sublime at the end of the poem leads inevitably to thoughts that "yearn" not merely for the author's friends and family but "for human kind" (232).

More might be said about the relation between these two conversation poems and about their connection to the aesthetic valences of queer and cosmopolitan theory discussed above, aesthetic valences that repeatedly emphasize political regeneration through shared identity. In one sense, the poems draw different circles of obligation in the space of their meditations—in "The Nightingale" around the family, and in "Fears," around a widened set of international relations with France and "distant tribes." But in both works the commitment to intimacy and the commitment to a more cosmopolitan affiliation to "human kind" are characterized by a shared aesthetic vantage point. They reject the logic of beauty, with its dependence on inheritance and replication, and instead embrace the logic of the sublime. This aesthetic vantage point, furthermore, rejects the notion of community formed through attractive models of virtue replicated through sympathy; in fact, both poems openly compromise and satirize that view of shared affect as the basis for social union. Instead, the sublime vantage point on justice designates a specific kind of relationship between individuals and the larger patterns of socialization to which they commit themselves. In both poems the speaker, who is both physically and mentally separated from domestic space and from the shared attitudes and beliefs that traditionally accompany that space, pursues a reformed sense of association. Appreciating this combination of separation and connection could aid us in interpreting a great many other Romantic writings that either reconfigure domestic relations (e.g., Percy Shelley's *Epipsychidion*, 1821) or pursue justice beyond the nation's boundaries (e.g., Mary Shelley's *The Last Man*, 1826). While acknowledging the possibility of disagreement, in "The Nightingale," or sheer hostility, in "Fears in Solitude," the poems broadly insist on the well-being of others and on the penalties that might arise from injuring them. Moreover, it's only *because* of that disagreement that the claim to justice can, with any confidence, be made.

CHAPTER 4

Biopolitics and the Sublime

Recent political theorizing has taken a surprising, often unrecognized interest in the legal and political innovations of the late eighteenth century. Michel Foucault certainly brought attention to the disciplinary technology of prisons—and their pervasive, intriguingly transferable social structures—many years ago. But his still later interest in biopolitics—which shifted emphasis from the disciplinary work on bodies to the biological functions of and within bodies—has inspired yet another wave of fascinating thought about the evolution of modern institutions. And with even more force than the disciplinary model, his thought has renewed interest in the problems surrounding the notions of political right that served as the foundation of liberal and radical political and legal discourse during the French Revolution and its aftermath.

If *biopolitics* is the name for the interpenetration of law and the body to become what Foucault called "a governmental naturalism,"[1] Giorgio Agamben locates, if not the birth of that notion, at least its apogee in the French Declaration of the Rights of Man and of the Citizen of 1789. In that document, Agamben finds political right to be identified with the sovereign constituting power of the "nation," a relationship defended by the Abbé Sieyès and codified in the Declaration itself.² Right is always already subsumed under the power constituted by and through the national body. What is relevant in Agemben's account is not simply that some persons are included in the nation and some are excluded but that all political subjectivity is tied to the formation of the bios—the naturalized, biologized community formed by drawing a boundary of inclusion and exclusion. By that logic there can be a connection between eighteenth-century conceptions of citizenship and modern understandings of political subjectivity as the biological control over life and death.

Agamben's claim about rights echoes in, or at least fortuitously coincides with, some accounts that do not openly proclaim a debt to Foucault but nevertheless view the acquisition of such rights as inseparable from the mechanisms of a deeply embodied sense of sympathy that in turn forms the basis for a political body. The vast literature on the role of sympathy in antislavery discourse in the eighteenth century—exemplified in the work of critics such as Charlotte Sussman and Debbie Lee—is one of the more obvious examples, and it is particularly pertinent to the discussions in this chapter. Slavery comes to be associated with the evils of foreign trade; abolition, conversely, becomes a possibility because of a compassionate claim of likeness between blacks and whites. That claim can, in turn, support a vigorous assertion of virtuous national identity.³

But what is particularly interesting for our purposes here is that the total absorption of right by biopolitical administration is considered inevitable by many of today's critics and theorists. Indeed, the openly avowed ontological project in Agamben's work culminates in a vision of biopolitics, not as the product of a particular historical moment, but rather as the "original activity of sovereign power."⁴ Hannah Arendt, in *The Origins of Totalitarianism* (1951)—an acknowledged influence on Agamben's project—offers a somewhat different perspective. Agamben rightly sees in Arendt an account of the equation (again, in the French Declaration) between political right and nationality that paves the way for later totalitarian regimes. But Arendt's very attempt to describe the loss of "significance" that results from the association between right and nation does not seem like an ontological claim, but rather like a political one; that is, hers is an attempt to identify a problem with the way humans are made significant under modern regimes of power. The problem she identifies is specifically located within the nation's defeat of the law's priority in the affairs of state, the disintegration of law as equal protection in favor of the protection of particular people.⁵ But the problem is not irreversible for Arendt: her argument about the dependence of human rights on the unequal protections offered by nation-states implicitly calls for a more capacious commitment to those rights. Arendt's text encourages us to seek a political remedy in order to address the harms she identifies.⁶

Arendt's work might encourage us to question the direction of Agamben's interpretation, which construes her argument to say that biopolitics is the ontological foundation of right. But if it is indeed the case that Arendt is incorrectly interpreted by Agamben, we might question Arendt's account in order to see whether her argument against the logic of the nation-state has a precedent in the very historical moment in which Arendt claims that this structure of the nation-state's authority arose. That question, in other words, could be addressed by turning, or rather returning, to address Romanticism and its legacy.

I am not advocating a complete alternative political history that would seek to rewrite our knowledge of revolutionary and counterrevolutionary political movements that swept across Europe in the late eighteenth and nineteenth centuries. I am more interested in a critical stance toward the pulsions of those movements that so frequently directed their attentions to the nation-state. I also emphasize, in order to capture the drift of that critical stance, the importance of biopolitical imperatives as intertwined aesthetic and political discourses and practices in which right is threaded through, and furthered by, an aesthetic norm identified with the proper limits of belonging.

If it is true, as suggested above with the example of slavery and abolition, that the philosophical discourse of sympathy easily tethered itself to a larger project of identifying rights with the administration of bodies, we could cast our view even wider to see how crucial it has been for critics and historians to see eighteenth-century literature as a reinforcement of the logic through which rights are linked to sympathetic attachments. It is hardly surprising that Lynn Hunt (in *Human Rights*, 2007) points out how novels like Samuel Richardson's *Pamela* (1740) and Jean-Jacques Rousseau's *Julie* (1761) generate reciprocal sympathies among and for their characters and thus provide the primary aesthetic argument for a significant, sympathy-based account of rights (Hunt, like Arendt and Agamben, traces that account—without Arendt's or Agamben's critical reflection—to the French Declaration).⁷ Hunt's work essentially echoes the work of Martha Nussbaum in *Poetic Justice* (1997), where Nussbaum argues, using Charles Dickens's *Hard Times* (1854) as one of its most prominent instances, for the force of literature as a prompt to "compassion" that yields justice. Compassionate feeling is "called into being" by literature and recommended, by provoking "identification and sympathy," to the reader.[8]

By emphasizing the importance of literary *characters* as focal points for compassion and sympathy, and thus as sources of beneficial social impulses, such recent accounts emphasize a feature of eighteenth-century fiction that clearly relates to the connection eighteenth-century philosophical aesthetics makes between beauty and various forms of sociability. Such accounts, that is, echo (for the most part unwittingly) Reynolds's interest in the inheritable models of classical antiquity, as well as Burke's suggestion that beauty is the cause of "love, or some passion similar to it." In Burke's argument, love, in turn, is central for sexual reproduction—"the generation of mankind"—and for binding us to other humans and animals in harmony.[9] To these we could add Hume's resonant claims that judgments about beautiful objects always involve a sympathy with those intimately affected by those objects; those judgments are likened to judgments about virtue, which involve sympathy with those affected by our actions.[10] Moral sentiment is thus analogized to taste. All of these insights about beauty and sociability extend forward into Kant's claims that beauty can be social insofar as it summons us to "communicate our *feeling* to all other men."[11]

In this chapter I begin by arguing against the notion that political right depends upon the generation of sympathy for normatively constructed identities and urge that attention be focused on the aesthetic of the sublime. The sublime leads toward a more conflictual mode of configuring the relations between persons; it provides an aesthetic vantage point that highlights complaint, dissent, and disagreement in the midst of a larger scheme of social cooperation. I go on to reveal a striking contrast between this aesthetic mode and the predominating logic of biopolitical critique itself. Agamben, whose work has become increasingly influential in literary studies, in part because of his own frequent gravitation toward literary texts, is typical of contemporary biopolitical critique in his understanding of political conditions as ontological conditions (as opposed to changeable political conditions, as in Arendt). He is also typical of those who tend to find a remedy for those conditions in normatively constructed identities. The centrality of the aesthetic of beauty in postmodern biopolitical critique is telling in this regard. If, as I suggested in chapter 1, beauty is the aesthetic discourse of biopolitics, biopolitical critique simultaneously, ironically, generates disciplinary and biopolitical counter-norms. Thus the paragons of biopolitical critique—from Agamben to Slavoj Žižek—fight beauty with beauty;[12] they offer instances of biopolitical aesthetic logic even in their apparent resistance to it.

Charlotte Smith's *Beachy Head*: From Sublime to Georgic

I take my example on which to focus discussion of the sublime and biopolitics not from a treatise on politics and aesthetics but from something like a poetic treatise on both subjects, which we find in Charlotte Smith's extraordinary *Beachy Head* (1807), a locodescriptive poem of roughly seven hundred lines of blank verse published after Smith died in 1806.[13] In this poem, Smith—a prolific poet, author of ten novels, much admired in her time and increasingly in ours—directly confronts the predicament that postmodern theory knows as biopolitics precisely through her representation of the authority of the nation-state in the discourse of political right. This confrontation ultimately results in instructive complications directly as a consequence of Smith's commitment to seeing the sublime as an aesthetic stance in relation to justice that is more wide-ranging and inclusive than the biopolitical model can allow. In fact, the poem consistently dislodges its claims about the rights of individuals from its more obvious celebrations of national territory and internal social harmony. I do not mean that aesthetics simply provides a model for justice; indeed the poem self-consciously distances itself from such a naïve position. Nevertheless, the sublime mode offers a vital position from which claims about justice might be modified or evaluated, animated by a thoroughly promiscuous and adventurous extension of imagination.

The poem begins with a "sublime" encounter with landscape: the word *sublime* appears in the first line of the poem to describe the "stupendous summit" that looms over the English Channel and that is the "first land made," as the note to the lines asserts, when one crosses it.[14] The word of course refers directly to an object much in the way that Edmund Burke, in his *Enquiry*, speaks of vast rocks, towers, or mountains filling us with "astonishment" because of their "greatness of dimensions."[15] But the first lines also do something else, referring to the "summit" as a place where the speaker is physically situated and also as a place seen from yet *another* place, occupied by a hypothetical "mariner" who, approaching the English coastline from "half way at sea," hails the rock at "early morning" (2–3).

The very opening premise of the poem—that it is being composed on the shores overlooking the English Channel—is itself interesting, because it situates poetic meditation at a place of bordering and crossing. But still more striking is the way in which the first lines, by counting two obviously distinct perspectives within one, by hinging two nonidentical experiences together, anticipate one of the central formal achievements of the poem's representation of sublime vision. The scene rendered by the poet's "Fancy" comes from the poet-speaker, while it reveals its exterior lining, its shadowing by another observer. But that apparent division can be treated as a single experience. This is why the lines can go on, revealing the speaker's extended apprehension in order to mold natural imagery by her creative powers. Continuing on, thirty-six lines of blank verse emphasize the blending of perceptions into one whole: the union of Ocean and Heaven, the murmuring trace of the tides on the sand.

Up to this point, Smith's poem reminds us of the serene harmonies that predominate in the nature lyrics of Wordsworth and Coleridge, both of whom read and admired Smith's work. What truly sets it apart from their work, at least at the beginning, is the initial anxiety set in motion by the poet's own powers of invention. That anxiety is marked by the abrupt shift from the sublime mode to the georgic, to an account of the laborers who populate the land and sea just described. The emphasis on the powers of "Fancy" in the initial lines gives way to a concentration on the labor of struggling seamen on their distant fleet, and on the toil of the "slave" who dives for pearls beneath the "waves," pearls that in turn load the "ship of commerce" (42). We could speculate at length about exactly why Smith focuses on the slave as pearl diver rather than as harvester of tobacco or sugar. (Her husband was a disastrously unsuccessful West India merchant and director of the East India Company, so she would have been familiar with all aspects of slavery.) But central in her reasoning would have to be that in her poem the sea provides both a literal and a figurative covering for the slave's body, even while the slave herself finds precious adornment for the British consumer's body. For just as the depths submerge the divers who struggle for life away from the poet-speaker's view, the slant rhyme echoing or whispering the word "slave" in "waves" serves as a formal reminder that the sublimity of the poem—which centers on an encounter with the cliffs and the sea—might come at the cost of the slave's "perilous and breathless toil" (53).

We might say that in this shift of modes Smith reverses the transcending movement away from the georgic immersion in matters of everyday life, a movement that Kevis Goodman attributes to Romantic poems like Wordsworth's *Excursion* (1814).[16] And that reversal to georgic also baldly violates Kant's claim early on in the third *Critique* that aesthetic judgments, in order to secure our indifference to an "object of representation," cannot involve specific matters of consumption or production that arise around objects of perception (38–39). Here, in order to make the poem assert its attention to the conditions of others, Smith strains its vision to the point that the imaginative spell conjured in the poem's initial lines might appear to be compromised, if not completely shattered. And in fact, as the poem continues, the perspective jerks restlessly between Fancy's "Wandering sublime thro visionary vales" (86) and more concrete observations of the fishermen toiling on the shore, "from their daily task / Returning" (102–3), and of the "athletic crew" unloading the boat's cargo with a "busy hum" once the boat's keel "ploughs the sand" (107–8).

It might be said that the poem's politics are articulated precisely through a retreat from, and ironizing of, the sublime, which seems deaf to the sounds of laborers and blind to the existence of slavery, the latter deemed a violation of "sacred freedom" motivated only by the lust for trivial "gaudes and baubles" (59, 58). And the fanciful perspective of the opening lines is further impugned by the poem's personification of that perspective as a female figure of Contemplation, who sits "aloof" and "high on her throne of rock" (117–18) and is thus elevated to the status of a regal consumer of the very "gaudes and baubles" that oppress the slave. More congenial to this ironizing or retreating gesture is the poem's still further contraction of sympathies at this point, focusing less on the blending of disparate elements in the landscape and more on its particular geographical continuity and integrity.[17]

For now, in the beginning of a new paragraph of verse, even as Contemplation sits aloof, Memory accounts (in greater, more faithful detail) for the historical and cultural significance of the very shoreline that the poet-speaker has been observing all along. The aim is not simply to recount history but to arrive at a rousing defense of England. Once invaded by the Normans, England has since "redeem'd" (160) itself through noble action in order to guard its "integrity secure" from the "Presumptuous hopes" of "modern Gallia" and a "world at arms" (152, 143, 144, 153). This more or less conventional account of the English "Norman Yoke" ideology—in which foreign conquest looks like a sin against national purity—might leave some readers stymied, as Theresa Kelley is in her reading of the poem, by the circuitous route Smith's narrative takes from the moral-political defense of "sacred freedom" to this celebration of British national integrity.[18] But we might just as easily say that we have arrived at nothing less than the poem's biopolitical imperative. Defending the rights of laborers, slaves, and other outcasts means defending the rights of English people as a distinct race—or at least England as a distinct national culture—against foreign invasion (an invasion from France that seemed particularly threatening in 1798 but had loomed since England went to war against Napoleon's forces in 1793). England wrests its freedom from bondage by virtue of its (supposedly) entirely defensive military "triumph" over foreign enemies (159)—we must note at this point the distinction between Smith's poem and Coleridge's more cautious view of war in "Fears in Solitude." Thus Smith's poem might seem to perfectly demonstrate the general point that Arendt makes, and that Agamben takes to heart, by suggesting that the foundation of political right is identical to the purity of the nation. Indeed, the poem would also seem to provide one of the Romantic period's most eloquent illustrations of Foucault's account of the ideology surrounding the Norman Conquest, according to which, as he describes it in his genealogy of modern biopolitics, "the right of the English people . . . was bound up with the need to expel foreigners."[19]

There is still more to this argument as Smith pursues it. The narrative of Norman conquest and English redemption finds its local counterpart in the poem's glorification of "green beauty" (490) and humble rural life. The influence of Oliver Goldsmith's *The Deserted Village* (1770) registers palpably here not only in direct quotation from his poem but also in the praise of a country village's "humble happiness."[20] Goldsmith, however, shows himself to be the consummate Tory: he is primarily concerned with virtue, which decays with the desertion of his "sweet smiling village" of Auburn, whose population dwindles and corrupts because of "trade's unfeeling train."[21] Smith, in what seems at first like a more Whiggish fashion, makes rural life embody or instantiate English *freedom*: "Rude, and just remov'd from savage life / Is the rough dweller among scenes like these, / . . . / . . . But he is free; / The dread that follows on illegal acts / He never feels; and his industrious mate / Shares in his labor" (207–13). Explicitly distanced, at least at this moment, from any moral or legal prohibition, the "rude" laborer, like England itself, seems to be defined merely as self-sufficiency. Governed by strict but extralegal boundaries always already in place, the "rough dweller" occupies a region that is one step beyond savagery, while still blessed with the virtuous attributes of "content" and patience (236). To put it another way, the rude laborer in the poem demonstrates the basis for freedom in English "integrity" precisely through a tautological commitment to domestic integrity. Integrity is founded upon integrity.

That logic more or less obviously seems to inform the poem's overt opposition to a range of excesses. Luxury, scientific speculation, and military ambition turn out to be fruitless and limiting compared with England's celebrated national and domestic adherence to internal boundaries. The quest for luxury chases a happiness that is false, because it chases a pleasure that eludes our grasp (247); natural history pursues a knowledge that encourages only vanity and "vague theories" (394); military conquest seeks a power that is only transient, passing away "even as the clouds" (435). The Norman Conquest, once contextualized in these terms, looks more like a strange form of metaphysical delusion. The triumph of English national strength, meanwhile, emerges less as a matter of foreign policy—that is, as a matter of relating to others outside the nation—than as a conspicuous commitment to domestic enclosure. This triumph condenses in the literal conversion of ancient fortresses across the countryside into farmhouses, the portal and battlements into a "humbler homestead" (502), and "armed foemen" into "herds" that are "driv'n to fold" (505). Achieving English freedom means finding protection from foreign conquest, but it also means adhering to a logic of self-enclosure, according to which "herds" keep close within their "fold," just as free people remain bound to their "humbler homestead." England, in which domestic and national selfsameness describe and mirror each other, becomes a vast sheepfold.

Smith's poem, with all of these elegantly wrought symmetries, founds a notion of political right in English nationhood, and founds English nationhood in a normative English character, defined precisely as national integrity and enclosure. This line of poetic argument, jealously reserving freedom for England alone and casting "modern Gallia" as an enemy to that freedom, certainly makes sense given Smith's disenchantment with the fortunes of the French Revolution, to which she, like so many of her contemporaries, had once been sympathetic. Yet I think that this aspect of the poem belies many of the more complicated ways in which it also mounts a conjoined aesthetic and moral-political challenge to the very normative gestures that it at first glance seems to support.

Indiscriminate Poetry

Although I discuss Smith in order to address a larger issue within the context of Romantic notions of justice—the way in which justice advances, extends, and distributes freedoms attending legally granted right[22]—my reading is at odds with readings of Smith's work that focus on the poem's emphasis on locality as a privileged position from which Smith herself speaks, as well as with readings that focus on the importance of sympathy among Smith, her poetic subjects, and her readers.[23] At the same time, there is much that is relevant for my task in the work of Adela Pinch, who exposes Smith's keen attentions to the "literary" quality of even the most heartfelt emotions, even while Smith appears to insist upon the deeply "personal" authenticity of those emotions.[24] Pinch's work centers on Smith's *Elegiac Sonnets* (1784–97), with their more obvious concentration on the inwardness of the lyric speaker, but her emphasis on literary fictions has something in common with my argument that the very conception of the nation itself in Smith's work submits to an expansive and mobile aesthetic pressure. That pressure in turn connects with a new kind of moral-political crosscurrent against the priority of the nation-state as the foundation of right.[25]

Moving in this direction attunes our reading at the very outset to the blatantly figurative texture of Smith's foundation of English right in English nationality, that is, to the full implications of the purely tautological foundation of freedom on integrity. It is an integrity further founded on domestic integrity, which finally can be emblematized only with reference to a *representation* of such integrity, an archetypal piece of rural domestic architecture—a sheepfold (a "fold," we might add, re-formed or re-worked and turned inward from other materials once functioning as battlements). But much more can be said about the way Smith contradictorily invests rural labor and natural landscape with flights of imaginative and figurative excess, which are altogether distinct from the beautifully laconic facticity that we find, for instance, throughout Dorothy Wordsworth's *Grasmere Journals*, the bible of Romantic naturalistic observation.[26] Natural imagery constantly and entirely unexpectedly associates with luxurious trappings: roses are "robes of regal state" (336); the root of the wood sorrel is "like beaded coral" (363); anemones are a "crown" made of gold and ivory (365, 367).

Is the crown for the head of "regal Contemplation"? Or perhaps it is the product of Contemplation itself? Why does natural imagery so quickly shift into self-consciously artificial and luxurious imagery, of the kind that Smith seemed to resist in the logic of national self-enclosure? The persistent direction of the metaphors and similes seems to challenge the claim that bare subsistence leads to happiness, since the very idea of subsistence seems to aspire to the markers of luxury and ambition that rural life and rude labor seem to critique. If we view this kind of excess as an indication of a restless imaginative power through which even the humble natural objects in the poem are metaphorically extended and thus redefined, then we can see that that logic echoes, rather than merely undermines, the sublime mode and wandering Fancy with which the poem began. And we can also see how utterly inaccurate it is for critics to see Smith's emphasis on natural scenery and rural labor merely as a celebration of local, domestic histories.

Even though Smith in this poem cites Goldsmith and dedicates her poem *The Emigrants* to William Cowper, the great English sage of domestic happiness and tranquility, she pays homage to these figures only to turn aesthetic imperatives quite radically against them. For while the English landscape in *Beachy Head* is home to the humble "tiller of the soil" (500), it's also the occasion for something that is still more consistent: a sublime vision that encompasses a "wide view" that itself "melts away" in the distance and "mingles indiscriminate with the clouds" (81–84). Perhaps the fact that Smith's own reading practices were conducted "indiscriminately," according to the memoir published by Sir Walter Scott in 1829,[27] points to the importance of the word *indiscriminate* for describing an aesthetic strategy generated throughout the poem and for describing the initial lyrical motivation behind it. That strategy, for instance, implicitly challenges the domestic economy of English national sovereignty, which had seemed (at first glance) to be central to Smith's ideological moorings. London, "the mart / Of England's capital," with its multiple "domes and spires," is acknowledged but made invisible to the poetic eye, which cannot see "so far" (484–85). The capital asserts itself here only as an absence, an inability to exert a controlling presence over the wide-ranging vision asserted within the poem. Similarly, the "distant range / Of Kentish hills" dissolves in a "purple haze" (486–87). No matter where the speaker turns, whether in country or in city, the "view" offered up in Smith's lines is most striking for its ability not merely to attend to or celebrate intimate detail but, at the same time, to cross over it and willfully blur its outlines.

What are we to make of these moments of excess that appear both at the level of rhetorical configurations and at the still broader level of the formal attributes of poetic vision itself? At one level, these formal aspects of the poem lend themselves to a more profound and persuasive argument against war and conquest aside from those that Smith mentions more openly. Conquest meets the speaker's opposition in the poem not only because of the violence that it imposes upon populations, and not only in order to shore up a strong English resistance against its former foreign opponents, but also because conquest, with its emphasis on the possession of other nations and other peoples, contradicts the flagrant promiscuity and "wide view" of sublime vision (481). The sublime, as Smith represents it, challenges the integrity of the nation itself, which blurs into the lustrous hazy atmosphere (487).

This is why the poet-speaker finally resists not only conquest but also its extreme opposite, a retreat into idyllic solitude. There is a story of a lovesick youth that appears late in *Beachy Head*; the youth's very idea of retreating to an idyllic and separate place, with "baffled hope" and eyes "intently fixed" on one place in the vale below, is viewed as a delusion, a bliss that "can never be" (653). But at this very moment, the gloss on the troubled youth takes an important turn that tells us still more about the poem's aesthetic stakes. The poet-speaker proceeds to speculate on "future blessings he may yet enjoy" and even seeks to provide imaginative completion for the very "hope" that, in the youth, is currently "baffled" (528). The imagination fills out a new space for the youth in the form of an "island in the southern sea," where his happiness can be realized rather than abandoned (663).

It's easy to be misled by this passage. The repositioning of the youth on an island—something that happens within the mind of the poet, who thinks of the island retreat as something that the youth may "haply build" for himself (664)—is not an attempt at escapism, a Rousseauian fantasy of *l'homme naturel* that simply replicates the youth's own hopeless fixity. The ability to figure a new place for him is precisely an index of the role imagination repeatedly takes in this poem in order to find redress for its lost, hopeless, estranged, or otherwise disadvantaged persons. Any person's ability to respond to the plight of others in this poem must come not from a restricted and domesticated viewpoint but from a widely extended one, and this is why it is finally in the mode of the sublime that Smith renders her most articulate perspectives for an account of justice and right.

Turning again to the slave passage, we find yet another convincing and even more explicit demonstration of the logic I'm tracing out—more explicit precisely because of its connection between the extensiveness of sublime vision and the building of new protective structures. Slaves in her poem, after all, are not visible from Beachy Head. Like the hypothetical mariner toward the beginning of the poem, they can only be imagined. The capacity to imagine them, furthermore, is understood in the slave passage in a truly extraordinary and unexpected way. For if it is an "erroneous estimate" to appraise the slave's life beneath the "gaudes and baubles" that slaves fetch from under the waves, the ability to offer the right estimate of the slave by valuing his or her "sacred freedom" is actually *not* tied to seeing the world according to any normative standards of measurement or correctness, and not even to any account of shared feeling with the slave.

Instead, that estimate correlates with the ability of those with "unadulterated taste" to posit "harmony" in nature (65–66). Those who underestimate the slave care only about predetermined indices of economic and cultural value—"the brightest gems, / Glancing resplendent on the regal crown, / Or trembling in the high born beauty's ear" (68–70). Those who properly estimate the slave send forth "aspiring Fancy," which ultimately grasps nature precisely by unleashing itself from an empirical account of its details. Aspiring Fancy "fondly soars, / Wandering sublime thro' visionary vales, / Where bright pavilions rise, and trophies, fann'd / By airs celestial; and adorn'd with wreaths / Of flowers that bloom amid elysian bowers" (85–89).

In these lines, even more so than in the passage on the hopeless lonesome youth, the poet-speaker insists on something paradoxical in her commitment to the slave's freedom. In one sense, that commitment gains expression in the speaker's wandering and "sublime" flight, culminating in a moment of purely "visionary" experience. That visionary experience is a departure or dissent from conventional standards of value. In yet another sense, that "visionary" and freely associative logic in the passage coagulates into a sense of hierarchical order and hypotactic organization, in which pavilions rise on vales, trophies rise above pavilions, and wreaths of flowers adorn trophies. The powerful poetic assertion here—that attending to the slave demands an unbounded and wandering imagination—cannot be separated from the sense that the product of the sublime is also a moment of sheltering and protection in the mind's visionary pavilions, just as the imagined "trophy" (a monument, it seems, perched on the mind's pavilions) looks like a thoroughly imaginary acknowledgment of the slave's breathless toil. The entire passage construes nature according to this similarly free-ranging but hypotactic structure and likewise makes it look like a kind of shelter against its own violence, to which the slave is exposed: the clouds shade the sun's "insufferable brightness" (79), and all of nature serves as an "ethereal canopy" (84). Nature, in effect, arranges itself into a defense against the slave's bodily injury.

In Smith's poem, then, the aesthetic mode of the sublime proposes a moral-political stance that involves extension and rebuilding beyond the quandaries of sympathy. Here and in other works—such as in her poem *The Emigrants* (1793), which attends to the rights of French immigrant clergy in England following the revolution—Smith asserts that "the vain boast / Of equal Law is mockery" (38). In the earlier poem the very skepticism about the power of law contrasts with the power of the poem itself to do justice to those who cannot find it already at hand in the nation's existing resources. *Beachy Head* follows that line of thinking by rendering the moment of sublime vision as a poetically generated aesthetic stance toward legal redress. For the insistent claim pervading Smith's verse is that the ranging power of the imagination would be the requirement for its pursuit of justice, since justice is construed rigorously and consistently as a commitment to reshaping a protection—aesthetically posited as an architectural structure—that would extend to the slave and the slave's claims on "sacred freedom." In *Beachy Head*, the possibility of extending a right to the slave has very little to do with any claim about the speaker's identity with the slave's plight, although Cowper, reflecting on Smith's financial condition, described the author herself as "chained to her desk like slave to his oars."[28] More pertinent to the poem's logic is the speaker's extension of a right through a structural principle; the poem addresses the problem of the slave by making room for her.

In these lines I've been discussing in the slave passage, Smith—with a great deal of economy—ends up saying something very profound about a much larger trend in the Romantic period of writing poems about slavery and the slave trade: works (by the likes of Hannah More and Ann Yearsley) that either provided searing details of a slave's suffering or even ventriloquized the slave's anguished thoughts and words. The point that I attribute to Smith is quite different from the drift of Ian Baucom's argument (in line with numerous other accounts noted earlier) about the importance of sympathy in abolitionism. Baucom's account is particularly relevant because of his emphasis on aesthetics: he views abolitionist discourse as a sympathetic, "interested" sublime (in the tradition of Longinus), in contrast to the abstraction of the Kantian sublime (which, I have been arguing, has an abstraction that is not nearly as unforgiving and unyielding as some have believed).[29] In contrast, Smith suggests that the interest in doing justice to the suffering of slaves in European colonies in the Indies and elsewhere has less to do with claiming any essential sympathetic connection between the white European's identity and the slave's and more to do with a claim that poetic form itself might mobilize—through the sublime—new commitments, duties, and patterns of affiliation.

But what is especially striking about Smith's poem, connected though it may be to other works of her day, is the regularity with which it argues for the centrality of the sublime in multiple contexts, as if the supposed geographical location for the poem at the border of the nation were an occasion to provide a figurative remapping, in multiple directions, of the territories embraced by the speaker's commitments to "sacred freedom." The end of the poem reinforces the scope of that remapping. There, Smith describes and pays homage to what might be called the poem's ideal figure: Darby, the "hermit," who, a note to line 675 explains, charitably saved "shipwrecked mariners" off the coast, although on one of these missions "he himself perished." While he is poised on the coastline, the hermit's attentions to the clouds, the sky, the cliffs, the wind, and the sea echo the poet's own perspective. At the same time, moreover, this aesthetic doubling of the poet-speaker's position fastens itself to an explicit moral-political perspective, with explicit consequences. As a poem, as a work of imagination, Smith's work can't necessarily *do* anything; it can't act in the world. But through the hermit, Smith is able to craft a figure that embodies both the aesthetic perspective of the poet and a specific commitment to action. That is, the hermit is "feelingly alive to all that breathed," thus appearing to double the poet's promiscuously roving sublime vision (688). But that articulation of aesthetic feeling is turned toward a moral-political position. The hermit, while "outraged . . . in sanguine youth, / By human crimes" (689–90), registers his disappointment with the world's injustices, just as the narrator exhibits her own dismay at crimes against the slave. Furthermore, he commits himself to battling waves to help drowning shipwrecked mariners, "helpless stranger[s]" (716) lost in the "roaring surge" (704). Thus, by "hazarding" his own life, which in his own eyes is "too valueless" (701), he embodies something like a corrective position on the "human crimes" against those deemed too "valueless"—the slaves—for protection earlier in the poem.[30]

What attracts our notice to the hermit is that he is less forceful as a literary character recommended for the reader's imitation than as an embodiment of the poem's legal and poetic formalism. Smith's final stanza asks the reader to see the very "mournful lines" of the poem "chisel'd within the rock" (727) as a memorial to the hermit; the poet does justice to the hermit even as the hermit has done justice to the helpless strangers "buffeting for life" (704) in the waves before him. In his intriguing reading of *Antigone*, Patchen Markell speaks of how Antigone commits herself, not to the *oikos* over politics, but to a political "impropriety" beyond the family's normative borders.[31] The argument is relevant for us here. At every moment of the poem—in its representations of characters and finally in its commitment to its own narrative position as memorializing the strange and solitary hermit—Smith makes the "helpless stranger" outside the *oikos* the focus for multiple commitments to justice.

It must be added that that the poem's reference to its chiseled lines obviously harkens back to the epigrams of Theocritus, which provide a possible beginning point for a genealogy of poems as "inscriptions" on objects leading to Thomas Gray, Smith, and Wordsworth. That tradition might be significant to Smith for many reasons, and Geoffrey Hartman has spoken on that tradition more resonantly than anyone.[32] But surely Smith's willingness to jettison the epigrammatic quality of inscription, and hence its entirely illusory status as a text attached to a material object (the center of Hartman's discussions), attracts our notice most immediately here. It is more or less improbable, if not absurd, to imagine finding more than seven hundred lines of poetry on a rock, even if that rock happens to be a large cliff on the English Channel. (Of course, "these mournful lines" might possibly refer to the last sixty explicitly about the hermit [671–731], although that boundary is far from clear.)

The improbability might contribute to the brilliance of the poem's closing, however. For even in this brief yet entirely self-conscious attention to poetic form, Smith imagines the work not merely as a memorial attached to specific beings and objects at the level of human scale but rather as a highly mobile creation of new, artificial accommodations. Its claim to be written on the rock cannot dissuade us from our suspicion that the inscription must also exceed it, just as the claim that the poem memorializes one person cannot make us forget that it has extended its view to many other helpless strangers who lie under its sheltering gaze.

The biopolitical move in the poem, as we can now see, fitfully emerges as a defense of anti-Norman ideology that finally cannot be sustained under the pressure of a competing and more pervasive aesthetic paradigm. That paradigm undercuts not only the embedding of rights within the nation, of polis within bios, but also the general set of imperatives that would seek to found justice within an account of recognition of groups, whether hegemonic or nonhegemonic. While in one sense the poem asserts right on identitarian terms by suggesting that right is found in England and that English rights are rights by virtue of selfsame culture or birth, it more consistently makes right into a more thoroughly politicized right that might be extended transnationally into new places, and new situations, with protections fostering newly included persons—right for those without rights.

Beauty and Biopolitics

To account for the aesthetic of the sublime in Smith's poem is to appreciate its historically specific way of looking at transnational or international law. Her view of a sublime accommodating architecture is quite different from international law or human rights according to the kind of majoritarian conception of mutual agreement that Samuel von Pufendorf argued for in his *Two Books of the Elements of Universal Jurisprudence* (1660). But her view does in fact circuitously connect with—even while departing from—the view of law as collected wisdom or common sense, as in the work of Hugo Grotius. Grotius relied upon the notion of justice to foreigners in his *Rights of War and Peace* (1625) as a common stock of knowledge inherited from the Bible, literature, natural law, and simple appeals to moderation; Smith's work intriguingly accentuates the fictionality inherent in Grotius's approach in order to emphasize the importance of justice as an artificial structure of protections.[33]

To account for this direction in Smith's work is also to appreciate an even more trenchant contrast between its strategies and Agamben and other recent theorists' view of the evolution of modern political structures in ontological terms, terms that inform their political prescriptions and the aesthetic commitments that both illustrate and mobilize them. I take several examples here, from the work on modern biopolitics by Agamben, Michael Hardt, Eric Alliez, Antonio Negri, and Slavoj Žižek, all of whom develop arguments that, even when they criticize unjust social or economic conditions, avoid solutions that involve correcting or repairing conditions; they propose instead the adoption of new individual or collective identities. In other words, rather than applying criticism in order to make a system different, biopolitical critique asks us to become different people following a replicable model. Focusing on the generation of imitable identities thus enlists the aesthetic of beauty in order to conjure its political vision. Whereas beauty discourse appears to be the quintessential aesthetic discourse of biopolitics, even biopolitical critique is entirely invested, it turns out, in the aesthetic of beauty.

My aim here is not a complete survey or thoroughgoing critique of writing on biopolitics; it is, rather, to point to a continuity in its strategies that connects it to the political-aesthetic discourses of the eighteenth century. If the problem with biopolitics is to be located (as Roberto Esposito has it) in the tendency to place politics "within the grip of biology without being able to reply,"[34] biopolitical critique constitutes the basis of a reply by picturing, as Agamben would have it, a new "form of life," one that serves as an alternative to rigid and seemingly inescapable biologization. This new form of life captures an indistinction between the public and the private, natural and political life. This indistinction, in turn, would be the basis for all future "research,"[35] as well as for a new identity that Agamben understands to lie at the crux of an ideal "ethical subject."[36]

Readers of Agamben thus must attune themselves to the way that his texts, even in their critique of the exposure of bare or naked life to the polis, so frequently resolve themselves with a set of recommendations for behaviors or modes of being that, in a sense, emblematize and recommend indistinction. Paradoxically, that is, nonidentity or refusal of identity is the basis for a new kind of identity.[37] In my view, it is right for Alison Ross to emphasize that Agamben's work repeatedly locates the focal point for its analytical pressure in particular limit cases, such as the concentration camp, that emblematize the structure of modern institutions even in their apparent marginality to them.[38] We might add that those limit cases begin to provide what Ross says is a movement from analysis to prescription; that is, they provide models for thinking and being that themselves accumulate political gravity. In *The Open* (2002), Agamben speaks of unsettling biopolitics with a specific kind of attitude—a particular kind of "blessed life"—that we might adopt; this is a position of "abandonment," or *desoeuvrement*, characterized by sensual pleasure and a renunciation of human "mystery," that avoids both the human mastery of the animal and reduction of humans to the animal in biopolitical regimes.[39] Agamben's use of Jean-Luc Nancy's notion of abandonment is telling here. For if Nancy understands abandonment as a freedom of existence prior to any legal freedom (similar to Derrida's location of an "alterity" prior to any claim of sovereign right), Agamben makes a slightly different point with the same term.[40] Here abandonment, like *desoeuvrement* (another important term in

Nancy's work),[41] is an imitable way of life; thus, once again, Agamben makes nonidentity—a refusal to identify life as either animal or human—resolve itself into an identity, or at least a very coherent set of beliefs about the nature of animals and humans that is as specific as any religion. The essentially poststructural methodologies of Agamben's writing are thus repeatedly directed to the formation of normative beliefs and attitudes; they compellingly instantiate biopolitical mechanisms of power rather than contest them. As Catherine Mills helpfully summarizes this position, which she traces to Agamben's early interest in abandonment and in the state of infancy, "It is at the extreme limit of abandonment that humanity is redeemed . . . it is here that 'happy life' finds its realization."[42]

It is hardly surprising, from that perspective, that the problem with Agamben's work in biopolitics is quite similar to the problem with cosmopolitan politics, which might itself be considered a particularly compelling instance of biopolitical thinking. In Agamben and in many writers on cosmopolitanism, the complication, multiplication, or disruption of unitary identities repeats a common mode of argument in poststructuralist thought, making identity into a play of identity and difference and making political redemption seem like a heightened state of that play. But this general line of argument, whatever form it takes, merely reinforces a politics of replicable identity, because the apparently complicated version of identity looks like something that we should adopt for ourselves. And, as with cosmopolitans, it is not clear what we are to do with those people who have less complicated identities, that is, people who tend to understand themselves in ways that don't coincide with postmodern philosophical insights.

This last point about the common ground between Agamben and cosmopolitan theorists helps to underline the complicity of biopolitical critique with the aesthetic champion of biopolitics—the discourse of beauty. Beauty's only justification for itself, after all, is that it already exists and is ready for replication. Someone already has it, and someone will recognize it and repeat it. Even as Agamben makes identity look like the replicable type of a theoretical commitment to nonidentity, he simultaneously seeks out types of the figures that he holds up for admiration or imitation. The mobilization of literary or quasi-literary characters is central in his work and does not seem to have been awarded nearly enough attention in commentary. The infant, as Mills notes, is an early instance of this logic through which abandonment coalesces within a representative figure; there are many more to follow. The figure of the *Musel-*

mann in the death camps, for instance—actually Primo Levi's representation of the *Muselmann*—embodies an indistinction between human and inhuman, law and nature, that Agamben sees as a site of possible resistance. This is because the *Muselmann* becomes a remnant, or "garbage," that is recognized to be, as J. M. Bernstein writes, "in each of us."[43] In *The Open*, Agamben thinks of abandonment as an attitude that is both rendered in and inspired by an "image" of the "life" he recommends.[44] Walter Benjamin's "To the Planetarium," the apocalyptic closing section of his 1928 *Einbahnstrasse*, by illustrating a play between nature and its mastery supplies one such image; Titian's mysteriously conjoined but indifferent figures in his 1570 *Shepherd and Nymph* cleave neither to enchanted nature nor to disenchanted knowledge and thus supply another image of what Agamben takes to be a "new and more blessed life."[45] And in *Profanations* (2005), the detached and impassive face of a porn star who defies the "conventions of the genre" of pornography provides precisely the instance of "profanatory" behavior that he has been seeking to describe throughout his text (91–92).

As in Steiner's account of Manet's *Olympia* (see chapter 1), images reinforce the logic of the beautiful by showing coherent identities that are to be shared by those who view or read them. The difference between Agamben's account and Steiner's might appear to be that Steiner is much more reliant on a more conventional sense of intimate psychological connection between images and viewers. For Agamben, the mutuality or reciprocity could be called intellectual and ideological; that is, he finds his own commitment represented in Benjamin and Titian and in turn offers up those representations for us to follow. But that should not obscure the real connection between their accounts, and it should not distract us from the more general way in which biopolitical critique, or at least this instance of it, immerses itself in the aesthetic of beauty.

Is it at all surprising that the very indistinction that Agamben's images capture is itself, as he puts it, a mark of "specialness," with *special* relating to *species*, which in turn relates to *specious* or, in its obsolete definition, *beautiful* (58)? And that elsewhere he identifies these images with "beauty" itself?[46] We could remark similarly about a whole range of biopolitical critique from Antonio Negri to Slavoj Žižek, that is, about a collection of writings that propose a response to biopolitics based upon replicable personal types—of attitudes, ideologies, or locations. While it may be initially striking that Negri and Eric Alliez, following Agamben, see "aesthetic acts" as central to a response to the biopolitical condition of sovereign decisionism—which has caught the fabric of modern societies within a permanent state of war—what is more interesting still is the particular mode in which aesthetic responses are framed.[47] For Negri and Alliez, art that is resistant to biopolitics involves a rejection of the "obedience to the regulation of utterable and visible identities" and an embrace of "measurelessness," freed from the "transcendental barriers" set up by biopolitical regimes (114–15). While they insist that art must become an *"expression of indistinction"* (114), nonetheless Negri and Alliez, like Agamben, construe measurelessness or indistinction as curiously routinized within a new "paradigm" (116). Their claims are arranged according to a logic of replication—as a set of aesthetic directions for composing art in an era of tyranny and oppression (presumably a model for writers to follow). And the *"work of peace"* is accomplished by embracing a "world without an outside" and "new spaces of commonality and cooperation" (115). This in turn must give rise to a peace characterized by a shared "tranquility of soul" (115).

What Negri and Alliez see as an aesthetic response to biopolitics becomes—more explicitly than in Agamben—the basis for collective activity and affect, and this logic predominates even more clearly in Michael Hardt and Antonio Negri's *Multitude* (2004), where the aesthetic assumes a crucial function as a coordination of the "multitude" (the dispersed subjectivities in a biopolitical regime) as "relationships in common."[48] Elsewhere, Hardt and Negri have taken some care to distinguish themselves from Agamben's position, which, because of its "blank refusal" of biopolitics, seems to leave no room for political action on the part of the poor and dispossessed.[49] The project of *Multitude* centers relentlessly, then, on the "creation and reproduction" of "subjectivities of resistance"; subjectivities enable a "biopolitical" resistance to regimes of "biopower" (66, 65). The argument against Agamben, because of its emphasis on expanding subjectivity into subjectivities, magnifies the problems with Agamben's political aesthetics. While Hardt and Negri are careful to make it clear that subjectivity consists in maintaining "singularities"—that is, the persistence of difference—in their account of the common they still insist on the importance of the very logic of normative replication that they seem more overtly to forswear (99). The enduring promise of biopolitical resistance lies in the "immaterial labor" of society, which in turn resides not merely in the "economic domain" but also in networks of "ideas, knowledges, and affects" that form the "multitude" (66). While "multiple," the multitude nonetheless "designates an active social subject" based on what singularities "share in common" (100). The "striving for democracy" that Hardt and Negri attribute to all movements of resistance, furthermore, is not merely a striving to alter the political or economic conditions; it takes the form of a "construction of a new society" by mobilizing the multitude's collaborative and affective relationships (69, 66).

While Hardt and Negri may say that the multitude is not based on "identity or unity," it nevertheless is based on shared identity features that allow the multitude to "rule itself" (100) and to strive for democracy. The precise mechanisms for and effects of this sharing become evident when we take into account both the aesthetic valences of the text and their particular instrumentality. *Multitude*—like *Empire* (2004) before it and *Commonwealth* (2009) after it—teems with references to great art and literature. It praises artists such as Diego Rivera, José Orozco, and David Siqueiros, who capture the "grand movement" of revolutionaries "so beautifully in their immense murals" (71). The multitude, the authors explain, ultimately distances itself from problematic aspects of the revolutionary armies and their dependence on hierarchical political military leadership. The admiration for murals comports with a general reliance on mobilizing images in the service of the creation and reproduction of subjectivity. What Hardt and Negri find beautiful about revolutionary murals is the possibility of providing a commonality among revolutionary subjectivities that depends upon mutual recognition and imitation. This emphasis on commonality and reciprocation explains why the aesthetic mobilization of subjectivity throughout the text is understood most consistently through the notion of the icon. Subcomandante Marcos, of the Zapatista movement in Chiapas, for instance, achieves significance in the argument of *Multitude* less because of specific actions or achievements than because of his ability to serve as an "icon," an imitable and replicable model of authority combined with subordination (85). It is precisely through the mobilization of iconic images that subjectivities form themselves, through mutual recognition, into the relationships in common that constitute the resistant "multitude." And although icons are local—each movement has its own—the history of the icon reveals an underlying connection among them. The mode of "aesthetic representation" at work in Byzantine icons provides the subject with "a way to participate in the sacred and imitate the divine"; with their "element of hope and salvation," they serve—because of the ethos of participation they depict—as the paradigmatic "vehicle" for "political representation" (325, 327). Still other icons abound in Hardt and Negri's text, enacting and recommending a similar commitment to participation, cooperation, and love. These include the golem, Frankenstein's monster (10–12), the swarming insects of Rimbaud's "beautiful hymns to the Paris commune" (92), and the migrant poor themselves with their quasi-poetic "creativity and inventiveness" (134). All of these serve as imitable models of properly insurgent identities; far from being merely local icons particular to a political movement, they aesthetically represent a mode of conduct common to all insurgent subjects.

Hardt and Negri declare that their inspiration is derived by turning "back to the eighteenth century" (306). That inspiration is to be found not merely in theories of radical democracy, as they claim, but also in the aesthetic of beauty, which provides a representation and recommendation for "a strong notion of community convention" (310). And this community, bypassing, as it does, the traditional formations of sovereign power, has the affective content of "love" (351). If in Burke beauty is a cause of love, in Hardt and Negri it is, in a related but more complex maneuver, love's effect and cause. Beautiful iconic aesthetic representation serves to galvanize the "strong notion of community convention" even while it serves as the "vehicle" of that community convention; that community, in turn, achieves the status of a "new race" or "new humanity" (356). One might say that the appeal to a new race and a new humanity is *Multitude*'s most potent aesthetic representation, acting both as the supposed result of political commonality and also as an iconic stimulation for the further imitation and replication of subjectivities.

Although Slavoj Žižek criticizes Hardt and Negri for assuming that the "multitude" can simply be set free to govern itself democratically, without thought to the "form" that democratic governing institutions might take, his critique neglects the way in which the interconnected aesthetic, affective, and racial dimensions of the argument stand in for claims about structures or procedures.[50] Žižek, by ignoring the aesthetic dimension of Hardt and Negri's argument, makes it seem that the problem with their account of "proliferating multitudes" is that it gives no account of how those multitudes can be mobilized.[51] Hardt and Negri, however, conceptualize the formation and mobilization of the multitude through the logic of the icon.

The lack of acknowledgment of this part of Hardt and Negri's position perhaps leads to some vagueness about the actual connection between Žižek's own position and theirs. Arguing against the mere fantasy of a reversal of biopolitical regimes through a determinate negation, Žižek seeks a politics that is founded upon a more complete embrace of the antagonism put at bay in the accounts he criticizes. This must consist in an "authentic" political act that stands in a critical relationship to biopolitics; its authenticity is defined by its purely excessive character, inaccessible to the level of "strategic-pragmatic interventions."[52] Indeed, so hostile is Žižek to the notion of resistance as a strategy that in his view the very fact that a group might be tolerated enough to achieve any political acknowledgment would invalidate their actions; "the very form of negotiation" deprives those groups of their "universal political sting."[53]

In a purely negative sense, authentic political acts lie beyond any individual intention, deliberation, or negotiation. Thus—at first glance, at least—they are unassimilated to the strategies of replicated identities as they appear in Agamben, Alliez, Hardt, and Negri. In more positive terms, what defines the authenticity of a political act, finally, is its proximity to the "Real," that is, to what comes about because it "cannot be resisted"; it is beyond judgment (520). Žižek takes special relish in the act that must be done even though it is "terrible" (521). The excessive, the irresistible, the terrible are signatures of the Real itself, an echo of Burke's empirical sublime.[54] This is the foundation for political action not because it guides any moral or utilitarian calculation, and not because it engages with any set of conditions that might be changed as a result of an action, but only because such actions designate a proximity to the Real. Or, more precisely, rather than seeking out a response to biopolitics in identity, Žižek finds it in "the Real of a drive whose injunction cannot be avoided" (521). Still, each description of the Real emphasizes an aspect of his critique that in fact binds his account ever more securely to Agamben's *Homo Sacer* and Hardt and Negri's *Multitude*, despite its apparent differences. If Žižek avoids assigning legitimate political action to a specific identity, he nevertheless assigns it to a specific drive, and the drive translates into behaviors and character types. This explains why his work has most recently become an inverted mirror image of eighteenth-century conduct literature, arbitrating, as he does in *In Defense of Lost Causes* (2008), between true and false forms of "civility" with a scrupulous attention that would rival Lord Chesterfield's *Letters to His Son* (1774–75).[55] And this also explains why Žižek's argument is repeatedly reinforced with a layering of aesthetic representations of what the Real really looks like—Wagner's Wotan, Brecht's Four Agitators, and so on (518, 520). These are all "difficult to sustain as a literal model to follow," we are warned (512). But the difficulty of following the model cannot detract from the way Žižek holds characters and typical actions up as potential models nevertheless: they are examples, in a sense, of the empirical sublime, securely converted into the logic of beauty.

Romanticism and the Boundaries of Justice

Biopolitical critique that has emerged in recent years invokes not merely replicable identities but identities of a specific *kind* deemed suitable for replication, such as the infant (Agamben), the loving outcast monster (Hardt and Negri), and the apostle of spontaneity or authenticity (Žižek). All are often considered to be quintessentially Romantic figures. But it is worth noting precisely how such figures are uniformly interpreted under the auspices of biopolitical critique. Literary works are about privileged characters, and privileged characters are in turn the occasion for the production (by viewers or readers) of beautiful replications, imitations, and symmetries; they serve more or less consistently as *models* for subjectivity. This strategy links biopolitical critique not with Romantic aesthetics in general but more particularly with the aesthetic of beauty reminiscent of writers such as Reynolds and Burke.

To be sure, the normative claims in biopolitical critique, while connected with these paradigmatic Romantic figures, do not usually hinge upon a suggestion that such figures themselves are connected with any accompanying Romantic political discourse or political prescriptions (beyond Hardt and Negri's nod to earlier revolutionary discourse). It is more clearly the case that those figures are retrieved by the biopolitical theorist in order to reanimate them for exemplification within a present that could not have been anticipated by the Romantics themselves. The explanation for this pervasive de-historicizing gesture seems clear enough when we turn back to the bland but specific way in which the political significance of the late eighteenth century is often characterized: as the uninterrupted triumph of racist nationalism, against which a resistant biopolitical reproduction of subjectivity arranges itself. Biopolitical critique in this respect dutifully follows in the footsteps of a time-honored tradition in political theory. When postmodern political theorists such as William Connolly refer to a conservative "nostalgia for a nineteenth-century image of the nation," they are speaking of a supposedly Romantic attachment to fictive unities based on equally fictive appeals to common descent, language, and values.[56]

The wonderful irony is that biopolitical critique depends upon the logic of replication and imitation that stands close to the heart of the biopolitical regimes it opposes. Beyond this irony, however, the dependence on the political aesthetic of beauty comes at the cost of neglecting a different significance for these marginalized or outcast figures, to which biopolitical critique so frequently attaches itself. In Smith's *Beachy Head*, the point of representing marginal figures in the poem, from the poet herself to the figure of the hermit, is not to provide imitable models for the reader. Rather, such figures are utterly estranged from others at the same time that this estrangement enables their commitment to protection, a commitment that lies beyond any coherent claim to shared identity. The solitary hermit's complaint against the world's injustices, registered by his saving the life of a voiceless but struggling stranger in the waves, echoes the equally estranged narrator's acknowledgment of the suffering slave, an acknowledgment figured within a sheltering though entirely figurative architecture.

We observe a double movement here, an oscillation between the inward turning of the solitary figure and the outward turn toward protection and affiliation. The outward movement has its own complexity, furthermore. On the one hand, it is a shift across isolated persons that blurs or obscures boundaries between persons or communities. On the other hand, that blurring or obscuring eventuates in a redefined structure of relations that emphasizes the connection between justice and the creation of new political and institutional frameworks.[57] The logic is carried forth in a range of Smith's work. Her 1794 novel *The Banished Man* amounts to nothing less than an obsession with the protection of strangers; the problem with Jacobinism, embodied in the threatening figures of the sans-culottes throughout the novel, seems to be understood as the denial, through "tyrannical anarchy," of that protection in the quest for national purity.[58] And in her very last poem, "To my lyre" (published posthumously by Sir Walter Scott in 1829), she thinks of her lyre—that is, the instrument of lyric poetry itself—as both the accompaniment of the author's "solitude" (37) and an instrument acknowledged by others who "own thy power" to soothe (33). The lyre's song is motivated by a complaint from an "anguished bosom" (5), but the song is *not* a "power" owned solely by the author. It is also the property of others who may not resemble the author at all but nonetheless share in her "fond attachment" to the lyre's music.

To make this argument about Smith, and to argue that her commitment to the sublime connects her to a range of other Romantic writers discussed in this volume, is not entirely to discount the attractions of the politics of beauty well into the Romantic age. One could easily turn to the idea of "spiritual assimilation" in Novalis to see the continuation of Burke's politics of the beautiful; Novalis was among the most fervent admirers of Burke's "revolutionary book against the Revolution."[59] Josef Chytry's *Aesthetic State* (1989) summarizes the continued interest that writers had in grounding the polis in beautiful bodies.[60] Still, the alternative that Smith and other Romantics provide to biopolitical critique is striking. As we have already seen, Smith's view of the significance of marginal figures in her poetry departs in remarkable ways from the widespread dependence on replicable identities in writers from Agamben to Žižek. The sublime removal of these figures is inseparable from a larger moral-political logic that differs from and even openly critiques the policies of biopolitical regimes. Those figures, that is, are connected to alternative ways of imagining affiliation that do not easily fall into the category of racist nationalism, so often viewed as the hallmark of the Romantic period. After all, *Beachy Head* turns out to oppose the xenophobic logic of the "Norman Yoke" ideology, to which it might at first seem to subscribe, even as it—just like her other works—opposes what Smith sees as the contemporary instantiation of that ideology in the French Revolution.

This leads us to note a further contrast between the logic of the sublime in Romantic writing and the appropriation of Romantic figures in biopolitical critique. There is a contrast at stake here between two legacies of Romantic writing. For biopolitical critique, the emblematic figures of an earlier age are passed down according to a genetic logic. Their meaning is not to be found in the relationships they establish within given texts; rather it is isolated within the figures themselves as mimetically replicable, predetermined patterns. The legacy for the logic of the sublime in its standpoint on justice urges against the logic of legacy. To the extent that we might view Romanticism as setting an example for the present, its example might militate against the logic of exemplification itself. Romantic texts may not provide models for identity any more than they recommend that we go out to view mountains or oceans to be more just. But their moments of sublimity convey an aesthetic vantage point on a contentious mode of belonging to which we might still aspire, on our own terms.

CHAPTER 5

Aesthetics and Animal Theory

Thus far I have been examining the consequences of beauty's privilege, because of its emphasis on symmetry, balance, and resemblance, as a model for justice or other political virtues. This aesthetic approach to social relations not only dominates writing on beauty but also inspires a whole range of critical theory and literary criticism. In the contrasting approach that I have been tracing out, while commitments to justice do need to depend upon aesthetic experience, in that we explain to people what we want the world to look and feel like, justice can't be adequately addressed through the discourse of beauty and the sympathetic identifications that beauty represents, enforces, and recommends. In Charlotte Smith's writing (chapter 4) we find a counterexample to the political aesthetic of beauty: the speaker's withdrawal from society accompanies an even greater commitment to it by extending a protection to new participants. The importance of architecture in Smith's poem can be discerned in the poem's association between attention to the slave and an inclusive structure. And although this way of "making room" for the slave is not identical to any act of law or set of laws, it describes a general commitment to allowance and accommodation that articulates what I identify as a pervasive Romantic aesthetic vantage point on justice.

This position might be related to the one found in the work of some theorists of justice, such as John Rawls. At least one point on which Rawls's position has been vulnerable, however, is the requirement that participants be "reasonable" beings if they are to be included within structures of social cooperation. Critics of Rawls's position tend to overemphasize the degree to which his account of justice requires conformity; but Rawls extends Kant's position precisely in its commitment to disagreement and complaint, which I see at the center of the account of justice explored in the previous chapters. In this closing chapter, I continue to examine this account of justice but acknowledge and explore its limits.

Perhaps one kind of limit can be approached by posing the following questions: How can new members be included within the scope of justice? What is the basis for that inclusion? Consider the case of slavery. In Smith's *Beachy Head*, slaves are always already included within the scope of the speaker's sublime vision, always already part of her community. In his own discussion of slavery, Rawls says that his constructivist approach yields the most persuasive argument against the injustice of slavery, because the "political conception of justice as fairness"—which entails the political virtues of "toleration and respect"—conflicts with slavery, which "allows some persons to own others as their property and thus to control and own the product of their labor."[1] But perhaps there is something dissatisfying about this kind of claim precisely because slaves, far from being outcasts or subhumans, are preregistered in the social contract. They are beneficiaries of the rights and duties that follow from the tolerant and respectful relations that Rawls describes. In his view, slavery involves only depriving persons of their rights rather than judging them as non-persons. Thus he might seem to sidestep the issue of how (and by whom) the enslaved are considered complete persons, capable of the arguments and deliberations that lead to justice.

I turn now to the question of animal rights, which—as commentators routinely point out and as my examples show—at least since the time of Jeremy Bentham and John Stuart Mill, and in the present with Stephen Wise, has been connected in crucial ways with the issue of slaves, women, and other members of society marginal to the protections of just institutions.[2] The treatment of animals in particular serves as an exemplary instance of the problem of justice toward beings that are not given the opportunity to occupy the corrective standpoint described earlier. Moreover, the problem of animals might even be said to magnify the problems of other marginal beings. It at once highlights the importance of a shared discourse in matters of political inclusion according to the Kantian account of the public, "in the truest sense of the word," even while it points to the limits of that perspective when applied to new species or to anything *considered* to be a non- or subhuman species. Although some recent writing tends to emphasize the opportunities for communication between humans and nonhuman animals and even likens human-animal exchange to "translation,"[3] such arguments struggle against the severe constraint on a shared discourse that would let animals "speak for themselves," as Catharine MacKinnon puts it.[4] In light of that constraint, a range of theoretical positions on animals places an increasing emphasis on the importance of identity features shared with human beings that require or demand our sympathy. For the issue of animal treatment routinely drifts toward an emphasis on physical and affective similarity as a way of compensating for what many interpret as an absence of modes of interaction based on reasoning and autonomy.[5] Because of this absence, Rawls simply cannot include animals within the scope of his understanding of justice. He instead concludes that "political justice does not cover everything" and therefore "needs always to be complemented by other virtues."[6]

Because it is beyond the scope of this chapter to describe fully the extensive theoretical work on animal life, I emphasize some of the more striking positions that have emerged in the past half-century. Although they cannot be classified uniformly as animal "rights" discourse, they can be broadly understood as animal theory or animal studies. Indeed, they diverge quite significantly when it comes to determining how and whether commitments to animal welfare or human-animal relations might resolve themselves into a commitment to rights. Some theorists, such as David Favre and Martha Nussbaum, have attempted to extend the insights of Rawls's theories even while limiting them to what they consider to be the appropriate capacities of animals. Favre advocates animal rights based upon an animal's "self-ownership" and "equitable title."[7] Nussbaum's modification of this approach—in order lend more precision to a sense of distinction between humans and animals—claims to be able to determine for a given animal what is needed in order for it to flourish according to its "capabilities."[8] By tailoring specific capabilities to specific animals, she modifies what she takes to be Rawls's "idealized rationality."[9]

A common critique of these and other rights-based approaches is that in their attempt to codify similarities and differences between humans and animals they are insensitive to nuances. Not that this vein of critique is heedless of the well-being of animals—few today argue against the notion of animal well-being altogether, although commitments to it vary—but it tends to argue that an adequate sensitivity to animal being is wrongly conceived according to codified rights. In a particularly succinct account of this view, Matthew Calarco accuses animal-rights discourses of depending upon an "isolationist" logic of "identity politics" even while they make the case for animal rights inevitably depend upon "anthropocentrism" and "speciesism." While assuming that animals constitute a unique identity, that is, animal rights, again quoting Calarco, determine "animality and animal identity according to human norms and ideals."[10]

It is easy to feel the force of this argument against animal-rights-based approaches, in part because the claims underline the difficulty of communicating with animals and thus the difficulty of establishing a relationship in which animals might "speak for themselves," or as Jean-François Lyotard puts it in *The Differend* (1983), might find an "expression" for a "wrong" by altering the construction of "rules" and the "formation . . . of phrases."[11] We might come to see, for instance, that Nussbaum's view of different capacities for animal well-being is simply an example of what Cary Wolfe calls "philosophical humanism," an extension of what we understand human well-being should be.[12] When animal-rights activists argue that animals should be protected according to their "mental abilities" or their access to "self-awareness," the problem only becomes more acute, since protection of animals appears to depend upon judging animals' mental abilities against the standard of human abilities.[13]

At the same time, the response to rights-based approaches often seems to accentuate, rather than eliminate, the problems that arise through sympathetic "anthropocentric" identification. The problem of uniform identity, which Calarco seems to critique at one level, merely emerges at another: the criticism of rights questions the distinction between human and animal in order to produce a more complex play of identities and differences without entirely ridding itself of the anthropocentrism with which it quarrels. Vicki Hearne, for instance, argues that a rights relationship can be known and attained only within the most intimate relationship between an animal and an owner or trainer, because this is the only relationship in which a condition of mutuality occurs that in turn enables "animal happiness."[14] What Calarco calls an "alternative ontology" of human-animal life renders the issue of sympathetic identification with animals more complex and localized in order to avoid a codification of rights, but this logic still does not eliminate the degree to which the concern for animals resolves into the "endless loops of sameness and difference" that MacKinnon associates with all liberal animal-rights theory.[15]

Deconstruction's important impact on discussions of animal justice is particularly revealing in this regard; this influence complements the impact it has had on notions of shared identity as justice in queer and cosmopolitan theory. Jacques Derrida's work on animals, for instance, takes aim at the likes of Jacques Lacan for supposing that the human can be separated from the animal, with an inviolable difference, as culture is separate from nature.[16] Derrida, for his part, questions absolute differences between human and animal life by showing that both are subject to a "trace beyond the human"[17] and thus share a profound vulnerability. Derrida aligns himself—even while seemingly setting himself apart from traditional humanist arguments—with commitments to "sympathy" for nonhuman animals generated through the experience of "suffering, pity, and compassion."[18] In this deconstructive vein, Akira Lippit starts with the premise that language itself is unable to control the division between human and animal being; it is thus the job of the animal theorist to "remember" the animal traces within the human.[19] Donna Harraway's work on "interspecies dependencies," approvingly noting Derrida's questioning of distinctions between humans and animals, follows a similar line of reasoning. Harraway's correction of Derrida is simply that despite all his expressions of sympathy and compassion, he does not get *close enough* to the animal: despite his curiosity, Derrida does not wonder enough about what animals are actually thinking or feeling.[20]

The critique of the supposed inflexibility of the rights-based approaches might seem to raise questions about its own motives and purposes. If theorists tend to oppose rights-based approaches for their tendency to solidify or codify identities, what is to be gained by opposing the language of rights more generally? What is the unstable affiliation, through identity and difference, supposed to do for the animal? Some critics have unsettled the boundary separating human and animal but distance themselves from any specific "advocacy" whatsoever.[21] J. M. Coetzee's now-famous book *The Lives of Animals* (1999) takes a different route, suggesting that there may be a way of advocating for animals even though that advocacy may be deeply conflicted or even contradictory. Elizabeth Costello, the fictional main character of his novella, gives a series of lectures on animal rights but then troubles rights with her own practices. Espousing vegetarianism while adorned with shoes and purse made from animal hides, she implicitly questions the possibility of any coherent position on animal justice. Coetzee (through his protagonist) declines to offer any position beyond living with unstable "degrees of obscenity" in our relations with animals.[22] Coetzee, by lodging philosophical polemic in a flawed, inconsistent *character*—accentuated in his novel *Elizabeth Costello* (2003), of which the two parts of *The Lives of Animals* form a part—ends up favoring instability (which is at the heart of Coetzee's understanding of the human) over an impossible logical purity. Is it the case that in the place of rights the critique of rights can at best only offer wavering sympathy—extended from the human to the animal in order to offer it inconsistent protection?[23]

Perhaps offering merely inconsistent protection in the place of rights may seem like an especially weak way of securing the welfare of animals, if that is a worthwhile goal. But even while this position explicitly abandons what it takes to be the insufficiently nuanced language of justice for animals, it may also, in its very instability or vagueness, point to something significant about the line of argument deployed within accounts of human-animal relations. Arguments like Coetzee's demonstrate a pervasive tendency in animal theory to address questions of treatment of other beings in terms of our fleeting, unstable, and inconsistent identification or lack of identification with them. And thus it may be that this tendency—a critique of sympathetically forged identity that ends up reinstating it—functions as a gloss on the problem of animal rights or animal treatment among diverse theoretical perspectives across the field of approaches to human-animal relations. This field appears to be continually bound up with what Susan McHugh calls "the disciplinary structures of the human subject."[24] Perhaps the nearly compulsive drive toward sympathetic identification with animals—from the rights perspective and from the critique of rights—points to a particular challenge that has routinely conditioned the coordinates within animal theory.

Animals and the Problem of Sympathy: Barbauld, Trimmer

As in the previous chapters, I shall look back to a cluster of works from the Romantic period. Here, however, my aim is not to offer a decisive alternative to the logic of mutually reinforcing identities that is so often presumed to lay the groundwork for postmodern understandings of justice but to expose the particular problems surrounding the issues of rights for and care of animals—problems that in a sense provide a genealogy for today's struggles. It would be possible to extend an account of the attention to the treatment of animals much further back than the eighteenth century. Praise for vegetarian diets can be found at least as far back as Hesiod's *Works and Days* (ca. 700 BC), and Virgil speaks vividly of animal life and sentience in the *Georgics* (ca. 29 BC). But the late eighteenth century is particularly important, as David Perkins points out, because of the prominent public attention devoted to the condition of animals for their own sake. In the English context, this public attention resulted in progressive legislation for protecting animals (a bill in 1822 passed to protect cattle) and in the founding of the Society for the Prevention of Cruelty to Animals in 1824.[25] The period is also of particular interest here because it demonstrates combating rather than entirely consistent perspectives on the issue of animal protection and rights, which help us to grasp the limiting contours of animal-rights discourse at the moment of its triumph.

In many instances, the concern for animals is generated by sympathy set in motion by calibrations of proximity and distance between humans and animals. This logic looks forward to Giorgio Agamben's problematizing of distinctions between humans and animals in *The Open*, as well as to the analogous way in which deconstructive theorists like Derrida and Lippit have approached the issue. In Anna Laetitia Barbauld's poem "The Mouse's Petition" (1773), for instance—one of her most popular since its first publication—a trapped mouse pleads for liberty, echoing but also differing from a human plea. Barbauld frames the mouse's petition as an incitement to the reader to feel "compassion" for the imprisoned creature.[26] The problem of justice to animals in this poem is initially addressed by assuming an identity among all living things, so that even a worm would seem to carry within it something that is like "men" so that it would command sympathetic feeling (46). But even though animals are said to be like humans, it makes sense to follow Kathryn Ready's advice not to press the analogy too far.[27] In fact, the poem implies that animals are not merely metaphorical for humans but also part of an implicit hierarchy. The poem thus looks forward to arguments such as Peter Singer's that animals deserve protection even though (in his opinion) they clearly do not deserve the same rights and protections as humans.[28] Commanding a position above all beings in the poem is the angel, who displays an idealized "compassion" by freeing the mortal beings (whether mouse or man) from the "hidden snare" that might cause their "destruction" (48, 45). The angel's kindness is significant because it is a human quality that the reader can imitate even though he or she may not quite reach the angel's perfection.[29] And while animals might have a "mind" or "soul" that is a human's, or at least like a human's (29, 34), the poem also argues for the mouse's *inferiority* to the human, just as the human is inferior to the angel. For instance, there is no indication that the mouse's "frugal meals" made from the scraps of human feasts, while only a "slender boon," are somehow unfair to the mouse (18, 20). And thus the mouse, while pleading for his life with phrases that echo Thomas Paine's *Rights of Man* (1791), does not argue for the benefits of humanity that at first seemed to form the basis and motivation for his plea. The poem urges readers to exercise human compassion while also accepting a limit to it, a defining characteristic of what Agamben calls the "anthropological machine."[30]

Of course, we might argue that Barbauld's "Petition" risks making religious authority merely like a compulsive extension of human feeling, a feeling that generates sympathy even as it swallows up everything in its own impulses not only to humanize but also to create hierarchical categories among humans. This argument may only underline the degree to which literary works about freeing animals—Barbauld's "Epitaph on a Goldfinch" (1774), Laurence Sterne's *A Sentimental Journey* (1768), and Mary Robinson's "The Linnet's Petition" (1775) are other examples—make the freedom of animals part of an implicit code of human value and conventional hierarchy.

Sarah Trimmer's *Fabulous Histories* (1786) takes a different interest in animals in that her work does not merely argue for freedom as analogized to human freedom, any more than it suggests that the impulse to grant this freedom would come from an angel. Trimmer instead advocates a specific set of duties toward them. These depend even more clearly on carefully calibrated and codified degrees of sympathy, although Trimmer translates the hierarchy in Barbauld into largely material, class-based conditions.Trimmer's didactic book for children combines both allegory and realism, leading to significant tensions between birds as metaphorical representatives of the family and as beings metonymically connected to it. Frequently, that is, the happy family of robin redbreasts in the stories conveys messages to the Benson family's children (and to readers) about the value of family, personal responsibility, moderate appetite, and so on. At the same time, children are to learn "compassion" for animals, which is different from the compassion shown to other humans.[31] While birds and even insects are proper objects of concern and are entitled to protection from needless harm—Nussbaum would say that they are acknowledged to have specific capabilities—Mrs. Benson tells her children, Harriet and Fredrick, that hungry children and poor people should be fed before hungry birds (5). Higher in estimation are one's immediate "dependents" or servants, and higher still are friends and family (17). Trimmer's work thus makes it clear that care for birds appears to be motivated by a sense that birds are similar to humans; but birds are also different (and inferior), and this is why Mrs. Benson can justify keeping certain species in cages and eating birds as well (34).

The care for animals in *Fabulous Histories*, then, is the byproduct of Trimmer's larger arrangement of interconnected duties, some of which are transferable across classes and species and some of which are articulated according to each being's place in a legible economy of power. All beings, that is, can profit from the robins' lessons about simple virtue. But other duties are more specific and nontransferable. If the Bensons are taught not to produce "causeless pain" (57), pain and scarcity—just like the "compassion" at the center of Trimmer's text—are given a "cause" by humans, specifically by humans who belong to the "gentry" about whom Trimmer is writing (57). If legitimate pain is pain with a "cause"—that is, pain that is necessary or unavoidable—the lesson to be learned from Trimmer's text is that a specific class of humans is endowed with the capability of discriminating between pains that are necessary and those that are not, among both human and nonhuman animal creatures. They are taught when, and when not, to exercise "merciful" conduct toward lesser beings (59). Any failure to honor our relationship with nonhuman animals and other humans makes both children and their parents bad people, as the Benson children's numerous adventures throughout the *Histories*—with neglectful parents and naughty bird-hating children—amply show.

Whereas Barbauld makes it seem as if protection is lodged within an angelic power that responds to the mouse's petition and recommends a benevolent but imperfect course of action for humans, Trimmer considers that power to be lodged entirely within humans. Humans relate to one another according to specific duties one group owes another; our duties to animals are the result, not of divine mercy, but rather of the particular place animals occupy within a social hierarchy. Furthermore, whereas the values in Barbauld's poem seem only implicitly to depend upon human values translated from religious authority, Trimmer works in the opposite direction, secularizing and humanizing Barbauld. She makes apparently religious values patently dependent upon a structure of relations in which those with the most power offer their protection to those beneath them.

The Aesthetics of Duties: Cowper

Animals that are familiar in and around domestic space, while not necessarily pets, are frequently the focus of sympathy-based rights. There is a nearly tautological way in which domestic animals in the works described above become the focus for domestic virtue. Inhabiting spaces within and around the home makes them particularly susceptible to being treated as analogies to humans themselves and thus as magnets for varying degrees of sympathy. Most certainly, the London sensation of the "Learned Pig," a popular eighteenth-century entertainment in Charing Cross in which audiences—including Coleridge, Trimmer, and Wordsworth—could supposedly see a pig read, spell, count, and tell time, depended precisely upon this kind of analogical reasoning, although the wise Mrs. Benson in Trimmer's text warns that the pig's superficial imitations of human life are thoroughly "foreign to his nature" (60).[32] The Benson children are to understand that no matter how the Learned Pig might imitate human habits, the pig is just a pig.

Kant argues that in fact this kind of sympathetic relationship with animals defines, and confines, our duties toward them. He argues that all animals can be considered analogies to humans but that since they are only analogies, we can only have "indirect" duties toward them. Because they lack "self-consciousness," we cannot conceive of them as ends in themselves but only as analogues to humans, who are ends.[33] As beneficiaries of only indirect duties, animals are seen by us as providing occasion for, practice for, or indications of, our duties to humans. The notion of an indirect duty—a duty that is not itself completely ethical but is analogous to ethics (as the examples of Barbauld and Trimmer show)—is intimately connected with the long history that Harriet Ritvo traces in relation to the use of domestic animals and pets in nineteenth-century literature, a history in which animals' representation of human conduct is accompanied by their simultaneous "marginalization."[34] But the idea of indirect duty is also intimately connected with claims that today's animal theorists likewise make about our relations with animals, which are understood to be governed through our sympathetic and compassionate attitudes toward them. Marginalization and compassion are two sides of the same coin.

The quasi-ethical position outlined in Kant begins to take on a specific aesthetic gravity because of its ability to provide an image of what it would be like to act ethically, although here the ethical action toward animals seems more or less obviously aesthetic in its very specific and restricted relation to *beauty*—its attractive and tender similarity to our equally tender treatment of humans. Indeed, it might even be said that the moral and aesthetic deployment of indirect duties stands close to the center of the utterly contradictory and problematic use of the animal in literary and philosophical representations from the eighteenth century on. For even as animals are analogous to humans, the very emphasis on likeness that mobilizes analogy also mobilizes a corresponding unlikeness and distance, a distance forbidding (or at least significantly curtailing) the kind of duty that we owe to humans.

We could turn to virtually any of the texts on animals from the period just surveyed to note the prevalence of the language of beauty. Here, as in previous chapters, the centrality of this language to the representation and motivation of political commitment should be noted. The birds to be cultivated in *Fabulous Histories* are not to be considered "alien playthings" but "beautiful little creatures" (59). The emphasis on the beauty of animals in Trimmer is a commonplace in other texts. Animals captured in Africa and Asia and displayed in London were repeatedly described in broadsides in terms of "beauty," "delicacy," and "regularity" of features; the "laughing hyaena" advertised in 1796 was said to have a "cry" that "resembles the human voice."[35] Ritvo points out how frequently, well into the nineteenth century, the defenders of certain kinds of animals, such as dogs, lions, and elephants, cherished them for their "beauty" precisely insofar as they demonstrated the courage and intellect supposedly possessed by humans.[36] George IV, having heard reports of the "beauty and symmetry" of a Southdown wether, demanded that the sheep be brought to Brighton "so that the King could see it before it was slaughtered."[37]

Is it any wonder that the eighteenth-century aesthetic logic of beauty, so crucial for rendering visible a proper ethical relationship to animals, also vividly asserts itself in today's writing on animals and animal-rights theory? A brief survey of animal studies shows how dominant the discourse of beauty has become in our own day as a way of aesthetically recommending a certain form of human-animal relationship. It is impossible to read these texts without suspecting that they emerged in the same climate as the prominent work on beauty with which I began this book. It is impossible, that is, to read them without the impression that they have been informed by beauty as a dominant political-aesthetic paradigm even while they lend that paradigm considerable force.

The aesthetic of beauty is central to animal theory's logic, in which the beauty of animals mobilizes a sympathy that is based upon recognition, resemblance, and symmetry. In *Empty Cages* (2004), Tom Regan speaks of the educational value of images that convey the "beauty and dignity, grace and mystery" of animals, which helps to counteract the "tragic truth" of humans who exploit them.[38] Regan speaks still more broadly elsewhere about how a respect for animals reinforces "the integrity, stability, and beauty of the biotic community," treating *integrity*, *stability*, and *beauty* roughly as synonyms.[39] The philosopher Cora Diamond urges her readers to acknowledge the "wonder" and "beauty" that characterize the similarity and distance between humans and animals, and this aesthetic standpoint is inseparable, in her view, from an emphasis on a shared disposition with animals—a shared "vulnerability" to death.[40]

The emphasis on beauty cuts across claims attached to quite different viewpoints on animal rights and animal care. From a more deconstructive perspective, one that champions a skeptical position on distinctions between humans and animals, Steve Baker's *Postmodern Animal* (2000) overlaps in remarkable ways with Wendy Steiner's work. He criticizes the exclusion of animals in modern art's abstractions in the same way that Steiner criticizes the exclusion of beauty; including animals in postmodern art, he says, emphasizes "awkward conjunctions of human and animal (identity)."[41] His book's quest for a new form of postmodern "beauty" encourages "openness to the animal."[42] While arguing for the importance of training in developing a relationship between animals and humans, Vicki Hearne, who consistently opposes animal rights, argues that good horse-training techniques lead to "the development or enhancement of the horse's beauty." This is because the trainer's commands allow the horse to achieve a "congruence and contact with . . . splendor," with that splendor defined in terms of "classically pure" movements.[43] Donna Harraway, echoing Hearne's account, describes the kind of "interspecies" relationship she analyzes and recommends in her work as "increasing the stock of beauty in the world," as if producing beauty were (as it is in Elaine Scarry's work) conformable to a reproductive paradigm.[44] Paul

Patton more directly builds upon Hearne's account when he explains that "the beauty of that of good riding is a beauty that belongs to the nature of a horse."[45] But even Patton admits that the "nature" of the horse is itself conditioned by human notions of what is appropriate animal training.

If beauty has been, and continues to be, so central in the aesthetic representation of animals, what about the sublime? William Cowper insists on a profound aesthetic distinction between appropriate poetic responses to the death of animals and appropriate poetic responses to the death of slaves; this translates into a distinction between indirect and direct duties as they are schematized in poetic speculation. When Cowper writes about the death of birds in poems like "On a Goldfinch starved to Death in his Cage" (1782) and "On the Death of Mrs. Throckmorton's Bullfinch" (1789), he personifies an animal and grieves its death as if it were a human. But whether a bird is starved or (like Mrs. Throckmorton's bird) eaten by a rat, it can *only* be mourned. The poet's aim is not to outline a contrasting obligation to the bird. Indeed, the very pathos generated by the animal's death seems to be inspired in part by a shared sense that a short life with a violent death is nothing other than the norm for a bird. Thus domestic confinement excites an ethical concern that comfortably comports with the imposition of violence. Cowper is consistent with Trimmer in this regard. For when little Frederick Benson in *Fabulous Histories* accidentally kills one of his birds by feeding it too quickly, he is taught that his tears, while certainly appropriate, should be dried quickly so that he can move along with his other obligations (95). Mourning for dead animals can be sustained only until it is unsettled by the reminder that birds are fundamentally different from humans, who present us with more substantial ethical claims.

With Cowper's treatment of the slave, however, the situation is different. The aim of a poem like "The Negro's Complaint" (1793) is, in a sense, to appeal to the white reader's "affection" as he or she reads the poem and hears the plight of the enslaved African who speaks in its lines.[46] But the crucial difference here lies in the way that the speaker forms his lines in terms of a "complaint" that vividly contrasts with the "petition" of Barbauld's mouse. If the birds in Cowper's poems suffer a misfortune that is only consistent with their nature, and if the mouse in Barbauld's poem petitions only to escape death without altering his living conditions, the speaker in Cowper's poem does something more: he urges a radically different treatment of the slave, asking his master to desist from mechanisms of torture like "knotted scourges" and "blood-extorting screws" (29–30). The speaker's aim, that is, is not merely a mystifying escape—of death, or even of legal punishment—but to *revise* a system of laws so that it no longer inflicts undue pain on himself and on other captives.

Such a revision can only come from the "one who reigns on high" (26), and this ending for the poem is significant in relation to its political-aesthetic vantage point. "The Negro's Complaint" ends with a sublime scene of retribution in which an imagined providential power—through "Wild tornados" and "whirlwinds" (33, 40)—exacts punishment for the crimes of murder and torture associated with slavery and named earlier in the poem. While the "Complaint" in a powerful and affecting way connects the slave's complaint with a revision of retributive justice, it consequently, and simultaneously, questions the very strength of the appeal to sympathy that at first sets the poem in motion. To seek a resolution to the problem of retributive justice only outside this world—from the one "on high"—is to underline the weakness in the logic of sympathy with its appeal to mutual "affection" between slaves and white slave owners or slave traders. Thus Cowper's poem could be said to provide a vivid contrast to the logic at work in both Barbauld and Trimmer. The operations of Providence, in his poem, are far less significant for articulating a merciful attitude that the speaker or reader might adopt for him- or herself. Instead, these operations point to a revised structure of justice even while they skeptically remove the achievement of justice from the sphere of human relations.

Animals and the Sublime: Coleridge

By invoking the sublime in relation to Cowper's poem, I am pointing to the poem's ability to invoke an aesthetic sense of what it would be like to follow a just law. That just law dramatically contrasts with the play of sympathies that more obviously characterize the poet's works on the deaths of birds, sympathies that are elegiacally set in motion but then quickly exhausted. What would it be like for a poet to conjure a more direct sense of duty toward animals? In Coleridge's poetry, I would suggest, it is possible to see an aesthetic approach to the world of animals that complicates Perkins's exclusive focus on sympathy and compassion as the sole bases for animal rights in the Romantic period. In Coleridge's poems, the sublime mode fleetingly captures a view of animals not merely as objects of sympathy but as free beings in an extended and inclusive order of justice presiding over human and nonhuman animals.

When Diamond argues against Singer's view of animal rights as justified entirely according to a tenuous calibration of how much animals do or do not feel pain, she approaches a perspective that could be useful for understanding the kind of view I want to describe in relation to both Coleridge and Shelley. Although in one sense Diamond appears to be advocating a sense of shared experience between humans and animals, her position turns out to be more complicated than that. Her claim that a human might see an animal, without any simplistic assumption about similarity or difference, as a "fellow creature" that exists in "the same boat" is conducive to the thinking we find in some writers of the Romantic age. This is because her "non-biological" account of "life" avoids the "anthropomorphic" and "sentimental" claims to similarity between different beings.[47] For Diamond, appealing to the notion of an animal as a "fellow creature" means imagining a structure of protections by which animals—different though they may be—are sheltered from abuse and harm.[48] Both the reasoning behind that claim and its attendant problems are the focus of the remainder of this chapter.

To approach the place of animals in Coleridge's poetry is to acknowledge that the poet insistently criticizes, even satirizes, conventional sympathetic relationships between humans and animals. Consider, for instance, Coleridge's insistence in "Fears in Solitude" that there is a remarkable difference between harming humans and harming nonhuman beings. The poem's diatribe is directed toward those who "would groan to see a child / Pull off an insect's leg"[49] even while they hear of England's war against France and do nothing about it. Or even worse, they invent "dainty terms for fratricide" (113), mere "abstractions, empty sounds to which / We join no feeling and attach no form" (115–16). Coleridge implies here that grieving over a creature as insignificant as an insect logically coincides with the "abstraction" from actual harms to which "Fears" raises an alarm, an alarm calling the poet's fellow English citizens to become aware of their harmful actions and to withdraw from armed conflict.

Of course, another point that Coleridge makes in "Fears" has to do with the way the *child*, after all, is depicted dismembering an insect with the tacit permission of the parent, as if the child's love of cruelty were utterly consistent with the adult's impulse toward abstract compassion. Certainly the moment in "Fears" echoes the keen eye of William Hogarth in *The Four Stages of Cruelty*

(1751) in which the young man Tom Nero's early torture of dogs and horses leads to theft and murder; with an ironic twist, Coleridge suggests that the torture of insect life is culturally consistent not only with cruelty in adult life but also with a hypocritical sympathy that attempts to mask it—unsuccessfully, thanks to the poem itself. In Coleridge's drama *Osorio* (1797) the insect is not merely an inferior being that attracts an abstract, meaningless sympathy compared with that shown to more compelling human objects of attention. When the play's hero, Albert, attempts to impress guilt upon his brother Osorio for his attempted murder of Albert, Osorio tries to get Albert to drink from a goblet of poisoned wine. Albert responds, as he does consistently throughout the play, by attempting to inspire a "terror" in Osorio of killing other living things: "Yon insect on the wall," he says, "Has life . . . life and thought," and thus "Saw I that insect on this goblet's brink, / I would remove it with an eager terror."[50] Thus Albert's point isn't simply that he won't drink the wine and kill himself; it is that Osorio should have respect for all living things, all of which have a "miraculous will" directed to "pleasurable ends."[51]

Some comment might be made here about the connection between animals like mice and birds—which, even if not entirely domesticated, live within and around the home—and insects and spiders. The distance of humans from lower forms of life emerges frequently even in the most passionate defenses of animal rights. That we do, or should, care more about dogs and cats than about insects and spiders is explained in contemporary animal theory by the imposition of a two-tiered hierarchy on nonhuman life. Stephen Wise is one of many who explain that some animals have a more developed consciousness than others. This advanced level of consciousness, firmly grounded in empirical measures of intelligence, designates a greater "practical autonomy" than found in lower beings, thus justifying our choice to protect some nonhuman beings and not others.[52]

This distinction between life that is suitable for protection and life that is not is worth mentioning only to provide a contrast with the complexity of Coleridge's position, which treats even those forms of life that are most estranged from familiar domestic existence as a specific kind of poetic opportunity to claim affiliation. Coleridge gestures toward the way that insects attract a strange and fanciful sympathy when he critiques those who "groan" to see the pain of an insect but have no care for injuries to human beings. Conversely, *Osorio*'s logic clearly unfastens itself from the notion that a concern for other creatures demands a claim to likeness or mutual understanding; all creatures are guided by a miraculous will toward their own separate ends (this is part of Coleridge's understanding of the "One Life"). When Coleridge addresses a familiar farm animal in "To a Young Ass" (1794), the point of the speaker's hailing the oppressed and tortured animal as a "BROTHER" (26) is not to assert a similarity between the speaker and the animal but simply to express a concern for its needs, for health and plentiful grass for food. And even the nightingale, while certainly one of the most familiar of birds to an English reader, is extracted in Coleridge's poem "The Nightingale" from its familiar meanings, as if to make a domestic bird improbably wild.

Coleridge's "The Rime of the Ancient Mariner" (first published in *Lyrical Ballads* in 1798) builds upon notions of justice that are at work in *Osorio*; both play on the logic in "Fears in Solitude" by applying the notion of "filial fears" that the speaker voices at the end of the poem more widely to the entire realm of living creatures. In a sense, the lines toward the poem's end affirm the importance of an even more broadly gauged understanding of the poetic speaker's "filial fears," which the "Rime" applies to all living things:

> He prayeth well, who loveth well
>   Both man and bird and beast.
>
> He prayeth best who loveth best
>   All things both great and small:
> For the dear God who loveth us,
>   He made and loveth all.   (612–16)

There is one way of reading the poem that accentuates the degree to which Coleridge, as Christine Kenyon-Jones points out, imbibes the popular emblems and fables scattered throughout the era's popular conduct books for children.[53] According to this reading, the travails of the Mariner and his crew can be seen as the eventual (but hardly predictable) result of the Mariner's killing the albatross. The hermit at the end of the poem shrieves the Mariner in a process necessary for his penance. Thus suffering and penance for the Mariner's killing of the bird form part of the divine retributive law that governs "All things both great and small." This reading is only accentuated in the poem's rewritten argument for the 1800 edition of *Lyrical Ballads* and in the gloss added in the 1817 *Sibylline Leaves* version, which, in an almost humorously laconic and moralizing fashion, codifies the law toward which the poem gestures elsewhere (in the gloss, the mariner pays "penance" by "travel[ing] from land to land"). Both reinforce the poem's events as a narrative of crime and punishment.

And yet at the same time, as Frances Ferguson has argued, the causal relations are consistently and intriguingly blurred as if to defy the meanings that seem to be imposed upon them by the supposedly clear meaning of the bird and the equally clear consequences of killing it.[54] "Fears" asserts the possibility of a just form of revenge that others might take against Britain's injurious actions; thus the poem appears to assert a wider and more inclusive form of justice. In the "Rime," though, the very assertion of a causal link between the albatross and good fortune—its presence on the ship and the cracking of the ice, the rising wind in the ships sails—is pronounced upon confidently in the gloss at line 71: "And lo! The Albatross proveth a bird of good omen." But the gloss, trumpeting its devotion to conventional religious values, seems, when compared with the verse itself, only to emphasize the limitation of that view, which is gradually exposed in the poem's relentless ambiguation of cause and effect. After all, the very attribution of the albatross as an omen is not stated as a truth; it is the result of a collective religious *belief* in the bird as the embodiment of a soul: "As if it had been a Christian soul, / We hailed it in God's name" (65–66). And the entire account of supernatural vengeance that follows the killing of the bird likewise depends upon the fact that "all averred" (93)—that is, the crew claimed or believed—that the killing of the albatross was a crime against God's law.

The poem, in a manner reminiscent of Cowper's treatment of retributive justice for slavery in "The Negro's Complaint," asserts a higher law governing all creatures great and small and then questions the clarity and legibility of that law. The Mariner's narration demonstrates the height of sublimity by insisting on his departure or dissent from conventional wisdom; as the 1800 argument puts it, he acts "in contempt of the laws of hospitality." In an action that goes against the beliefs and assurances of the crew, he shoots the bird that is hailed in God's name and that supposedly brings good fortune. At the same time, this sublime separation comports with the Mariner's affirmation of a sense of lawfulness that is not merely conventional. Although Raimonda Modiano seems right to say that the Mariner's narrative gives his experience a "coherence and meaning that it did not originally possess," the poem is not merely a skeptical account of a "vastly nebulous universe."[55] Instead, it seems to dramatize the Mariner's struggle to envision a coherent cosmic order, even though that order cannot be fully articulated by any of the poem's human agents. The Mariner can only gesture toward a mightier set of forces beyond his comprehension—the "tyrranous" forces of nature (42), the "spirit" that appears to plague and follow the Mariner's ship (132), the mysterious appearance of the "spectre-bark" (202).[56]

These arresting features of the poem, even while gesturing to a higher source of authority, fail to coalesce into the kind of learning or doctrine that aligns with or informs the crew's judgments and the gloss's occasional reinforcement of them. They gesture instead toward *some* coherent organization of the universe without concretely providing a notion of what that organization might be. (And in this sense the poem pits two sublime modes against each other—the Kantian formal sublime and the Burkean, natural sublime, legible only as an illegible terrifying otherness.) This structure produces a certain kind of limitation: even though the poem is clearly invested in representing the animal world—while also clearly addressing the issue of the transatlantic slave trade—the laws that rule over conventionalized assertions and beliefs cannot actually be known; they are not even open to the poetic fantasy of coherent retributive justice to be found in Cowper.[57] Still, the poem's sum total of supernatural effects converts this ontological limitation into poetic strength. While the supernatural elements in the poem are only traces of an authority that cannot be cognized, they are simultaneously an apprehended concatenation of indelible images, clearly distinguished from the transience and uncertainty of the crew's beliefs and from the learned gloss. Images like the specter ship, in contrast, are surely the most *poetic* aspects of the poem, luxuriantly described with every rhetorical resource at the poet's disposal; poetic authority is an echo or trace of divine authority that nevertheless forcefully asserts itself as a substitution for it.

Shelley, Beauty, Animal Life

The way that Coleridge poetically conceives the relations between humans and animals as governed by a higher power beyond the vagaries of affect could be contrasted with Wordsworth's line of argument in poems such as "Hart-Leap Well" (1800) and "Peter Bell" (1819). In both poems, the animal world is subject to injury and abuse that violates a protective relationship between nature and "sympathy divine"; that sympathy is in turn cultivated by the poet in his reader, who is taught a proper concern or "kind commiseration" for "the meanest thing that feels."[58] Coleridge's understanding of what he called a "brotherhood" (in a letter to Francis Wrangham) between human and nonhuman animals is possible, not because of an exchange of sympathy between divinity, nature, poet, and reader, but precisely and paradoxically because of a withdrawal or disruption of that sympathy.[59]

The higher power governing all creatures in the "Rime" becomes, in Shelley's work, nothing other than poetry itself: a power of schematizing, creating, and asserting new relationships between humans and animals. In Shelley's ambitious *Queen Mab; A Philosophical Poem* (1813), his first long poem in verse, the Fairy Mab speaks to the spirit, or soul, of Ianthe of the "progress" of "Man" or "human things," a progress that will enable humans and animals to live in harmony. In the Fairy's vision of the future, war and vengeance have given way to an absolute peace among all things in which "the flame / Of consentaneous love inspires all life."[60] All animals are at peace with one another: "The lion now forgets to thirst for blood: / There might you see him sporting in the sun / Beside the dreadless kid" (8.124–26). And man himself has abandoned all impulses to kill and enslave other human and animal beings. "All things are void of terror: man has lost / His terrible prerogative, and stands / An equal among equals" (8.225–27).

The politics and aesthetics of the poem are realized as a future that appears as a *vision* of Mab, that is, a vision of a fairy who is already a Shakespearean literary character, as if to underscore the notion of human progress as a possibility enabled only through an aesthetic moment.[61] All of these resonances contribute to a vision of justice that lies at a decided remove from the human, even as it outlines justice as the outcome of the progress of human kind. For the progress of human being is one in which humans participate rather than one they merely direct; the "human being stands adorning" the earth (8.198); the earth "gives suck" to all who "grow beneath her care" (1.109–10). And even "love" itself is a flame that "inspires" life rather than the outcome any living being (8.107–8).

This isn't the complete picture, however. *Queen Mab* consistently—even in the Fairy speaker's vision of human progress, which would include all beings equally—tilts the scale against man's equality with nonhuman animals. The poem, that is, sees man as "chief" among all things, not simply one among equals, since "he . . . can know / More misery, and dream more joy than all" (8.134–35). Mab thus speaks of a potential for man that is currently "stunted" and that has "Marked him for some abortion of the earth, / Fit compeer of the bears that roamed around" (8.152, 153–54). In other words, the lost potential that Mab sees in man registers in his loss of preeminence over nonhuman animals. Surely this must bring us to a reconsideration of Timothy Morton's overly optimistic sense that the poem shows a reformed world with no objects, only a utopian "interpenetrating subjectivity."[62] Only by acknowledging this aspect of *Queen Mab* can we grasp its full force. The poem attempts imaginatively to envision human progress as the possibility of embracing all human and nonhuman animals, even though the very impetus for this progress, and the vision it puts into place, lies quite squarely in the intellectual superiority of man above his fellow beings.

The crucial end point for progress in *Queen Mab*—the sublime, all-inclusive vision of a world protecting all things even while it is superintended by the very human force it claims to organize—also informs Shelley's poem "The Sensitive-Plant," the first of the "Miscellaneous Poems," published in 1820 in the same volume as *Prometheus Unbound*. The poem conjures a vision of nature in a lushly proliferating garden tended by a "Lady" who offers all the "innocent" creatures her protection (2.5, 49). Her death is followed by the decay and death of the garden; the poem, however, entertains the thought that she is the embodiment of a "Spirit" (2.17) that, the poem acknowledges, may live beyond human life or death. "Love, and beauty, and delight" are not the property of human being; "their might / Exceeds our organs—which endure / No light—being themselves obscure" (conclusion, 21, 22–24). Love and beauty, the poem ultimately wants to say, may not live and die with the "Lady" and her "gentle mind" (conclusion, 5); they may instead describe a "form" that protects, and ensures the growth of, all things.

Stuart Curran, noting the play of idealism and skepticism throughout "The Sensitive-Plant," keenly observes that the closing lines of the poem tread a middle ground between them. "The result is at once to honor the eternity of our imaginative ideals and to temper our compulsion for their gratification."[63] Perhaps Curran's commentary can lead us to say something more specific about Shelleyan beauty and its role in the treatment of humans and the nonhuman world in Shelley's poem. Beauty, for Shelley, is not quite the beauty of the eighteenth century—the beauty of symmetries and resemblances. Beauty is something more complex and ambiguous in his writing, and we would do well to heed Angela Leighton's suggestion that Shelleyan beauty "pushes toward the sublime."[64] Shelley constantly draws attention to beauty as the product of human finitude. Beauty is a human "form" that strives to be more than human and seeks to encompass the full range of human and nonhuman living things. The closing lines of "The Sensitive-Plant" bear witness to that aspiration without erasing the status of Shelleyan beauty precisely *as* an aspiration, an aspiration to endure beyond the limits of human animal endurance.

Still more can be said about "The Sensitive-Plant" and its grandly capacious imaginative forms. The poem is very particular about the kinds of beings that are contained within the garden. Warm-blooded animals seem only peripheral to it, for example. Birds are mentioned only late in the poem; elsewhere the poem mentions human and nonhuman animal life only in metaphorical terms. A flower that opens toward the brightening sky resembles an infant smiling on her mother (1.59–60); the sensitive-plant itself is likened to a "doe" (1.11). What is the significance of these maneuvers? Although commentary on the poem (contained, for instance, in the Norton Critical Edition's note on the work's title) usefully points out that in Shelley's day the sensitive-plant was considered to be a plant that might be "a bridge between the animal and vegetable kingdoms," it is still crucial to see that Shelley's mode of representing the range of living beings in the garden—and his mode of representing the "love" in which those beings might participate—excludes animal life even while it suggests that attaining the status of human and nonhuman animal life might be a product of poetic figuration. The Lady's loving attention to the garden, that is—her ability to nourish it and make it flourish—may be consistent with a distinctively poetic form of attention that transforms plants and flowers into animals and infants. The work of poetry itself conspicuously awards living things with ever more animate modes of being.

This poetic potential is, of course, what links the Lady in "The Sensitive-Plant" to the Fairy in *Queen Mab*. And yet we must acknowledge the aspect of "The Sensitive-Plant" that accords with *Mab*'s emphasis on the intellectual superiority of man over the very creatures that appear to be granted justice within *Queen Mab*'s scheme of moral-political progress. In "The Sensitive-Plant," Shelley depicts the Lady, even though she is the guarantor of life and flourishing "as God is to the starry scheme" (2.4), as one who sustains through rigorous and vigilant protection and exclusion. Thus she removes "all killing insects and gnawing worms / And things of obscene and unlovely forms" into the "rough woods" in a basket (2.41–42, 43). They are "banished insects, whose intent, / Although they did ill, was innocent" (2.47–48), in contrast to the bees, flies, and moths, which, because they do good to and for the plants in the garden, are made into her "attendant angels" (2.52).

Shelley accomplishes something significant with the Lady's godlike presence, undercutting any notion that the poem represents merely a symbiotic relationship between the human and nonhuman worlds.[65] If Coleridge's "Rime" refers to an unfathomable divine order that can be located only within the space of the poem, "The Sensitive-Plant" situates that order—which at first appears to be imagined as a form beyond the reach of all beings who live and die—within the realm of the Lady's making. Particularly relevant for the discourse of animal rights, then, is this aspect of the poem: it provides the possibility for flourishing among all creatures, while it also inscribes precise limitations upon its ability to think widely about what flourishing actually is. The poem's resonance with so many forms of literary paradise—from Spenser to Milton to Blake—strains under the pressure of its status as an unavoidably anthropomorphic construction.[66]

In its effort to expand a notion of care for the animal world, as well as in its imposition of a limit upon it, "The Sensitive-Plant" accords with Shelley's prose work on vegetarianism, *A Vindication of Natural Diet* (first published as a note to the eighth canto of *Queen Mab* in 1813). At one level, the essay views the consumption of animals by humans as an act of violence that is metonymically connected to violence, criminality, corruption, and greed throughout society; it views the cause of "natural diet," or vegetarianism, as supporting the "liberty and pure pleasures of natural life."[67] This is more or less the logic that animates the claim, eccentric though it may be, that the militarism of Napoleon Bonaparte would have been all but extinguished had he been a vegetarian (86).

The argument about Napoleon does not imply that murdering animals is like murdering humans. It does, however, suggest that violence is systematically imposed, and that a spirit of nonviolence in one context might induce nonviolence in another context. At an entirely different level of argument, though, Shelley proceeds in another direction. He urges vegetarianism not because of a specific concern with animals or with a generally peaceful and just order of beings but because of a concern with a more restricted kind of human life and human culture. Eating animal flesh rather than vegetables, Shelley argues, indulges an "unnatural craving" that simultaneously misconstrues the harms of animal flesh, and the benefits of vegetables, to humankind. If in the first line of reasoning Shelley anxiously asserts a kinship among all living things, in the second he insists on inviolable distinctions based upon more and less powerful similarities between living beings. Humans, for instance, more closely resemble (in their biological constitution) animals that eat vegetables than they do animals that eat flesh; they resemble the "orang-outang" but "no carnivorous animal" (84). Humans that eat vegetables, moreover, would be further separated from other humans that do not; the English, if they followed a "natural diet," would cease to "depend upon the caprices of foreign rulers," since they would not need to import goods such as wine and spices to accompany their consumption of flesh (87). The project of the essay is to focus not merely on humans, in other words, but also on a purified nationalism. Thus the progress that Shelley's essay imagines for mankind—a progress toward increasing justice toward all beings—must necessarily result in unjust relationships between humans and animals and among humans themselves.

Like the essay, "The Sensitive-Plant" risks imposing the rights of nonhuman beings as a sympathetic and limited extension of a *human* right. The requirements for a full life are always only inferred as a result of sympathetic understanding, and sympathy can so easily turn into a repetition of an already entrenched sense of convention or prejudice. At the same time, even though sympathy poses an obstacle, it remains the only way that new rights can be imagined and obtained, since humans are continually engaged in the problematic enterprise of speaking for the rights of other beings—that is, of producing justice for them. Thus, the cosmic energies at the end of Shelley's "The Sensitive-Plant" are framed as a might that "exceeds our organs." And yet the superhuman power envisioned in these lines is also a highly limited power, as we have seen, that sets up determinate and conventionalized limits. These limits determine that some beings will be treated as angels, while others will be banished, depending upon what forms of life are to be considered most valuable, what forms are to be saved and nurtured at the expense of others.

In Shelley's work, then, the question of the animal is significant because it opens up a frontier for justice. The impulse to extend protection proposes an ideal that is simultaneously opened to qualification, exposing both the value and the importance of the more capacious dissenting approach to justice explored elsewhere in this book and also its potential limitations. Shelley's work can thus lead us to reflect on a certain strain in animal theory that, like Diamond's work, aims to depart from a codified discourse of rights, as well as from a merely sympathetic and sentimental opposition to those rights. But it also leads us to reflect on the point of resistance beyond which it cannot reach. Shelley affords at least two layers of insight. First, claims that humans and animals are in the "same boat" or (as other animal theorists suggest) exist in a community shaped by "mutual respect" or participate in "entanglements" beyond sympathy often emerge as engaging and enduring poetic fictions. These fictions generously expand the scope of just relationships with other beings beyond those that share similar human or animal features.[68] Second, Shelley reveals that the aesthetic and political logic of this very ambition for protection of nonhuman animals is also a potential (but not predetermined) means of exclusion. It is the human animal that constructs the account of the boat, the respect, the entanglement. It's true, then, that humans may watch and listen for new languages from beings they don't currently understand. But it's also true that humans, even with all their efforts to find mutuality and a common language among all living things, will have the first, and the last, word.

Notes

Introduction

1. Mary Shelley, *Frankenstein* (New York: Collier Books, 1961), 49 (hereafter cited in text).

2. Paul Youngquist, *Monstrosities: Bodies and British Romanticism* (Minneapolis: University of Minnesota Press, 2003), 28–56. For the racial dimensions of this exclusion, see H. L. Malchow, *Gothic Images of Race in Nineteenth-Century Britain* (Stanford, CA: Stanford University Press, 1996), 17–40; and Anne K. Mellor, "Frankenstein, Racial Science, and the Yellow Peril," *Nineteenth-Century Contexts* 23 (2001): 1–28. Feminist interpretations such as Sandra Gilbert's have seen monstrosity as a symbol of femininity. See Gilbert, "Horror's Twin: Mary Shelley's Monstrous Eve," *Feminist Studies* 4 (1978): 48–73.

3. Although many critics have favored the 1818 edition of the novel, I agree with James O'Rourke's suggestion that some critical directions are strengthened in the revision. See O'Rourke, "The 1831 Introduction and Revisions to *Frankenstein*: Mary Shelley Dictates her Legacy," *Studies in Romanticism* 38 (1999): 365–85.

4. My account resembles—while adding an aesthetic dimension to—Colleen Bentley's "Family, Humanity, Polity: Theorizing the Basis and Boundaries of Political Community in *Frankenstein*," *Criticism* 47 (2003): 325–51.

5. See, e.g., David Marshall, *The Surprising Effects of Sympathy: Marivaux, Diderot, Rousseau, and Mary Shelley* (Berkeley and Los Angeles: University of California Press, 1988), 178–227; and Anne K. Mellor, *Mary Shelley: Her Life, Her Fiction, Her Monsters* (New York: Methuen, 1988), 38–51.

6. Plato, *Laws*, in *The Collected Dialogues of Plato*, ed. Edith Hamilton and Huntington Cairns (Princeton, NJ: Princeton University Press, 1961), 1254.

7. Sir Joshua Reynolds, *Discourses*, ed. Pat Rogers (Harmondsworth, UK: Penguin, 1992), 79 (hereafter cited in text).

8. George Gordon, Lord Byron, *Manfred*, in *Byron: Poetical Works*, ed. John Jump (Oxford: Oxford University Press, 1990), 3.4.123–24 (hereafter cited in text; references are to act, scene, and line).

9. Terry Eagleton, *The Ideology of the Aesthetic* (Oxford: Blackwell, 1990); Theodor W. Adorno, *Aesthetic Theory* (Minneapolis: University of Minnesota Press, 1997). For an extended view of the history of the proximity of aesthetics to politics,

see J. M. Bernstein, *The Fate of Art: Aesthetic Alienation from Kant to Derrida and Adorno* (University Park: Pennsylvania State University Press, 1992).

10. Sheldon Wolin, *Politics and Vision: Continuity and Innovation in Western Political Thought*, expanded ed. (Princeton, NJ: Princeton University Press, 2006), 19.

11. Stuart Hampshire, *Justice Is Conflict* (Princeton, NJ: Princeton University Press, 2001).

12. See Wendy Brown, "Suffering the Paradoxes of Rights," in *Left Legalism/Left Critique*, ed. Wendy Brown and Janet Halley (Durham, NC: Duke University Press, 2002), 420–34; and Mary Ann Glendon, *Rights Talk: The Impoverishment of Political Discourse* (New York: Free Press, 1991).

13. Lynn Hunt, *Inventing Human Rights: A History* (New York: Norton, 2007), 15–34; Michael Sandel, *Justice: What's the Right Thing to Do* (New York: Farrar, Straus, and Giroux, 2009).

14. Martha C. Nussbaum, *Poetic Justice: The Literary Imagination and Public Life* (Boston: Beacon, 1995), 10.

15. Iris Marion Young, *Justice and the Politics of Difference* (Princeton, NJ: Princeton University Press, 1990), 167, 119.

16. Jacques Derrida, "The 'Mystical Foundation of Authority,'" in *Deconstruction and the Possibility of Justice*, ed. Drucilla Cornell, Michel Rosenfeld, and David Gray Carlson (New York: Routledge, 1992), 16. For the enormous influence of Derrida throughout literary studies, see, e.g., Wai Chee Dimock, *Residues of Justice: Literature, Law, Philosophy* (Berkeley and Los Angeles: University of California Press, 1996); and Thomas Keenan, *Fables of Responsibility: Aberrations and Predicaments in Ethics and Politics* (Stanford, CA: Stanford University Press, 1997).

17. Michael Ignatieff, *Human Rights as Politics and Idolatry*, ed. Amy Gutmann (Princeton, NJ: Princeton University Press, 2001), 20.

18. Young, *Justice and the Politics of Difference*, 142; Judith Halberstam, *In a Queer Time and Place* (New York: New York University Press, 2005), 99ff.

19. René Wellek, *Immanuel Kant in England, 1793–1838* (Princeton, NJ: Princeton University Press, 1931).

20. William Godwin, *Enquiry Concerning Political Justice, and its Influence on Modern Morals and Happiness*, ed. Isaac Kramnick (Harmondsworth, UK: Penguin, 1976), 383.

21. Claude-Adrien Helvétius, *De L'Esprit, or Essays on the Mind and Its Several Faculties* (London: J. M. Richardson, 1809), 125.

22. Mary Wollstonecraft, *An Historical and Moral View of the Origin and Progress of the French Revolution* (London: Joseph Johnson, 1794), 4.

23. John Penn, *Further Thoughts on the Present State of Public Opinion* (London: W. Bulmer, 1800), 49.

24. The emphasis in my account contrasts with the emphasis in W. R. Johnson's on the privacy of the Romantic lyric *I*, which he associates with cultural fragmentation and disintegration, in *The Idea of Lyric: Lyric Modes in Ancient and Modern Poetry* (Berkeley and Los Angeles: University of California Press, 1983), 7.

25. John Keats, "Sleep and Poetry," in *John Keats: Complete Poems*, ed. Jack Stillinger (Cambridge, MA: Harvard University Press, 1978), 69, 161–62.

26. Although Martin Jay doesn't place any particular emphasis on the sublime in his account, my view shares his more general attempt to re-assess the political value of aesthetic judgments in "'The Aesthetic Ideology' as Ideology; or, What Does It Mean to Aestheticize Politics?" *Cultural Critique* 21 (1992): 41–61.

27. Carl Schmitt, *Political Romanticism*, trans. Guy Oakes (Cambridge, MA: MIT Press, 1986), 128; Hannah Arendt, *The Origins of Totalitarianism* (Cleveland, OH: Meridian, 1958), 67–302.

28. Theresa Kelley, *Wordsworth's Revisionary Aesthetics* (Cambridge: Cambridge University Press, 1988).

29. Jon Mee, *Romanticism, Enthusiasm, and Regulation: Poetics and the Policing of Culture in the Romantic Period* (Oxford: Oxford University Press, 2003), 10.

30. Denise Gigante, *Life: Organic Form and Romanticism* (New Haven, CT: Yale University Press, 2009), 36; and also Alan Richardson, *The Neural Sublime: Cognitive Theories and Romantic Texts* (Baltimore: Johns Hopkins University Press, 2010), which understands the sublime as an "antisublime" (25) pointing to the regularities of human corporeal reaction and interaction.

31. Orrin N. C. Wang, "Romantic Sobriety," *Modern Language Quarterly* 60 (1999): 479.

CHAPTER ONE: Beautiful People

1. Wendy Steiner, *Venus in Exile: The Rejection of Beauty in 20th-Century Art* (New York: Free Press, 2001), 140 (hereafter cited in text). The quotation is from Peter Schjeldahl's "Beauty is Back: A trampled aesthetic blooms again," *New York Times*, 29 September 1996, 161. For a detailed account of the revived interest in beauty in the 1990s, see Arthur Danto, *The Abuse of Beauty: Aesthetics and the Concept of Art* (Chicago: Open Court, 2003), 8–15.

2. Elaine Scarry, *On Beauty and Being Just* (Princeton, NJ: Princeton University Press, 1999), 112 (hereafter cited in text).

3. *Oxford English Dictionary*, 2nd ed., s.v. "symmetry."

4. For James Merrill's quite different reading of the palm—one that emphasizes abandonment, loss, and recovery in the interrupted lineage from Valéry to Rilke to the author—see his poem "Lost in Translation," in *Divine Comedies: Poems* (New York: Atheneum, 1976), 4–10.

5. Elsewhere, Scarry magnifies this problem to such an extent that "deliberative thinking" is conceptually indistinguishable from the habitual repetition of rules and patterns. See *Thinking in an Emergency* (New York: Norton, 2011), 7.

6. John Rawls, *A Theory of Justice* (Cambridge, MA: Belknap Press of Harvard University Press, 1971), 4.

7. To a certain extent, the difference is attributable to Scarry's dependence on Kant's pre-critical *Observations on the Feeling of the Beautiful and Sublime* and Steiner's interest in the *Critique of Judgment*.

8. See Tobin Siebers, "Kant and the Politics of Beauty," *Philosophy and Literature* 22 (1998): 31–50.

9. Although desire does not occupy a central place in Scarry's account, we must assume that it's necessary in order to "bring children into the world" in the way that she envisions (i.e., through heterosexual coupling).

10. Jerome McGann is the latest to celebrate the banishment of beauty as artifice in the works of Byron and Poe, in "Beauty, the Irreal, and the Willing Assumption of Disbelief," *Critical Inquiry* 30 (2004): 734–38.

11. Wendy Steiner, *The Real Real Thing* (Chicago: University of Chicago Press, 2010), 4.

12. For a discussion of the place of the black female body and its relation to the "(re)productive performance of 'white' sexuality," see Jennifer DeVere Brody, "Black Cat Fever: Manifestations of Manet's Olympia," *Theater Journal* 53 (2001): 105.

13. Peter de Bolla, *Art Matters* (Cambridge, MA: Harvard University Press, 2001), 18, 137 (hereafter cited in text). See also de Bolla's argument in "Toward the Materiality of Aesthetic Experience," *Diacritics* 32 (2002): 19–37.

14. Although de Bolla does refer to the sublime in his account, he accepts Barnett Newman's account of sublimity as an exaltation of "our feelings." See Barnett Newman, "The Sublime is Now," in *Art in Theory, 1900–2000: An Anthology of Changing Ideas*, ed. Charles Harrison and Paul Wood (Oxford: Blackwell, 1992), 582.

15. Isobel Armstrong, *The Radical Aesthetic* (Oxford: Blackwell, 2000), 41, 79.

16. Tobin Siebers, *Disability Aesthetics* (Ann Arbor: University of Michigan Press, 2010), 3. See also Anita Silvers, "From the Crooked Timber of Humanity, Beautiful Things Can Be Made," in *Beauty Matters*, ed. Peg Zeglin Brand (Bloomington: Indiana University Press, 2000), 197–221.

17. Dave Hickey, *The Invisible Dragon: Four Essays on Beauty* (Los Angeles: Art Issues, 1993), 62, 59, 57.

18. John Armstrong, *The Secret Power of Beauty: Why Happiness is in the Eye of the Beholder* (2004; repr., London: Penguin, 2005), 72, 48.

19. Elizabeth Prettejohn, *Beauty and Art, 1750–2000* (Oxford: Oxford University Press, 2005), 29, 195.

20. Jeremy Gilbert-Rolfe, *Beauty and the Contemporary Sublime* (New York: Allworth, 1999), 69–71. Gilbert-Rolfe's terms echo those in misogynistic rhetoric from the early church fathers to Chaucer. See Howard Bloch, "Medieval Misogyny," *Representations* 20 (1987): 1–24. I thank Mary Beth Rose for pointing out this connection.

21. Eleanor Heartney, "Foreword: Cutting Two Ways with Beauty," in Brand, *Beauty Matters*, xiv.

22. Douglas Mao, "The Labor Theory of Beauty," in *Aesthetic Subjects*, ed. Pamela R. Matthews and David McWhirter (Minneapolis: University of Minnesota Press, 2003), 223.

23. For recent accounts of the connection between aesthetics and nationalism—accounts that are less interested in particular modes of the aesthetic than mine—see

Marc Redfield, *The Politics of Aesthetics: Nationalism, Gender, Romanticism* (Stanford, CA: Stanford University Press, 2003); and Paul Youngquist, *Monstrosities: Bodies and British Romanticism* (Minneapolis: University of Minnesota Press, 2003).

24. Sir Joshua Reynolds, *Discourses*, ed. Pat Rogers (Harmondsworth, UK: Penguin, 1992), 109 (hereafter cited in text).

25. Sir Joshua Reynolds, *The Works of Sir Joshua Reynolds, Knight*, 3 vols. (London: T. Cadell, 1809), 2:226.

26. Francis Hutcheson, *An Inquiry into the Original of Our Ideas of Beauty and Virtue*, ed. Wolfgang Leidhold (Indianapolis: Liberty Fund, 2004), 28.

27. Ibid., 114.

28. John Barrell makes a similar point but claims that Reynolds's nationalism conflicts with his "civic humanism." See *The Political Theory of Painting from Reynolds to Hazlitt: The Body of the Public* (New Haven, CT: Yale University Press, 1986), 69–162. I would suggest instead that civic humanism, insofar as it involves a fantasy of politics as an inheritance from the ancients, is perfectly consistent with racism and nationalism.

29. On Burke's apparent influence on the *Discourses*, see Elbert N. S. Thompson, "The Discourses of Sir Joshua Reynolds," *PMLA* 32 (1917): 357–58.

30. Edmund Burke, *A Philosophical Enquiry into the Origin of our Ideas of the Sublime and Beautiful*, ed. James T. Boulton (Notre Dame: University of Notre Dame Press, 1968), 64–66 (hereafter cited in text).

31. Edmund Burke, *Reflections on the Revolution in France*, ed. Conor Cruise O'Brien (Harmondsworth, UK: Penguin, 1968), 172.

32. Ibid., 178, 120–21, 164. My account echoes but also adjusts the priority of Tom Furniss's, which sees aesthetics as controlled by (rather than producing, as in his account) politics, in *Edmund Burke's Aesthetic Ideology* (Cambridge: Cambridge University Press, 1993), 17–40.

33. Immanuel Kant, *Critique of Judgment*, trans. J. H. Bernard (New York: Hafner, 1951), 139 (hereafter cited in text).

34. Paul Guyer investigates this aspect of the third *Critique* in *Kant and the Claims of Taste* (Cambridge, MA: Harvard University Press, 1979). See also Denise Gigante's resonant account of the centrality of the "Man of Taste" to the Western "civilizing process" in *Taste: A Literary History* (New Haven, CT: Yale University Press, 2005), 18, 24.

35. There are exceptions, of course, including Bill Beckley, ed., *Sticky Sublime* (New York: Allworth, 2001). But even in that volume, many of the contributors are more concerned with rejecting the sublime in favor of other categories of pleasure, such as the beautiful or the "primordial" (192), than with analyzing it.

36. Peter de Bolla, *The Discourse of the Sublime: Readings in History, Aesthetics, and the Subject* (Oxford: Blackwell, 1989), 70; Howard Caygill, *Art of Judgment* (Oxford: Blackwell, 1989), 345, 387.

37. De Bolla's *The Education of the Eye* (Stanford, CA: Stanford University Press,

2003) reinforces this line of aesthetic argument, as it concentrates on "gestures, attitudes, [and] psychic modes or modalities" that constitute a "culture" of viewing visual art (5).

38. While not situating itself explicitly in any scholarly tradition, recent writing does in fact bear an unacknowledged and untheorized resemblance to the kind of phenomenological account running from Hegel to Gadamer and defended by Paul Crowther in *Art and Embodiment: From Aesthetics to Self-Consciousness* (Oxford: Clarendon, 1993). But it is also connected in a profound way to deconstruction, as I explain in chapter 3.

39. Stuart Hampshire, "Public and Private Morality," in *Public and Private Morality*, ed. Stuart Hampshire (Cambridge: Cambridge University Press, 1978), 23.

40. Stuart Hampshire, "Morality and Pessimism," in ibid., 4.

41. Ibid., 17.

42. Hampshire, "Public and Private Morality," 35.

43. For an excellent account of the politics of aesthetics in the 1960s and 1970s, see Carter Ratcliff, "The Sublime Was Then: The Art of Barnett Newman," in Beckley, *Sticky Sublime*, 211–39.

44. Ronald Paulson, *Representations of Revolution (1789–1820)* (New Haven, CT: Yale University Press, 1983), 57–87.

45. Harold Bloom, *The Anxiety of Influence: A Theory of Poetry* (Oxford: Oxford University Press, 1973), 15.

46. Thomas Weiskel, *The Romantic Sublime: Studies in the Structure and Psychology of Transcendence* (Baltimore: Johns Hopkins University Press, 1976), 4.

47. Neil Hertz, "A Reading of Longinus," in *The End of the Line: Essays on Psychoanalysis and the Sublime* (New York: Columbia University Press, 1985), 14; this essay was first published in French in *Poétique* 15 (1973). Jonathan Lamb discusses the substantial variation in accounts of the sublime in treatments of the politics of the sublime in "Longinus, the Dialectic, and the Practice of Mastery," *ELH* 60 (1993): 545–67.

48. Denis Donoghue, *Speaking of Beauty* (New Haven, CT: Yale University Press, 2003), 7–9.

49. Eve Kosofsky Sedgwick, *Tendencies* (Durham, NC: Duke University Press, 2003), 109–10.

50. Denis Donoghue, *The Practice of Reading* (New Haven, CT: Yale University Press, 1998), 11; idem, "In My Time," in *American Council of Learned Societies Occasional Paper* 44, http://archives.acls.org/op/op44dono.htm.

51. Bill Readings, *The University in Ruins* (Cambridge, MA: Harvard University Press, 1996); Masao Miyoshi, "'Globalization,' Culture, and the University," in *The Cultures of Globalization*, ed. Fredric Jameson and Masao Miyoshi (Durham, NC: Duke University Press, 1998), 247–70.

52. Miyoshi, "'Globalization,'" 264.

53. Eric Cheyfitz, "The Corporate University, Academic Freedom, and American Exceptionalism," *South Atlantic Quarterly* 108 (2009): 719.

54. I use *postmodern* to describe a political-economic condition rather than an intellectual (i.e., *poststructuralist*) one, although I revise this point in chapter 3.

55. John Guillory, *Cultural Capital: The Problem of Literary Canon Formation* (Chicago: University of Chicago Press, 1993), 176–265. David Shumway speaks of the limits of academic stars in "The Star System in Literary Studies," *PMLA* 112 (1997): 85–100.

56. Danto, *Abuse of Beauty*, 116.

57. Jerome Christensen calls this commercializing gesture a symptom of "corporate populism" in "From Rhetoric to Corporate Populism: A Romantic Critique of the Academy in an Age of High Gossip," *Critical Inquiry* 16 (1990): 459.

58. Umberto Eco, *History of Beauty*, trans. Alastair McEwan (New York: Rizzoli, 2004).

59. Ian Stewart, *Why Beauty Is Truth: A History of Symmetry* (New York: Basic Books, 2007); Alexander Nehemas, *Only a Promise of Happiness: The Place of Beauty in World Art* (Princeton, NJ: Princeton University Press, 2007).

60. David Harvey, *A Brief History of Neoliberalism* (Oxford: Oxford University Press, 2005), 69.

61. Stewart, *Why Beauty Is Truth*, ix; Denis Dutton, *The Art Instinct* (Oxford: Oxford University Press, 2009).

62. Leo Bersani and Ulysse Dutoit, "Beauty's Light," *October* 82 (1997): 17–29; Crispin Sartwell, *Six Names of Beauty* (New York: Routledge, 2004), 67.

63. Matthew Arnold, "The Function of Criticism at the Present Time," in *Essays in Criticism* (London: Macmillan, 1889), 37.

64. Ibid., 11.

65. Matthew Arnold, *Culture and Anarchy: An Essay in Political and Social Criticism, and Friendship's Garland* (London: Macmillan, 1883), 20.

66. Arnold, "Function of Criticism," 23.

67. Ibid., 16.

68. For a discussion of the relationship between Arnold's account of culture and representative democracy, see David Lloyd and Paul Thomas, "Culture and Society or 'Culture and the State'?" *Social Text* 30 (1992): 27–56.

CHAPTER TWO: Justice and the Romantic Sublime

1. For some effective and balanced critiques of his positions, see Robin May Schott, ed., *Feminist Interpretations of Immanuel Kant* (University Park: Pennsylvania State University Press, 1997).

2. Howard Caygill, *Art of Judgment* (Oxford: Blackwell, 1989), 103–6; idem, "Kant and the Age of Criticism," in *A Kant Dictionary*, ed. Caygill (London: Blackwell, 1995), 7–34.

3. John Baillie, *An Essay on the Sublime* (London: R. Dodsley, 1747), 12–13.

4. Immanuel Kant, *Critique of Judgment*, trans. J. H. Bernard (New York: Hafner, 1951), 84, 89 (hereafter cited mainly in text).

5. Frances Ferguson, *Solitude and the Sublime: Romanticism and the Aesthetics of Individuation* (New York: Routledge, 1992), 32.

6. Edmund Burke, *A Philosophical Enquiry into the Origin of our Ideas of the Sublime and Beautiful*, ed. James T. Boulton (Notre Dame: University of Notre Dame Press, 1968), 64–66.

7. See John Locke, *An Essay Concerning Human Understanding*, ed. Peter H. Nidditch (Oxford: Clarendon, 1975), 55; and David Hartley, *Observations on Man, His Frame, His Duty, and His Expectations* (1749; repr., London: Joseph Johnson, 1791), iii.

8. I quote here from the King James version, which Burke misquotes.

9. Immanuel Kant, *Lectures on Ethics*, ed. Peter Heath and J. B. Schneewind, trans. Peter Heath (Cambridge: Cambridge University Press, 1997), 9, 96.

10. Although Guyer in *Kant and the Experience of Freedom: Essays on Aesthetics and Morality* (Cambridge: Cambridge University Press, 1993) stresses the equal importance of the beautiful and the sublime in considerations of the moral, Guyer's own characterization of the beautiful as a "symbolization" of morality indicates a more rigorous separation from the sublime, since the latter, unlike the beautiful, does not provide a "bodily manifestation" of the morally good (*Critique of Judgment*, 72). See also William Connolly, *Why I Am Not a Secularist* (Minneapolis: University of Minnesota Press, 1999), 172–73. Paul Crowther sees the sublime's failure to display morality with an "aesthetic concept" as a shortcoming. See Crowther, *The Kantian Sublime: From Morality to Art* (Oxford: Clarendon, 1989), 135.

11. Michel Foucault, *Politics, Philosophy, Culture: Interviews and Other Writings, 1977–1984*, ed. Lawrence D. Kritzman, trans. Alan Sheridan et al. (New York: Routledge, 1988), 49.

12. José Esteban Muñoz, *Disidentifications: Queers of Color and the Performance of Politics* (Minneapolis: University of Minnesota Press, 1999), 145.

13. See Joseph Priestley, *A Course of Lectures on Oratory and Criticism* (Dublin: William Hallhead, 1781), 187.

14. Rodolphe Gasché, "Linking onto Disinterestedness, or the Moral Law in Kant's *Critique of Judgment*," in *Between Ethics and Aesthetics: Crossing the Boundaries*, ed. Dorota Glowacka and Stephen Boos (Albany, NY: SUNY Press, 2002), 62. See also Gasché's *The Idea of Form: Rethinking Kant's Aesthetics* (Stanford, CA: Stanford University Press, 2003).

15. George Gordon, Lord Byron, *Manfred*, in *Byron: Poetical Works*, ed. John Jump (Oxford: Oxford University Press, 1990), 1.2.44; 1.1.28; 1.2.56 (hereafter cited in text; references are to act, scene, and line).

16. William D. Melaney, "Ambiguous Difference: Ethical Concern in Byron's *Manfred*," *New Literary History* 36 (2005): 465.

17. Peter Martin, *Byron: A Poet before His Public* (Cambridge: Cambridge University Press, 1982), 113. Martin's account coincides with Bertrand Evans's view of *Manfred*'s citation and internalization of gothic imagery, in "Manfred's Remorse and Dramatic Tradition," *PMLA* 62 (1947): 752–73.

18. Melaney, "Ambiguous Difference," 471. See also Stephen Behrendt, "*Manfred*

and Skepticism," in *Approaches to Teaching Byron's Poetry*, ed. Frederick W. Shilstone (New York: Modern Language Association, 1991), 120–25.

19. See, e.g., Friedrich Nietzsche, *On the Genealogy of Morals and Ecce Homo*, ed. Walter Kaufman (New York: Vintage, 1967), 245.

20. William Duff, *An Essay on Original Genius* (London: Charles Dilly, 1767), 162. I give a different account of enthusiasm here, one that contrasts with Shaun Irlam's account of self-regulated passion in *Elations: The Poetics of Enthusiasm in Eighteenth Century Britain* (Stanford, CA: Stanford University Press, 1999).

21. Immanuel Kant, *Groundwork for the Metaphysics of Morals*, ed. Allen W. Wood (New Haven, CT: Yale University Press, 2002), 57 (hereafter cited in text). Reference to the operations of the moral law and sublimity can also be found throughout Kant's *Critique of Practical Reason*, ed. Lewis White Beck (New York: Macmillan, 1956), 90.

22. Some feminists have found Kant's position congenial to their theorizing. See Marcia Baron, "Kantian Ethics and Claims of Detachment," in Schott, *Feminist Interpretations of Immanuel Kant*, 145–70.

23. Kant, *Critique of Practical Reason*, 103.

24. My account in general supports Barbara Herman's argument against Bernard Williams's claim that Kant's morality compromises the integrity of the self. See Herman, *The Practice of Moral Judgment* (Cambridge, MA: Harvard University Press, 1993). Williams's claim is related to Jean-François Lyotard's constrained account of reason as a "holy law" that is "not [the subject's] own" in *Lessons on the Analytic of the Sublime*, trans. Elizabeth Rottenberg (Stanford, CA: Stanford University Press, 1994), 189, and to Eagleton's claim that Kant inhabits two "contradictory" worlds, the bodily and the abstract. Terry Eagleton, *The Ideology of the Aesthetic* (Oxford: Blackwell, 1990), 83.

25. Richard Rorty, "Justice as a Larger Loyalty," *Ethical Perspectives* 4 (1997): 139–51.

26. David Lloyd, "Kant's Examples," *Representations* 28 (1989): 34–54.

27. The point of view might also be God's, according to Kant's account of the virtuous disposition "well-pleasing to God" in *Religion within the Limits of Reason Alone*, trans. Theodore M. Greene and Hoyt H. Hudson (New York: Harper and Brothers, 1960), 161. But in the *Critique of Judgment* the evidence that the perspective is juridical outweighs the evidence that it is theological.

28. For a more extended account of the aesthetic dimensions of toleration, see Mark Canuel, *Religion, Toleration, and British Writing, 1790–1830* (Cambridge: Cambridge University Press, 2002).

29. [Joseph Addison], *The Spectator* (London: Jones and Co., 1840), no. 413, 24 June 1712, p. 596.

30. Jeremy Waldron, *The Dignity of Legislation* (Cambridge: Cambridge University Press, 1999), 56.

31. Friedrich Schiller, *On the Aesthetic Education of Man: A Series of Letters*, trans. Reginald Snell (New York: Continuum, 1965), 139; idem, "On the Sublime," in *"On Naïve and Sentimental Poetry" and "On the Sublime"*, trans. Julius A. Elias (New York:

Frederick Ungar, 1966), 210. My view departs from those of Martha Woodmansee, *The Author, Art, and the Market: Rereading the History of Aesthetics* (New York: Columbia University Press, 1994), and David Aram Kaiser, *Romanticism, Aesthetics, and Nationalism* (Cambridge: Cambridge University Press, 2004), which understand Schiller as more of a prototype for Romantic aesthetics than I do.

32. Hannah Arendt, *Lectures on Kant's Political Philosophy*, ed. Ronald Beiner (Chicago: University of Chicago Press, 1992), 69.

33. Immanuel Kant, "On a Newly Arisen Superior Tone in Philosophy," in *Raising the Tone of Philosophy: Late Essays by Immanuel Kant, Transformative Critique by Jacques Derrida*, ed. Peter Fenves (Baltimore: Johns Hopkins University Press, 1993), 62.

34. Immanuel Kant, *The Metaphysics of Morals*, ed. Mary Gregor (Cambridge: Cambridge University Press, 1996), 95.

35. See Kant, *Lectures on Ethics*, 299.

36. Immanuel Kant, "Idea for a Universal History," in *Kant's Political Writings*, 45.

37. Ibid., 44–45.

38. Immanuel Kant, "An Answer to the Question: 'What is Enlightenment?'" in *Kant's Political Writings*, 56–57.

39. Ibid., 56.

40. Kant, *Metaphysics of Morals*, 98.

41. G. W. F. Hegel, *Philosophy of Right*, trans. T. M. Knox (London: Oxford University Press, 1952), 161; Thomas Hobbes, *Leviathan*, ed. C. B. Macpherson (Harmondsworth, UK: Penguin, 1968), 366.

42. While connected to his account, the *relational* aspect of combating perspectives contrasts with Jean-François Lyotard's understanding of justice as multiplicity in Lyotard and Jean-Loup Thébaud, *Just Gaming*, trans. Wlad Godwich (Minneapolis: University of Minnesota Press, 1985). See also Lyotard's account of the heterogeneity of language games in *The Postmodern Condition: A Report on Knowledge*, trans. Geoffrey Bennington and Brian Massumi (Minneapolis: University of Minnesota Press, 1984).

43. See, e.g., Peter Graham, "Byron, Negativity, and Freedom," in *Liberty and Poetic License: New Essays on Byron*, ed. Bernard Beatty, Charles Robinson, and Tony Howe (Liverpool, UK: Liverpool University Press, 2008), 50–59; Peter Manning, *Byron and His Fictions* (Detroit: Wayne State University Press, 1978), 81; and Anne K. Mellor, *English Romantic Irony* (Cambridge, MA: Harvard University Press, 1980), 35–37.

44. Peter Cochran, ed., *Byron's Alpine Journal*, 5, 6, 13, http://petercochran.files.wordpress.com/2009/03/alpine_journal.pdf.

45. *Hansard Parliamentary Debates*, 1st ser., vol. 21, 1812, col. 859.

46. George Gordon, Lord Byron, "Frame Work Bill Speech," in *The Complete Miscellaneous Prose*, ed. Andrew Nicholson (Oxford: Oxford University Press, 1991), 24.

47. Alan Richardson, *A Mental Theater: Poetic Drama and Consciousness in the Romantic Age* (University Park: Pennsylvania State University Press, 1988), 43.

48. C. Suetonius Tranquillus, *Lives of the Twelve Caesars*, Loeb Classical Library, 2 vols. (Cambridge, MA: Harvard University Press, 1914), 2:179.

49. Kant, *Metaphysics of Morals*, 176–77, 105–7.

50. Kant, *Lectures on Ethics*, 149.

51. Immanuel Kant, *Anthropology from a Pragmatic Point of View*, trans. Victor Lyle Dowdell (Carbondale: Southern Illinois University Press, 1978), 156.

52. Ibid.

53. Johann Wolfgang von Goethe, *Faust*, ed. and trans. Stuart Atkins (Princeton, NJ: Princeton University Press, 1984), line 11,937.

54. Jonathan Lamb, *The Rhetoric of Suffering: Reading the Book of Job in the Eighteenth Century* (Oxford: Oxford University Press, 1995), 11.

55. Sir Samuel Romilly, *Observations on the Criminal Law of England*, 2nd ed. (London: T. Cadell and W. Davies, 1811), 7–8.

56. William Wordsworth, *The Prelude*, in *William Wordsworth: 21st-Century Oxford Authors*, ed. Stephen Gill (Oxford: Oxford University Press, 1984), 10.80, 374, 379, 380.

57. Obviously, the idea of civil disobedience supposes a lawful resistance to law that is broader that Kant's, but in my view this does not seriously compromise the more basic point I am making here.

58. John Rawls, *John Rawls: Collected Papers*, ed. Samuel Freeman (Cambridge, MA: Harvard University Press, 1999), 182.

59. Ibid., 184–85. I am grateful to Stephen Engelmann for pointing out the centrality of civil disobedience in Rawls's view of "reflective equilibrium." See John Rawls, *Political Liberalism* (New York: Columbia University Press, 1993), 28 (hereafter cited in text). My view of this aspect of Rawls contrasts with Davide Panagia's account of Rawls's aesthetic of the beautiful, although I am in agreement with much of his argument in *The Poetics of Political Thinking* (Durham, NC: Duke University Press, 2006).

60. Stanley Cavell, *Conditions Handsome and Unhandsome: The Constitution of Emersonian Perfectionism; The Carus Lectures, 1988* (Chicago: University of Chicago Press, 1990), 101–21; Melissa Williams, "Justice toward Groups: Political Not Juridical," *Political Theory* 23 (1995): 67–91.

61. Loren King, "The Federal Structure of a Republic of Reasons," *Political Theory* 33 (2005): 646.

62. Stuart Hampshire, *Justice Is Conflict* (Princeton, NJ: Princeton University Press, 2000), 3–43.

63. David Hume, *Enquiries Concerning Human Understanding and Concerning the Principles of Morals*, ed. P. H. Nidditch, 3rd ed. (Oxford: Clarendon, 1975), 203.

64. J. G. Fichte, *Foundations of Natural Right: According to the Principles of the Wissenschaftlehre*, ed. Frederick Neuhauser, trans. Michael Baur (Cambridge: Cambridge University Press, 2000), 149.

65. Michael Sandel, *Justice: What's the Right Thing to Do?* (New York: Farrar, Straus, and Giroux, 2009), Kindle edition, 6601; Charles Taylor, "The Politics of Recognition," in *Multiculturalism: Examining the Politics of Recognition*, ed. Amy Gutmann, (Princeton, NJ: Princeton University Press, 1994), 59; Michael Walzer, *Spheres of*

Justice: A Defense of Pluralism and Equality (New York: Basic Books, 1983), 29. Will Kymlicka convincingly shows that communitarian arguments often presuppose that the Kantian commitment to practical reasoning is impossible. By insisting on shared beliefs as a limit to moral-political viewpoints, furthermore, communitarian arguments likewise insist (without significant acknowledgment) on excluding certain features from their designation of a common way of life. From Kymlicka's perspective, for example, communitarian arguments are unable to deal adequately with the rights of indigenous peoples. See his *Liberalism, Community, and Culture* (Oxford: Clarendon, 1989).

66. Norman Daniels, "Health Care Needs and Distributive Justice," *Philosophy and Public Affairs* 10 (1981): 158.

67. Michel Foucault, *The Birth of Biopolitics: Lectures at the Collège de France, 1978–1979*, ed. Michel Senellart, trans. Graham Burchell (Houndmills, UK: Palgrave Macmillan, 2008), 282–83.

68. Michel Foucault, "Kant on Enlightenment and Revolution," in *Foucault's New Domains*, ed. Mike Gane and Terry Johnson (London: Routledge, 1993), 18.

69. Judith Butler, *The Psychic Life of Power: Theories in Subjection* (Stanford, CA: Stanford University Press, 2004), 104. See also Foucault, *Birth of Biopolitics*, 300.

70. Susan Stewart, *The Open Studio: Essays on Art and Aesthetics* (Chicago: University of Chicago Press, 2005), 104.

71. For an account of the sublime as a resistance to generation and population, an account that has influenced my own, see Frances Ferguson, "The Nuclear Sublime," *Diacritics* 14 (1984): 4–10.

72. George Gordon, Lord Byron, *Childe Harold's Pilgrimage*, canto 2, line 88.

73. Percy Bysshe Shelley, "Mont Blanc," in *Shelley's Poetry and Prose*, ed. Donald H. Reiman and Sharon B. Powers, Norton Critical Edition (New York: Norton, 1977), 80–84.

74. Thomas De Quincey, *Confessions of an English Opium Eater and Other Writings*, ed. Grevil Lindop (Oxford: Oxford University Press, 1985), 46, 49.

75. Jean-François Lyotard, "The Sublime and the Avant-Garde," in *The Inhuman: Reflections on Time*, trans. Geoffrey Bennington and Rachel Bowlby (Stanford, CA: Stanford University Press, 1988), 89–107; Jean-Luc Nancy, *The Experience of Freedom*, trans. Bridget McDonald (Stanford, CA: Stanford University Press, 1993); Vivasvan Soni, "Communal Narcosis and Sublime Withdrawal: The Problem of Community in Kant's *Critique of Judgment*," *Cultural Critique* 64 (2006): 1–3.

76. Caygill, *Art of Judgment*, 347; Terry Eagleton, *The Ideology of the Aesthetic* (Oxford: Blackwell, 1990), 23.

77. Eagleton, *Ideology of the Aesthetic*, 23, 24. See also David Lloyd's account of Kant's enforcement of a "cultural ideal," a subordination of the individual to the universal," in "Kant's Examples," 35, 48.

78. Kant, *Metaphysics of Morals*, 153. My view, by insisting that there is no necessary connection between the sublime and questions of right, departs somewhat from Frances Ferguson's claim that "the sublime . . . constitutes an avowal of the rights of

man," in "Legislating the Sublime," in *Studies in Eighteenth Century British Art and Aesthetics*, ed. Ralph Cohen (Berkeley and Los Angeles: University of California Press, 1985), 141.

79. Jacques Rancière, "Ten Theses on Politics," *Theory and Event* 5 (2001), paras. 21, 32. See also the distinction between progress and emancipation in idem, *The Ignorant Schoolmaster: Five Lessons in Intellectual Emancipation*, trans. Kristin Ross (Stanford, CA: Stanford University Press, 1991), 113–22.

80. John D'Emilio, *Lost Prophet: The Life and Times of Bayard Rustin* (New York: Free Press, 2003); Melissa A. Orlie, *Living Ethically, Acting Politically* (Ithaca, NY: Cornell University Press, 1997). I am grateful to Kirstie McClure for directing me to Orlie's book.

81. Orlie, *Living Ethically, Acting Politically*, 152, 80. My claims bear some resemblance to Lyotard's linkage between the sublime, enthusiasm, and "cosmopolitical society" in *The Differend: Phrases in Dispute*, trans. Georges Van Den Abeele (Minneapolis: University of Minnesota Press, 1988), 170. I differ mainly by addressing the relationship between the sublime and justice rather than that between the sublime and a cosmopolitan "culture" (169).

CHAPTER THREE: The Reparative Impulse

1. Stanley Fish, *Save the World on Your Own Time* (Oxford: Oxford University Press, 2008), 8, 14.

2. For an account of the reading public that is more or less consistent with my own, see Andrew Franta, *Romanticism and the Rise of the Mass Public* (Cambridge: Cambridge University Press, 2007).

3. Eve Kosofsky Sedgwick, *Touching Feeling: Affect, Pedagogy, Perfomativity* (Durham, NC: Duke University Press, 2003), 150 (hereafter cited in text).

4. Lauren Berlant, "Two Girls, Fat and Thin," in *Regarding Sedgwick: Essays on Queer Culture and Critical Theory*, ed. Stephen M. Barber and David L. Clark (New York: Routledge, 2002), 88, 98, 103.

5. Judith Halberstam, *In a Queer Time and Place* (New York: New York University Press, 2005), 105.

6. Martha Nussbaum, *Cultivating Humanity: A Classical Defense of Reform in Liberal Education* (Cambridge, MA: Harvard University Press, 1997), 84.

7. Kwame Anthony Appiah, *Cosmopolitanism: Ethics in a World of Strangers* (New York: Norton, 2006), 133 (hereafter cited in text).

8. Sheldon Wolin, *Politics and Vision: Continuity and Innovation in Western Political Thought*, expanded ed. (Princeton, NJ: Princeton University Press, 2006), 19.

9. Neil Hertz, *The End of the Line: Essays on Psychoanalysis and the Sublime* (New York: Columbia University Press, 1985), 44; Jacques Derrida, *The Truth in Painting*, trans. Geoff Bennington and Ian McLeod (Chicago: University of Chicago Press, 1987), 140.

10. Derrida, *Truth in Painting*, 141, 142.

11. Paul de Man, "Kant's Materialism," in *Aesthetic Ideology*, ed. Andrzej Warminski (Minneapolis: University of Minnesota Press, 1996), 128.

12. Paul de Man, "Phenomenality and Materiality in Kant," in ibid., 87.

13. Neil Hertz, "Lurid Figures," in *Reading de Man Reading*, ed. Lindsay Waters and Wlad Godzich (Minneapolis: University of Minnesota Press, 1989); idem, "More Lurid Figures," *Diacritics* 20 (1990): 2–27. Although the consequences of my argument are different, some of my basic claims about deconstruction align with Walter Benn Michaels's *The Shape of the Signifier: 1967 to the End of History* (Princeton, NJ: Princeton University Press, 2004), 82–128.

14. Barbara Johnson, *Persons and Things* (Cambridge, MA: Harvard University Press, 2008), 125.

15. Paul Bové, "Variations on Authority: Some Deconstructive Transformations of the New Criticism," in *The Yale Critics: Deconstruction in America*, ed. Jonathan Arac, Wlad Godzich, and Wallace Martin (Minneapolis: University of Minnesota Press, 1983), 3–19.

16. For deconstructive accounts of justice as a commitment to alterity, the other, or singularity, see Jacques Derrida, "The 'Mystical Foundation of Authority,'" in *Deconstruction and the Possibility of Justice*, ed. Drucilla Cornell, Michel Rosenfeld, and David Gray Carlson (New York: Routledge, 1992), 17; and Derek Attridge, *The Singularity of Literature* (London: Routledge, 2004), 129.

17. Iris Marion Young, *Justice and the Politics of Difference* (Princeton, NJ: Princeton University Press, 1990), 119.

18. Ibid., 152.

19. Leo Bersani, *Homos* (Cambridge, MA: Harvard University Press, 1995), 149.

20. Halberstam, *In A Queer Time and Place*, 96. For an illuminating debate about the merits of these perspectives, see the summaries of conference presentations by Robert Caserio, Lee Edelman, Judith Halberstam, José Esteban Muñoz, and Tim Dean in "The Antisocial Thesis in Queer Theory," *PMLA* 121 (2006): 819–28.

21. Michael Warner, *The Trouble with Normal: Sex, Politics, and the Ethics of Queer Life* (Cambridge, MA: Harvard University Press, 1999) (hereafter cited in text).

22. Patchen Markell, *Bound by Recognition* (Princeton, NJ: Princeton University Press, 2003), 12. I tend to disagree with Markell's suggestion that Warner is an exception to this politics.

23. Lauren Berlant and Michael Warner, "Sex in Public," *Critical Inquiry* 25 (1998): 561.

24. Dwight A. McBride, *Why I Hate Abercrombie & Fitch: Essays on Race and Sexuality* (New York: New York University Press, 2005), 88–89. For a comparable critique of Eve Kosofsky Sedgwick's concentration on white queer subjectivity, see Marlon B. Ross, "Beyond the Closet as Raceless Paradigm," in *Black Queer Studies: A Critical Anthology*, ed. E. Patrick Johnson and Mae G. Henderson (Durham, NC: Duke University Press, 2005), 161–89.

25. Halberstam, *In a Queer Time and Place*, 97–124; David Eng, *The Feeling of Kin-*

ship: *Queer Liberalism and the Racialization of Intimacy* (Durham, NC: Duke University Press, 2010), 49.

26. Kathryn Bond Stockton, *Beautiful Bottom, Beautiful Shame: Where "Black" Meets "Queer"* (Durham, NC: Duke University Press, 2006), 16.

27. José Esteban Muñoz, *Cruising Utopia: The Then and There of Queer Futurity* (New York: New York University Press, 2009), 53; Tim Dean, *Unlimited Intimacy: Reflections on the Subculture of Barebacking* (Chicago: University of Chicago Press, 2009).

28. Whitney Davis, *Queer Beauty: Sexuality and Aesthetics from Winckelmann to Freud and Beyond* (New York: Columbia University Press, 2010), 27.

29. Eve Kosofsky Sedgwick, *Epistemology of the Closet*, updated with a new preface (Berkeley and Los Angeles: University of California Press, 2008), 222, 228.

30. D. A. Miller, *Jane Austen, or, the Secret of Style* (Princeton, NJ: Princeton University Press, 2003), 3.

31. Julia Kristeva, in "Foreign Body: A Conversation with Julia Kristeva and Scott Malcomson," *Transition* 59 (1993): 183.

32. Julia Kristeva, *Strangers to Ourselves*, trans. Leon Roudiez (New York: Columbia University Press, 1994), 136.

33. Stephen William Foster, *Cosmopolitan Desire: Transcultural Dialogues and Antiterrorism in Morocco* (Lanham, MD: Altamira, 2003), 169.

34. Scott L. Malcomson, "The Varieties of Cosmopolitan Experience," in *Cosmopolitics: Thinking and Feeling beyond the Nation*, ed. Pheng Cheah and Bruce Robbins (Minneapolis: University of Minnesota Press, 1998), 239-40.

35. Immanuel Kant, "Perpetual Peace," in *Kant's Political Writings*, ed. Hans Reiss (Cambridge: Cambridge University Press, 1970), 98, 112 (hereafter cited in text).

36. Martha Nussbaum, "Patriotism and Cosmopolitanism," in *For Love of Country: Debating the Limits of Patriotism*, ed. Joshua Cohen (Boston: Beacon, 1996), 6. See also Nussbaum's defense of specific qualities to be learned in order to become a "citizen of the world" in *Not for Profit: Why Democracy Needs the Humanities* (Princeton, NJ: Princeton University Press, 2010), 7.

37. Amartya Sen, *Identity and Violence: The Illusion of Destiny* (New York: Norton, 2006), 15 (hereafter cited in text); Ulrich Beck, "The Cosmopolitan Society and its Enemies," *Theory, Culture, & Society* 19 (2002): 18.

38. Amartya Sen, *The Idea of Justice* (Cambridge, MA: Belknap Press of Harvard University Press, 2009), 334.

39. Pheng Cheah, *Inhuman Conditions: On Cosmopolitanism and Human Rights* (Cambridge, MA: Harvard University Press, 2006), 114. See also David Harvey's analysis of cosmopolitanism as an awareness of tensions between globalization and local cultures, "Cosmopolitanism and the Banality of Geographical Evils," *Public Culture* 12 (2000): 529-64; and Timothy Brennan's assertion of the importance of locality and nationality over the global, "Cosmo-Theory," *South Atlantic Quarterly* 100 (2001): 659-91.

40. Bruce Robbins, "Comparative Cosmopolitanisms," in Cheah and Robbins, *Cosmopolitics*, 257.

41. Amanda Anderson, *The Way We Argue Now* (Princeton, NJ: Princeton University Press, 2005), 92.

42. Amanda Anderson, *The Powers of Distance: Cosmopolitanism and the Cultivation of Detachment* (Princeton, NJ: Princeton University Press, 2001), 71.

43. Bruce Robbins, "Cosmopolitanism, America, and the Welfare State," *Genre* 38 (2005): 255.

44. Seyla Benhabib, *Another Cosmopolitanism* (Oxford: Oxford University Press, 2006), 68, 74.

45. See Michael Warner, "Queer World Making: Annamarie Jagose Interviews Michael Warner," *Genders* 31 (2000), http://www.genders.org/g31/g31_jagose.html.

46. A different version of that weaker argument can be found in Bersani's attempt to gloss Foucault's ethics of "the homosexual mode of life" by imagining its "relationality" as a commitment to "replication" or a "reoccurrence of the same." Leo Bersani, "Genital Chastity," in *Homosexuality and Pyschoanalysis*, ed. Tim Dean and Christopher Lane (Chicago: University of Chicago Press, 2001), 351, 366.

47. Michael Warner, "Disruptions: In the Age of Alterity, the Rainbow is not Enuf," *Village Voice*, 21–27 June 2000, http://www.villagevoice.com/news/0025,warner,15823,1.html.

48. Melissa Orlie, *Living Ethically, Acting Politically* (Ithaca, NY: Cornell University Press, 1997), 80. For Warner's very brief connection between his project and the potential radicalism he locates in Kant, see Michael Warner, *Publics and Counterpublics* (New York: Zone Books, 2002), 44–46. See also Robert Kaufman's illuminating connections between Kantian aesthetics and "critical agency" in "Red Kant, or the Persistence of the Third *Critique* in Adorno and Jameson," *Critical Inquiry* 26 (2000): 682–724.

49. For an example of queer critique that emphasizes actions rather than identity, see Janet Halley, "Reasoning about Sodomy: Act and Identity in and after *Bowers v. Hardwick*," *Virginia Law Review* 79 (October 1993): 1721–80.

50. John Rawls, "A Kantian Conception of Equality," in *John Rawls: Collected Papers*, ed. Samuel Freeman (Cambridge, MA: Harvard University Press, 1999), 260.

51. Eric O. Clarke, *Virtuous Vice: Homoeroticism and the Public Sphere* (Durham, NC: Duke University Press, 2000); Andrew Elfenbein, *Romantic Genius: The Prehistory of a Homosexual Role* (New York: Columbia University Press, 1999); Richard Sha, *Perverse Romanticism: Aesthetics and Sexuality in Britain, 1750–1832* (Baltimore: Johns Hopkins University Press, 2009), 182.

52. Adriana Craciun, *British Women Writers and the French Revolution: Citizens of the World* (Houndmills, UK: Palgrave Macmillan, 2005); Peter Melville, *Romantic Hospitality and the Resistance to Accommodation* (Waterloo, ON: Wilfred Laurier University Press, 2007); Gerald Newman, *The Rise of English Nationalism: A Cultural History, 1740–1830* (New York: St. Martin's, 1987); Esther Wohlgemut, *Romantic Cosmopolitanism* (London: Palgrave Macmillan, 2009).

53. Wohlgemut, *Romantic Cosmopolitanism*, 3.

54. Mark Canuel, *Religion, Toleration, and British Writing, 1790–1830* (Cambridge: Cambridge University Press, 2002), 86–121.

55. Samuel Taylor Coleridge, "The Plot Discovered," in *Lectures 1795 on Politics and Religion*, ed. Lewis Patton and Peter Mann (London: Routledge and Kegan Paul, 1971), 313.

56. George McLean Harper, "Coleridge's Conversation Poems," in *English Romantic Poets: Modern Essays in Criticism*, ed. M. H. Abrams (Oxford: Oxford University Press, 1975), 190; Gene Bernstein, "The Recreating Secondary Imagination in Coleridge's 'The Nightingale,'" *ELH* 48 (1981): 347; Kelvin Everest, *Coleridge's Secret Ministry: The Context of the Conversation Poems* (Sussex, UK: Harvester, 1979), 197–290.

57. Samuel Taylor Coleridge, "To Charles Lloyd, On his Proposing to Domesticate with the Author," in *Samuel Taylor Coleridge: Poetical Works*, vol. 16, pt. 1, ed. J. C. C. Mays (Princeton, NJ: Princeton University Press, 2001), lines 17, 62, 59–60 (hereafter references to the poems are to this edition, by line).

58. Phil Cardinale, "Coleridge's 'Nightingale': A Note on the Sublime," *Notes and Queries* 49 (2002): 35–36.

59. Cuthbert Shaw, *Monody to the Memory of a Young Lady* (London: G. Kearsly, 1779), 23.

60. Immanuel Kant, *Critique of Judgment*, trans. J. H. Bernard (New York: Hafner, 1951), 157.

61. My reading of the role of the infant in the poem is amplified by the fact that Coleridge adapted many lines of this poem from the earlier "To the Nightingale" (1796), which places a greater emphasis on the domestic intimacy between the speaker and Sara, who "thrills me with the HUSBAND's promised name" (26).

62. William Wordsworth, *Selected Prose*, ed. John O. Hayden (Harmondsworth, UK: Penguin, 1988), 273.

63. Frederick Garber, "The Hedging Consciousness in Coleridge's Conversation Poems," *Wordsworth Circle* 4 (1973): 124–38; Lucy Newlyn, *Reading, Writing, and Romanticism: The Anxiety of Reception* (Oxford: Oxford University Press, 2000), 49–90; Charles Rzepka, *The Self as Mind: Vision and Identity in Wordsworth, Coleridge, and Keats* (Cambridge, MA: Harvard University Press, 1986), 118.

64. Melville, *Romantic Hospitality*, 111.

65. Although I criticize views of Coleridge's conversation poems that consider it merely as a support of conventional domesticity, I also take issue also with those accounts that see these poems as failed efforts at, or skeptical questionings of, community. See, e.g., Tilottama Rajan, *Dark Interpreter: The Discourse of Romanticism* (Ithaca, NY: Cornell University Press, 1980), 204–59; and William A. Ulmer, "The Rhetorical Occasion of 'This Lime Tree Bower My Prison,'" *Romanticism* 13 (2007): 24.

66. Mary Favret, *War at a Distance: Romanticism and the Making of Modern Wartime* (Princeton, NJ: Princeton University Press, 2010), 74, 196.

67. Ibid., 69.

68. Samuel Taylor Coleridge, *The Friend*, ed. Barbara E. Rooke, 2 vols. (New York: Routledge, 1969), 1:292 (hereafter cited in text).

69. Richard Holmes, *Coleridge: Early Visions, 1772–1804* (New York: Pantheon, 1989), 324n. My view contrasts with Mark Jones's account of the poem as a retreat from the public sphere in "Alarmism, Public-Sphere Performatives, and the Lyric Turn: Or, What Is 'Fears in Solitude' Afraid of?" *boundary 2* 30 (2003): 96–97.

CHAPTER FOUR: Biopolitics and the Sublime

1. Michel Foucault, *The Birth of Biopolitics: Lectures at the Collège de France, 1978–79*, ed. Michel Senellart, trans. Graham Burchell (Houndmills, UK: Palgrave Macmillan, 2008), 61.

2. Giorgio Agamben, *Homo Sacer: Sovereign Power and Bare Life*, trans. Daniel Heller-Roazen (Stanford, CA: Stanford University Press, 1998), 40–41.

3. Charlotte Sussman, "Women and the Politics of Sugar, 1792," *Representations* 48 (1994): 48–69; Debbie Lee, *Slavery and the Romantic Imagination* (Philadelphia: University of Pennsylvania Press, 2002), 9–28.

4. Agamben, *Homo Sacer*, 6.

5. Hannah Arendt, *The Origins of Totalitarianism* (Cleveland: Meridian, 1958), 302, 273, 90.

6. Nasser Hussain and Melissa Ptacek make this point in "Thresholds: Sovereignty and the Sacred," *Law and Society Review* 24 (2000): 495–515. See also Seyla Benhabib, "Kantian Questions, Arendtian Answers: Statelessness, Cosmopolitanism, and the Right to Have Rights," in *Pragmatism, Critique, Judgment: Essays for Richard J. Bernstein*, ed. Seyla Benhabib and Nancy Fraser (Cambridge, MA: MIT Press, 2004), 171–96.

7. Lynn Hunt, *Inventing Human Rights: A History* (New York: Norton, 2007), 35–69. Joseph Slaughter discusses the normative account of rights in the context of the Bildungsroman in *Human Rights, Inc.: The World Novel, Narrative Form, and International Law* (New York: Fordham University Press, 2007).

8. Martha Nussbaum, *Poetic Justice: The Literary Imagination and Public Life* (Boston: Beacon, 1995), 4–5.

9. Edmund Burke, *A Philosophical Enquiry into the Origin of our Ideas of the Sublime and Beautiful*, ed. James T. Boulton (Notre Dame: University of Notre Dame Press, 1968), 91,41.

10. David Hume, *Enquiries Concerning Human Understanding and Concerning the Principles of Morals*, ed. P. H. Nidditch, 3rd ed. (Oxford: Clarendon, 1975), 224–26.

11. Immanuel Kant, *Critique of Judgment*, trans. J. H. Bernard (New York: Hafner, 1951), 139.

12. I thank Stephen Engelmann for this felicitous turn of phrase.

13. Although the advertisement for the 1807 volume of Smith's poems announced that *Beachy Head* was "not completed," I follow Stuart Curran's suggestion that the poem "bears a remarkable coherence" in his introduction to *The Poems of Charlotte Smith*, ed. Stuart Curran (Oxford: Oxford University Press, 2003), xxvii.

14. Charlotte Smith, *Beachy Head*, in *The Poems of Charlotte Smith*, ed. Stuart Curran (New York: Oxford University Press, 1993), line 1 (hereafter references to the poem are to this edition and cited in text by line).

15. Burke, *Philosophical Enquiry*, 72.

16. Kevis Goodman, *Georgic Modernity and British Romanticism: Poetry and the Mediation of History* (Cambridge: Cambridge University Press, 2004), 106–43.

17. On the poem as a record of natural detail, see Donelle R. Ruwe, "Charlotte Smith's Sublime: Feminine Poetics, Botany, and *Beachy Head*," *Prisms* 7 (1999): 117–32.

18. Theresa Kelley, "Romantic Histories: Charlotte Smith and *Beachy Head*," *Nineteenth-Century Literature* 59 (2004): 304.

19. Michel Foucault, *"Society Must Be Defended": Lectures at the Collège de France*, trans. David Macey (New York: Picador, 2003), 101.

20. Oliver Goldsmith, *The Deserted Village*, in *Poems, Plays, and Essays of Oliver Goldsmith* (New York: Thomas Crowell, 1900), line 8.

21. Goldsmith, *Deserted Village*, lines 35, 63.

22. Although the relationship of the terms *freedom, justice,* and *right* can be difficult to define when they are submitted to some finer points of legal argument, my basic understanding of Smith's view of their relationship, in which justice is a protection of freedoms attached to legally protected rights, coincides with many standard accounts of these terms in legal theory. See, for a particularly coherent summary, Tara Smith, "On Deriving Rights to Goods from Rights to Freedom," *Law and Philosophy* 11 (1992): 217–34.

23. See, e.g., Sarah M. Zimmerman, *Romanticism, Lyricism, and History* (New York: State University of New York Press, 1999), 39–72.

24. Adela Pinch, *Strange Fits of Passion: Epistemologies of Emotion, Hume to Austen* (Stanford, CA: Stanford University Press, 1996), 51–71. See also Melissa Sodeman, "Charlotte Smith's Literary Exile," *ELH* 76 (2009): 131–52.

25. My argument here also differs from Adriana Craciun's emphasis on the cosmopolitan identities of characters in Smith's writing. See her *British Women Writers and the French Revolution: Citizens of the World* (Houndmills, UK: Palgrave Macmillan, 2005), 138–78.

26. Still, even Dorothy Wordsworth likens flowers to jewels. See her description of the anemone, which closely resembles Smith's, in her entry for 12 May 1802, in *The Grasmere Journals*, ed. Pamela Woof (Oxford: Oxford University Press, 1991), 98.

27. Sir Walter Scott, *Prose Works*, 28 vols. (Edinburgh: Robert Cadell, 1834), 4:32.

28. William Cowper, quoted in Judith Phillips Stanton, introduction to *The Collected Letters of Charlotte Smith* (Bloomington: Indiana University Press, 2003), v.

29. Ian Baucom, *Specters of the Atlantic: Finance Capital, Slavery, and the Philosophy of History* (Durham, NC: Duke University Press, 2005), 182.

30. I take issue with the view that the hermit undoes the earlier perspective by merely refusing its distance and detachment. See Kari Lokke, "The Figure of the Hermit in Charlotte Smith's *Beachy Head*," *Wordsworth Circle* 39 (2008): 39.

31. Patchen Markell, "Tragic Recognition: Action and Identity in Antigone and Aristotle," *Political Theory* 31 (2003): 22. This article appears as chapter 3 of Markell's *Bound by Recognition* (Princeton, NJ: Princeton University Press, 2003).

32. See Geoffrey Hartman, *The Unremarkable Wordsworth* (Minneapolis: University of Minnesota Press, 1987), 31–46.

33. Samuel von Pufendorf, *Two Books of the Elements of Universal Jurisprudence*, ed. and intro. Thomas Behme (Indianapolis: Liberty Fund, 2009); Hugo Grotius, *The Rights of War and Peace*, ed. and intro. Richard Tuck, 3 vols. (Indianapolis: Liberty Fund, 2005).

34. Roberto Esposito, *Bios: Biopolitics and Philosophy*, trans. Timothy Campbell (Minneapolis: University of Minnesota Press, 2008), 16.

35. Agamben, *Homo Sacer*, 187–88.

36. Agamben, *Profanations* (New York: Zone Books, 2007), 72 (hereafter cited in text).

37. See Andrew Norris, "Giorgio Agamben and the Politics of the Living Dead," *Diacritics* 30 (2000): 53.

38. Alison Ross, introduction to "The Agamben Effect," special issue, *South Atlantic Quarterly* 107 (2008): 4.

39. Giorgio Agamben, *The Open: Man and Animal*, trans. Kevin Attell (Stanford, CA: Stanford University Press, 2004), 87, 80, 87.

40. Jean-Luc Nancy, *The Experience of Freedom*, trans. Bridget McDonald (Stanford, CA: Stanford University Press, 1993), 8; Jacques Derrida, *Sovereignties in Question: The Poetics of Paul Celan* (New York: Fordham University Press, 2005), 108–34.

41. See Jean-Luc Nancy, *The Inoperative Community* (Minneapolis: University of Minnesota Press, 1991).

42. Catherine Mills, "Playing with the Law: Agamben and Derrida on Postjuridical Justice," *South Atlantic Quarterly* 107 (2008): 18.

43. J. M. Bernstein, "Intact and Fragmented Bodies: Versions of Ethics 'After Auschwitz,'" *New German Critique* 97 (2006): 44.

44. Agamben, *The Open*, 83.

45. For another instance of the aesthetics of biopolitics, see Roberto Esposito's commitment to "flesh" as a kind of reiterated deconstructive logic demonstrated in works like Francis Bacon's "indeterminacy" between human and animal in *Bios*, 169.

46. Giorgio Agamben, *Nudities*, trans. David Kishik and Stefan Pedatella (Stanford, CA: Stanford University Press, 2011), 82–90.

47. Eric Alliez and Antonio Negri, "Peace and War," *Theory, Culture & Society* 20 (2003): 113 (hereafter cited in text).

48. Michael Hardt and Antonio Negri, *Multitude: War and Democracy in the Age of Empire* (New York: Penguin, 2004), 336 (hereafter cited in text).

49. Michael Hardt and Antonio Negri, *Commonwealth* (Cambridge, MA: Harvard University Press, 2009), 58.

50. Slavoj Žižek, "*Objet a* as Inherent Limit to Capitalism: On Michael Hardt and Antonio Negri," http://www.lacan.com/zizmultitude.htm (accessed 1 August 2009).

51. Ibid.

52. Slavoj Žižek, "From Politics to Biopolitics . . . and Back," *South Atlantic Quarterly* 103 (2004): 510 (hereafter cited in text).

53. Slavoj Žižek, "Have Michael Hardt and Antonio Negri Rewritten the Communist Manifesto for the Twenty-First Century?" *Rethinking Marxism* 13/14 (2001), http://www.egs.edu/faculty/zizek/zizek-have-michael-hardt-antonio-negri-communist-manifesto.html.

54. This empirical aspect of the sublime registers also in Žižek's account of Hegel in *The Sublime Object of Ideology* (London: Verso, 1989), 201–31.

55. Slavoj Žižek, *In Defense of Lost Causes* (London: Verso, 2008), 21.

56. William Connolly, *Why I Am Not a Secularist* (Minneapolis: University of Minnesota Press, 1999), 112.

57. On the connection between justice and the construction of new "frames," see Nancy Fraser, *Scales of Justice: Reimagining Political Space in a Global World* (New York: Columbia University Press, 2009).

58. Charlotte Smith, *The Banished Man* (Whitefish, MT: Kessinger, 2010), 64.

59. Novalis, "Pollen," in *The Early Political Writings of the German Romantics*, ed. Frederick C. Beiser (Cambridge: Cambridge University Press, 1996), 19, 29.

60. Josef Chytry, *The Aesthetic State: A Quest in Modern German Thought* (Berkeley and Los Angeles: University of California Press, 1989).

CHAPTER FIVE: Aesthetics and Animal Theory

1. John Rawls, *Political Liberalism* (New York: Columbia University Press, 1993), 122.

2. See Steven Wise, "Animal Rights, One Step at a Time," in *Animal Rights: Current Debates and New Directions*, ed. Cass Sunstein and Martha C. Nussbaum (Oxford: Oxford University Press, 2004), 19–50.

3. Kari Weil, "A Report on the Animal Turn," *differences* 21 (2010): 8.

4. Catharine A. MacKinnon, "Of Mice and Men: A Feminist Fragment on Animal Rights," in Sunstein and Nussbaum, *Animal Rights*, 270.

5. James Rachels, "Drawing Lines," in ibid., 165.

6. Rawls, *Political Liberalism*, 21.

7. See David Favre, "A New Property Status for Animals: Equitable Self-Ownership," in Sunstein and Nussbaum, *Animal Rights*, 234–50.

8. Martha C. Nussbaum, *Frontiers of Justice: Disability, Nationality, Species Membership* (Cambridge, MA: Belknap Press of Harvard University Press, 2006), 327.

9. Ibid., 332.

10. Matthew Calarco, *Zoographies: The Question of the Animal from Heidegger to Derrida* (New York: Columbia University Press, 2008), 7–8.

11. Jean-François Lyotard, *The Differend: Phrases in Dispute*, trans. Georges Van Den Abeele (Minneapolis: University of Minnesota Press, 1988), 13.

12. Cary Wolfe, "Flesh and Finitude: Thinking Animals in (Post)Humanist Phi-

losophy," *SubStance* 117 (2008): 10. On the prevalence of humanist argument in animal rights, see also idem, *Animal Rites: American Culture, the Discourses of Species, and Posthumanist Theory* (Chicago: University of Chicago Press, 2003).

13. Wise, "Animal Rights," 27; Lesley Rogers and Gisela Kaplan, "All Animals Are Not Equal: The Interface between Scientific Knowledge and Legislation for Animal Rights," in Sunstein and Nussbaum, *Animal Rights*, 176.

14. Vicki Hearne, *Animal Happiness* (New York: HarperCollins, 1994), 196–217.

15. Calarco, *Zoographies*, 141; MacKinnon, "Of Mice and Men," 264.

16. Jacques Derrida, "And Say the Animal Responded," in *Zoontologies: The Question of the Animal*, ed. Cary Wolfe (Minneapolis: University of Minnesota Press, 2003), 121–46.

17. Jacques Derrida, quoted in Wolfe, *Animal Rites*, 93.

18. Jacques Derrida, "The Animal That Therefore I Am (More to Follow)," trans. David Wills, *Critical Inquiry* 28 (2002): 395.

19. Akira Lippit, *Electric Animal: Toward a Rhetoric of Wildlife* (Minneapolis: University of Minnesota Press, 2000), 26.

20. Donna Harraway, *When Species Meet* (Minneapolis: University of Minnesota Press, 2007), 20.

21. Michael Lundblad, "From Animality to Animality Studies," *PMLA* 124 (2009): 496–502.

22. J. M. Coetzee, *The Lives of Animals*, ed. and intro. Amy Gutmann (Princeton, NJ: Princeton University Press, 1999), 43–44.

23. In many ways, Coetzee's position echoes that in Emmanuel Levinas's "The Name of a Dog, or Natural Rights," in *Difficult Freedom*, trans. Seàn Hand (Baltimore: Johns Hopkins University Press, 1990), 151–55. The Levinas essay has been most eloquently studied by David L. Clark in "On Being 'the Last Kantian in Nazi Germany': Dwelling with Animals after Levinas," in *Animal Acts: Configuring the Human in Western History*, ed. Jennifer Ham and Matthew Senior (New York: Routledge, 1997), 42–74.

24. Susan McHugh, "Literary Animal Agents," *PMLA* 124 (2009): 489.

25. David Perkins, *Romanticism and Animal Rights* (Cambridge: Cambridge University Press, 2003), 19.

26. Anna Laetitia Barbauld, *Selected Poetry and Prose*, ed. William McCarthy and Elizabeth Kraft (Peterborough, ON: Broadview, 2002), line 26 (hereafter cited in text by line).

27. Kathryn Ready, "'What then, poor Beastie!': Gender, Politics, and Animal Experimentation in Barbauld's 'The Mouse's Petition,'" *Eighteenth Century Life* 28 (2004): 109.

28. Peter Singer, *Animal Liberation: A New Ethics for Our Treatment of Animals* (New York: New York Review of Books, 1975).

29. Colin Jager refers to this aspect of Barbauld's writing as the creation of an "analogical space" even though she does not insist on analogy yielding philosophical or religious certainty. *The Book of God: Secularization and Design in the Romantic Era* (Philadelphia: University of Pennsylvania Press, 2007), 93.

30. Giorgio Agamben, *The Open: Man and Animal*, trans. Kevin Attell (Stanford, CA: Stanford University Press, 2004), 33–43.

31. Sarah Trimmer, *Fabulous Histories, Designed for the Instruction of Children, Reflecting Their Treatment of Animals* (London: Longman, 1786), x (hereafter cited in text).

32. J. Jefferson Looney, "Cultural Life in the Provinces: Leeds and York, 1720–1820," in *The First Modern Society: Essays in English History in Honor of Lawrence Stone*, ed. A. L. Beier, David Cannadine, and James M. Rosenheim (Cambridge: Cambridge University Press, 1989), 493.

33. Immanuel Kant, *Lectures on Ethics*, ed. Peter Heath and J. B. Schneewind, trans. Peter Heath (Cambridge: Cambridge University Press, 1997), 210.

34. Harriet Ritvo, *The Animal Estate: The English and Other Creatures in the Victorian Age* (Cambridge, MA: Harvard University Press, 1987), 133.

35. *To All Lovers and Admirers of the Beauties of Nature* (Boston: Stainbank, 1796).

36. Ritvo, *Animal Estate*, 41.

37. Ibid., 55.

38. Tom Regan, *Empty Cages: Facing the Challenge of Animals Rights*, with a foreword by Jeffrey Moussaieff Masson (New York: Rowman and Littlefield, 2004), 5.

39. Tom Regan, *The Case for Animal Rights* (Berkeley and Los Angeles: University of California Press, 2004), 362.

40. Cora Diamond, "The Difficulty of Reality and the Difficulty of Philosophy," in *Philosophy and Animal Life*, by Stanley Cavell, Cora Diamond, John McDowell, Ian Hacking, and Cary Wolfe (New York: Columbia University Press, 2008), 62, 74.

41. Steve Baker, *The Postmodern Animal* (London: Reaktion Books, 2000), 24.

42. Ibid., 189.

43. Vicki Hearne, *Adam's Task: Calling Animals by Name* (1982; repr., New York: Harper Perennial, 1994), 135.

44. Harraway, *When Species Meet*, 229.

45. Paul Patton, "Language, Power, and the Training of Horses," in Wolfe, *Zoontologies*, 93.

46. William Cowper, "The Negro's Complaint," in *The Poetical Works of William Cowper* (London: Macmillan, 1921), line 15 (hereafter Cowper's poems cited in text by line).

47. Cora Diamond, "Eating Meat and Eating People," in Sunstein and Nussbaum, *Animal Rights*, 102.

48. Ibid., 104.

49. Samuel Taylor Coleridge, "Fears in Solitude," in *Samuel Taylor Coleridge: Poetical Works*, vol. 16, pt. 1, ed. J. C. C. Mays (Princeton, NJ: Princeton University Press, 2001), lines 105–6 (hereafter references to the poems are to this edition, by line).

50. Samuel Taylor Coleridge, *Osorio*, in ibid., vol. 16, pt. 3, ed. J. C. C. Mays and Joyce Crick, 5.161, 164, 168–69 (references are to act and line).

51. Ibid., 5.165, 167.

52. Wise, "Animal Rights," 38.

53. Christine Kenyon-Jones, *Kindred Brutes: Animals in Romantic-Period Writing* (Aldershot, UK: Ashgate, 2001), 76.

54. Frances Ferguson, "Coleridge and the Deluded Reader," in *Post-Structuralist Readings of English Poetry*, ed. Richard Machin and Christopher Norris (Cambridge: Cambridge University Press, 1987), 248–63.

55. Raimonda Modiano, "Words and 'Languageless' Meanings: Limits of Expression in The Rime of the Ancient Mariner," *Modern Language Quarterly* 38 (1977): 43.

56. My reading here agrees largely with Stanley Cavell's, although the region of meaning to which the poem gestures seems quite clearly to be the divine, not the unconscious, as Cavell argues. See Cavell, *In Quest of the Ordinary: Lines of Skepticism and Romanticism* (Chicago: University of Chicago Press, 1988), 47–48.

57. On the connection between the "Rime" and abolition, see J. R. Ebbatson, "Coleridge's Mariner and the Rights of Man," *Studies in Romanticism* 11 (1972): 171–206.

58. William Wordsworth, "Hart-Leap Well," lines 174, 190, and "Peter Bell," line 482, in *William Wordsworth: 21st-Century Oxford Authors*, ed. Stephen Gill (Oxford: Oxford University Press, 1984).

59. Richard Holmes, *Coleridge: Early Visions, 1772–1804* (New York: Pantheon, 1989), 82. Despite the contrast between Wordsworth and Coleridge that I make here, Wordsworth's account is complex. See Mark Canuel, *Religion, Toleration, and British Writing, 1790–1830* (Cambridge: Cambridge University Press, 2002), 161–204.

60. Percy Bysshe Shelley, *Queen Mab*, in *Shelley's Poetry and Prose*, ed. Donald H. Reiman and Sharon B. Powers, Norton Critical Edition (New York: Norton, 1977), 8.144–45, 9.134, 8.107–8 (hereafter Shelley's poems cited in text; references to *Queen Mab* are to canto and line, and those to "The Sensitive-Plant" are to part and line).

61. My reading of the poem differs from Cian Duffy's, which emphasizes natural processes as the origin of the sublime, in *Shelley and the Revolutionary Sublime* (Cambridge: Cambridge University Press, 2005), 18–48.

62. Timothy Morton, *Shelley and the Revolution in Taste: The Body and the Natural World* (Cambridge: Cambridge University Press, 1994), 99.

63. Stuart Curran, *Poetic Form and British Romanticism* (New York: Oxford University Press, 1986), 123.

64. Angela Leighton, *Shelley and the Sublime: An Interpretation of the Major Poems* (Cambridge: Cambridge University Press, 1984), 55.

65. Richard S. Caldwell, "'The Sensitive Plant': Original Fantasy," *Studies in Romanticism* 15 (1976): 221–52.

66. For Shelley's recollection of Edenic models, see Harold Bloom, *Shelley's Mythmaking* (Ithaca, NY: Cornell University Press, 1969), 148–64.

67. Percy Bysshe Shelley, *Shelley's Prose: Or, the Trumpet of a Prophecy*, ed. David Lee Clark (Albuquerque: University of New Mexico Press, 1954), 83 (hereafter cited in text).

68. Diamond, "Eating Meat and Eating People," 102; McHugh, "Literary Animal Agents," 490; Nigel Rothfels, "Zoos, the Academy, and Captivity," *PMLA* 124 (2009): 486.

Index

academy, 15, 33–35, 64
Addison, Joseph, 49
Adorno, Theodor, 6
aesthetics. *See* beauty; sublime
affect. *See* beauty
Agamben, Giorgio, 11, 94–95, 96, 97, 98, 101, 110, 111–13, 118, 120, 127
Alliez, Eric, 110, 113–14
Anderson, Amanda, 79
animal studies, 12–13, 121–45
anthropomorphism, 67, 87, 124
Appiah, Kwame Anthony, 9, 78, 79
Arendt, Hannah, 11, 51, 95–96, 101
Armstrong, Isobel, 26
Armstrong, John, 27
Arnold, Matthew, 38–39
art, 16, 20–26, 28–30, 44–45, 64, 78, 110–20
autonomy, 20, 46, 51, 53, 60, 71, 85, 123, 136

Bach, Johann Sebastian, 24, 26
Baker, Steve, 132
Barbauld, Anna, 13, 127–28, 129, 130, 134
Baron, Marcia, 155n22
Barrell, John, 151n28
Baucom, Ian, 107
beauty: affect and, 23–26, 86, 92; allegory and, 36, 87, 128; biology and, 18–19, 37, 94, 111, 143; biopolitics and, 26–39, 109, 110–20; as communication, 5, 22–23, 29–30, 42, 45, 51, 67, 74, 88, 97, 123–24; defined, 28; gender and, 21–23; justice and, 10, 14–39; literary characters and, 97, 111–13; morality and, 45; norms of, 2, 8–9, 15, 24, 37, 39, 58, 62, 64, 67–68, 69, 81, 97–98, 102, 110–18; race and, 11, 20, 23, 29, 116; as reciprocity and likeness, 2, 4, 20–23, 29–30, 60, 113, 115; as replication, 1–2, 5, 29, 110–20; sexuality and, 17–18; sociability and, 2, 25, 31, 35, 97; as symmetry, 15–20, 29; sympathy and, 1–2, 91, 103, 127–45. *See also* identity
Benhabib, Seyla, 80, 82
Benjamin, Walter, 113
Bentham, Jeremy, 122
Berlant, Lauren, 71
Bernstein, J. M., 113
Bersani, Leo, 37, 70, 162n46
biopolitics, 5, 11, 94–120. *See also under* beauty
Bloom, Harold, 33, 36
body and bodies, 15, 17, 22–23, 25, 28, 37, 66–67, 94–95
Bové, Paul, 68
Brennan, Timothy, 161n39
Brooks, Peter, 56
Brown, Wendy, 7
Burke, Edmund, 29–30, 43–45, 86, 97
Butler, Judith, 59
Byron, George Gordon, Lord, 46–47, 52–55, 60

Calarco, Matthew, 124
Caserio, Robert, 160n20
Cavell, Stanley, 56, 170n56
Caygill, Howard, 31, 61, 67
Cheah, Pheng, 79
Cheyfitz, Eric, 34
Chytry, Josef, 120
Clark, David L., 168n23
Clarke, Eric O., 83
Coetzee, J. M., 125–26
Coleridge, Samuel Taylor, 9, 12, 65, 82–93, 134–39, 140. Works: "Fears in Solitude," 89–93, 135; "Frost at Midnight," 88; "The Nightingale," 85–89; *Osorio*, 136; "The Rime of the Ancient Mariner," 137–39, 143; "To Charles Lloyd," 84–85; "To a Young Ass," 137

communitarianism, 58, 62, 157n65
community, 2, 4, 31, 51, 62, 72, 81, 84–85, 90, 116, 122, 132
Connolly, William, 45, 51, 118
conscience, 52, 91
cosmopolitanism, 8–9, 64–65, 66, 73–82, 83, 89, 91, 92, 112, 125
Cowper, William, 104, 107, 133–34, 138, 139
Craciun, Adriana, 83, 165n25
Crowther, Paul, 152n38, 154n10
culture, 20, 31, 34, 37, 38, 58, 64, 68, 70, 71–82, 92, 101, 110, 125, 143
Curran, Stuart, 141, 164n13

Daniels, Norman, 58
Danto, Arthur, 35
Dean, Tim, 74, 160n20
de Bolla, Peter, 5, 16, 23–26, 31, 35, 36, 60, 61, 67
deconstruction, 61, 66–68, 70, 125, 127, 132
D'Emilio, John, 61
de Man, Paul, 66, 67
De Quincey, Thomas, 60
Derrida, Jacques, 7–8, 66–67, 70, 111, 125, 127
Diamond, Cora, 132, 135
Dimock, Wai Chee, 148n16
disability, 26–27
dissent. *See under* sublime
Donoghue, Denis, 14, 33, 73
Duff, William, 47
Duffy, Cian, 170n61
Dutoit, Ulysse, 37
duty, 3, 51, 130–31
Dworkin, Andrea, 35

Eagleton, Terry, 6, 61, 155n24
Ebbatson, J. R., 170n57
Eco, Umberto, 14, 36
Edelman, Lee, 160n20
Elfenbein, Andrew, 83
embodiment. *See* body and bodies
Eng, David, 73
Engelmann, Stephen, 157n59, 164n12
enthusiasm, 12, 47–49, 51, 60, 62, 81
Esposito, Roberto, 111, 166n45

Favre, David, 123
Ferguson, Frances, 42, 138, 158n71, 158n78

Fichte, J. G., 57
form, 5, 12, 26, 42–44, 47, 66–67, 81, 89, 99, 104–6, 108–9, 141–42
Foucault, Michel, 45, 58–59, 94–95, 101
Franta, Andrew, 159n2
Fraser, Nancy, 167n57
freedom, 20, 31, 50, 51, 60, 63, 81, 82, 102, 103, 106, 107, 108, 111, 128, 165n22
French Revolution. *See* revolution
Furniss, Tom, 151n32

Gandhi, Mahatma, 62
Gasché, Rodolphe, 46, 59
Gendler, Ruth, 35
Gigante, Denise, 12, 151n34
Gilbert-Rolfe, Jeremy, 27
Glendon, Mary Ann, 6
Godwin, William, 9, 84
Goethe, Johann Wolfgang von, 55
Goldsmith, Oliver, 101
Gould, Glenn, 26
Gray, Thomas, 109
Grotius, Hugo, 110
Guillory, John, 35, 36
Guyer, Paul, 45, 51, 151n34, 154n10

Halberstam, Judith, 8, 73, 160n20
Halley, Janet, 162n48
Hampshire, Stuart, 7, 32, 34, 57
Hardt, Michael, 110, 114–17, 118
Harraway, Donna, 125, 132
Hartley, David, 44
Hartman, Geoffrey, 109
Harvey, David, 161n39
Hearne, Vicki, 124, 132
Heartney, Eleanor, 27
Hegel, G. W. F., 52, 57, 152n38
Helvétius, Claude Adrien, 9
Herman, Barbara, 155n24
Hertz, Neil, 33, 40, 61, 66, 67
Hesiod, 127
Hickey, Dave, 5, 27
Hobbes, Thomas, 52
Hobhouse, John Cam, 53
Hogarth, William, 135
Hume, David, 57, 97
Hunt, Lynn, 7, 96

Hussain, Nasser, 164n6
Hutcheson, Francis, 29

icon, 115, 116
identity, 5, 27–28, 37, 58, 64–65, 72, 74, 76–80, 92, 107, 108, 111–20, 123–30
ideology, 6, 11, 100, 101, 113, 120
Ignatieff, Michael, 8
imagination, 5, 6, 12, 30, 33, 42–43, 44, 47, 62, 66, 98, 104–5, 106–7, 108
Irlam, Shaun, 155n20

Jager, Colin, 168n29
Jay, Martin, 149n26
Johnson, Barbara, 67
Johnson, W. R., 148n24
Jones, Mark, 164n69
justice, 7–8, 50–52, 58. *See also under* beauty; sublime

Kaiser, David Aram, 155n31
Kant, Immanuel, 4, 5, 9, 21, 30, 40–62, 63, 75, 82, 122, 123. Works: "An Answer to the Question: 'What is Enlightenment?,'" 51–52; *Anthropology*, 55; *Critique of Judgment*, 5, 20, 30, 40–46, 47, 48, 49–50, 60, 62, 66–67, 86, 97, 100; *Critique of Practical Reason*, 5, 47; *Groundwork of the Metaphysics of Morals*, 5, 47–48, 100; *Lectures on Ethics*, 45, 130–31; *The Metaphysics of Morals*, 5, 50, 52; "Perpetual Peace," 75; *Religion within the Limits of Reason Alone*, 155n27
Kaufman, Robert, 162n48
Keats, John, 10–11
Keenan, Thomas, 148n16
Kelley, Theresa, 12, 101
Kenyon-Jones, Christine, 137
King, Loren A., 57
Kymlicka, Will, 157n65

Lamb, Jonathan, 55, 152n47
Law. *See* justice
Lee, Debbie, 95
Leighton, Angela, 141
Levi, Primo, 113
Levinas, Emmanuel, 168n23
Lewis, Matthew, 55

Lippit, Akira, 13, 125, 127
Lloyd, David, 49, 153n68, 158n77
Locke, John, 44
Lokke, Karri, 165n30
Lyotard, Jean-François, 61, 124, 155n24, 156n42, 159n81
lyric poetry, 10, 148n24

MacKinnon, Catharine, 123
Manet, Eduard, 23, 113
Mao, Douglas, 28
Markell, Patchen, 71, 109, 160n22
Martin, Peter, 46
McBride, Dwight A., 72–73
McGann, Jerome, 150n10
McHugh, Susan, 126
Mee, Jon, 12
Melaney, William D., 46
Melville, Peter, 83, 89
Merrill, James, 149n4
Mill, John Stuart, 122
Mills, Catherine, 112
Miyoshi, Masao, 33
Modiano, Raimonda, 138
Morality. *See under* beauty; sublime
More, Hannah, 107
Morton, Timothy, 141
Muñoz, José Esteban, 74, 160n20

Nancy, Jean-Luc, 61, 111–12
nationalism, 29, 89, 95–96, 100–102
nature, 3, 14, 24, 37, 43, 44, 46, 85–89, 91–92, 106–7, 113, 132–33, 139–41; culture and, 125, 130; state of, 75, 105. *See also* animal studies
Negri, Antonio, 110, 113–17, 118
Nehemas, Alexander, 36
neoliberalism, 37
New Historicism, 31–32, 67–68
Newman, Barnett, 24, 150n14
Newman, Gerald, 83
Nietzsche, Friedrich, 47
Norman Yoke, 100
Nussbaum, Martha, 7, 13, 76, 79, 123, 124, 161n36

Orlie, Melissa, 62, 81
O'Rourke, James, 147n3

Panagia, Davide, 157n59
Patton, Paul, 133
Paulson, Ronald, 32
Penn, John, 9
Perkins, David, 127, 134
Pinch, Adela, 103
Plato, 5
politics and the political, 4, 6, 32, 40–41, 61; and aesthetic form, 5, 6–7, 27, 28, 33–36, 38–39, 51, 63–82; and juridical form, 48–62. *See also* biopolitics; sublime, dissent and
pornography, 35
postmodernism, 5, 8, 11, 15, 35, 36, 38–39, 63–68, 73, 97–98, 112, 118, 127, 132, 153n54
Prettejohn, Elizabeth, 27, 36
Priestley, Joseph, 45
Ptacek, Melissa, 164n6
Pufendorf, Samuel von, 110
punishment, 52–55
purposiveness, 30, 43

queer theory, 8, 9, 45, 64–75, 76, 77, 79–81, 82, 83, 89, 92, 125

race. *See under* beauty
Rajan, Tilottama, 163n65
Rancière, Jacques, 61–62, 159n79
Ratcliff, Carter, 152n43
Rawls, John, 6, 7, 19, 56–57, 77, 82, 122–23
Readings, Bill, 33
Ready, Kathryn, 127
recognition, politics of, 2, 5, 69–71, 109–10, 115
Redfield, Marc, 150n23
Regan, Tom, 132
religion, 19, 38, 45, 48–49, 77, 90, 112, 128–30, 138. *See also* toleration
reparation, 6, 63–93
revolution, 9, 30, 38, 51, 56, 70, 94–95, 96, 102, 107, 115, 118, 120
Reynolds, Joshua, 5, 28–29, 45
rights, 6, 7, 8, 11, 12–13, 20, 50–59, 75, 82, 84, 91, 94–98, 101, 103, 105, 107, 109–10, 121–45, 158n78, 164n7, 165n22, 167n12
Ritvo, Harriet, 130
Robbins, Bruce, 79, 82
Robinson, Mary, 128

Romanticism, 10–12, 55, 83, 96, 107, 118–20
Romilly, Samuel, 56
Rorty, Richard, 48
Ross, Alison, 111
Ross, Marlon, 160n24
Rousseau, Jean-Jacques, 105
Rustin, Bayard, 62
Ruwe, Donelle, 165n17

Sandel, Michael, 7, 58
Scarry, Elaine, 5, 14, 16–20, 35, 58, 61, 132, 149n5, 150n9
Schiller, Friedrich, 51
Scott, Sir Walter, 104
Scruton, Roger, 5, 36
secularization, 49, 129
Sedgwick, Eve Kosofsky, 8, 33, 68–71, 72, 74, 79
Sen, Amartya, 9, 76
sexuality, *See* beauty; queer theory
Siebers, Tobin, 20, 26
Sha, Richard, 83
Shelley, Mary, 1–4
Shelley, Percy Bysshe, 12, 60, 139–45. Works: *Queen Mab*, 140–41; "The Sensitive-Plant," 141–43, 144; *A Vindication of Natural Diet*, 143
Singer, Peter, 127, 135
Slaughter, Joseph, 164n7
slavery, 95, 96, 99, 106, 107–8, 122, 133–34
Smith, Charlotte, 11, 98–120, 121. Works: *The Banished Man*, 119; *Beachy Head*, 98–110, 119, 122; *Elegaic Sonnets*, 103; *The Emigrants*, 107; "To My Lyre," 119
Smith, Tara, 165n22
Soni, Vivasvan, 61
Spinoza, Baruch, 47
Steiner, Wendy, 5, 14, 16, 21–23, 58, 113
Sterne, Laurence, 128
Stewart, Ian, 36
Stewart, Susan, 59
Stockton, Kathryn Bond, 74
sublime: community and, 3; as critique of custom, 41; defined, 41–42; dissent and, 33, 41–48, 49, 51–52, 56, 62, 69, 75–76, 85, 89, 90; justice and, 3–4, 6, 8, 9, 48–62, 90–93, 103–10, 118–20, 134–45; morality and, 45–48; New Historicism and, 31–32; normativity and, 49, 56, 62; political cri-

tique and, 105, 107; publicity and, 52, 63, 123; reason and, 6, 43; separateness and, 42, 88; strangers and, 108. *See also* form; imagination
Suetonius, 54
suicide, 54
Sussman, Charlotte, 95

Taylor, Charles, 58
Thomas, Paul, 153n68
toleration, 9, 49, 52, 62, 84. *See also* sublime, dissent and
Trimmer, Sarah, 13, 128–30, 133, 134

ugliness, 1–2
Ulmer, William A., 163n65

Vietnam War, 32, 33
Virgil, 127

Walzer, Michael, 58
Wang, Orrin, 12
Warner, Michael, 71–73, 80–82, 162n48
Weiskel, Thomas, 33, 61
Williams, Melissa, 56
Wise, Stephen, 136
Wohlgemut, Esther, 83
Wolfe, Cary, 124, 167n12
Wolin, Sheldon, 6, 65
Wollstonecraft, Mary, 9
Woodmansee, Martha, 155n31
Wordsworth, Dorothy, 103
Wordsworth, William, 56, 109, 139

Yearsley, Ann, 107
Young, Iris Marion, 7–8, 70
Youngquist, Paul, 2, 150n23

Žižek, Slavoj, 11, 98, 110, 116–18, 120, 167n54